Deana + Cin

NEW CONSCIOUSNESS
FOR A NEW WORLD

Hope you enjoy.
This is where our
consciousness is
today - Dipe

NEW CONSCIOUSNESS FOR A NEW WORLD

How to Thrive in Transitional Times
and Participate in the
Coming Spiritual Renaissance

KINGSLEY L. DENNIS

Inner Traditions
Rochester, Vermont • Toronto, Canada

Inner Traditions
One Park Street
Rochester, Vermont 05767
www.InnerTraditions.com

Text stock is SFI certified

Library of Congress Cataloging-in-Publication Data
Dennis, Kingsley.
  New consciousness for a new world : how to thrive in transitional times and
participate in the coming spiritual renaissance / Kingsley L. Dennis.
    p. cm.
  Summary: "A call for a paradigm shift in human thinking in recognition of the
interconnectedness of all things—a new mind for a new world"—Provided by
publisher.
  Includes bibliographical references (p.   ) and index.
  ISBN 978-1-59477-412-6 (pbk.)—ISBN 978-1-59477-809-4 (ebook)
  1. Spiritual life—Miscellanea. 2. Spirituality—Miscellanea. 3. Twenty-first
century—Forecasts. 4. Civilization—21st century. 5. Civilization—Forecasting.
6. Consciousness—Miscellanea. 7. Thought and thinking—Miscellanea. I. Title.
  BF1999.D37 2011
  303.49—dc23
                                                                    2011022810

Printed and bound in the United States by Lake Book Manufacturing
The text stock is SFI certified. The Sustainable Forestry Initiative® program
promotes sustainable forest management.

10 9 8 7 6 5 4 3 2 1

Text design by Virginia Scott Bowman and layout by Priscilla Baker
This book was typeset in Garamond Premier Pro with News Gothic, Legacy Sans,
and Copperplate used as display typefaces

To send correspondence to the author of this book, mail a first-class letter to the
author c/o Inner Traditions • Bear & Company, One Park Street, Rochester, VT
05767, and we will forward the communication.

Dedicated to my parents, Jeff and June Dennis,
for their unswerving support and unconditional love:
Always and in Everything.

My thanks to Ervin Laszlo for his many years of
inspiration and for his support on this project.

My appreciation and gratitude to everyone who
has been a part of my own journey: you may
or may not know who you are.

Life is an incredible entanglement—and unfolding.

CONTENTS

FOREWORD

To my mind, the key point to Kingsley Dennis's *New Consciousness for a New World* is the coming of a "worldshift"—not as a "perhaps" or an "if," but as an event that will come our way without question, well within the lifetime of most of us. He states: "Global society in the twenty-first century has entered a period of profound, fundamental, and unprecedented change. . . . Our planet is experiencing a major *transition stage.*"

Why so? Because "[G]lobal humanity has reached critical points in its equilibrium. It is at a point of dynamic critical vulnerability . . . not only for the future development of complex human societies but also for the future evolution of our entire species. . . . Human civilizations have in the past disappeared, and it now appears that our current patterns of global civilization are arriving at a similar crossroads."

One cannot be any clearer than this about the critical nature of the epoch we are now entering. Yet Kingsley tells us that the quasi-certainty of a coming worldshift should not inspire fear and despair, but rather should raise the question as to whether we are *ready* for this change.

That, indeed, is the question. The author offers vital compass points to orient our thinking, so as to help make the tipping point into an overture for global breakthrough rather than the prelude to worldwide breakdown. These compass points are fundamental and need to be read and pondered.

For my part, I will merely add a thought that came to me as I was reading Kingsley's deep yet highly readable book. What, indeed, is *the* most vital fact or factor you and I should take into account when getting ready for the tipping point? The following is what I have come up with.

The condition of humanity on this planet is decided in the interaction of two vast and now increasingly diverging systems: the system of nature—the biosphere—and the system formed by the now globally interacting human community. When we speak of the need for profound and urgent change, we should specify that this refers to the system of the human community and not to the system of nature. The biosphere needs to be conserved, its integrity safeguarded, its dynamic equilibria maintained and made more resilient. It is not to be pushed to a tipping point, for the dynamic regime into which it would then settle is not likely to be favorable to the persistence of the human community. After all, the human system has been built into the system of nature during the millennia that had elapsed since the last Ice Age. The human system could persist, and even thrive, because it was in harmony with the generative and regenerative capacities of the biosphere. This was always a delicate harmony, and it has been made more delicate by the magnitude and the resource-hunger of the human system. We are now a vast system of seven billion humans, with enormous technological powers and unprecedented demands.

The human–nature system mesh has precious little error tolerance in our day. We are dependent on a proper mesh for obtaining the basic resources of our life: air, water, food, habitable space, and the diverse mineral and biological resources on which we have now come to depend. And we are running out, or at any rate low, on most if not all of these resources.

Let us be very careful, then, about what change we are speaking of, and where. In regard to the system of nature, we can speak of safeguarding and maintaining, rebalancing, restabilizing, and making more resilient the current system, but we cannot speak of intervening in it to create change and transformation. Given the limitations of human knowledge, any change we would catalyze would be very likely detrimental to the web of life on Earth, including the ever more precariously balanced system of human life.

Precisely the opposite is the case in regard to the human system on the planet. This system has developed in the embrace of the nature system, but it has now overgrown that embrace. We have entered on mistaken paths of development and have disregarded their unintended consequences as "side effects" or "collateral damage." When they became painfully evident, we have resorted to technology to compensate for the negative effects. And we have continued to grow. We have artificially increased the fertility of soils and tapped energies beyond those that sustain the nature system. We have built enormous urban complexes and used the resources of vast hinterlands to sustain them. These and similar measures gave us the illusion of stability and progress, when in reality they have undermined the vital balances on which our very existence depends.

Now we had better learn to live within the embrace of the nature system, reintegrating ourselves within the limits and possibilities of the processes and equilibria of the biosphere. This requires a radical shift in the human system: a worldshift. Current attempts to restabilize or revitalize the dominant structures and processes of the present world are a grievous mistake. Success could only be temporary, and it would only postpone the day of reckoning, making it all the more dramatic, and possibly traumatic. The processes we have initiated in this system cannot be simply stopped—not population growth, not resource consumption, not the progressive degeneration of natural cycles and resources. Yet our political and business leaders speak of restabilizing and revitalizing our ailing social and economic systems as the way to solve our problems.

The bottom line is that we must change, but we must know *what* to change, and *how*. We know that the future will not be a linear continuation of the past. It will encounter a tipping point—a bifurcation in the evolutionary trajectory of the human system. It is our unique and very likely nonrecurring opportunity to orient the thinking of today's people, especially young people, so they can face the tipping point with a clear recognition that it is our world that needs to change, and change profoundly, whereas the system that supports life on the planet must be made more stable and resilient. A sustainable nature system can enable us to shift our world without a collapse of our population.

Seizing this opportunity calls for realizing that if we are to change the world—*our* world—we must first change ourselves. As the title of this book rightly suggests: we must change the way we look at ourselves and the world; change our consciousness.

ERVIN LASZLO

Ervin Laszlo, twice nominated for the Nobel Peace Prize, is editor of the international periodical *World Futures: The Journal of General Evolution* and Chancellor-Designate of the newly formed GlobalShift University. He is the founder and president of the international think tanks the Club of Budapest and the General Evolution Research Group and the author of 83 books translated into 21 languages. He lives in Italy.

INTRODUCTION

Standing at the Precipice of Change

Humankind is being led along an evolving course,
Through this migration of intelligences,
And though we seem to be sleeping,
There is an inner wakefulness
That directs the dream,
And that will eventually startle us back
To the truth of who we are.

RUMI, *THE DREAM THAT MUST BE INTERPRETED*

Humanity is asleep, concerned only with what is useless,
living in a wrong world.

SANAI OF AFGHANISTAN, 1130 CE

Global society in the twenty-first century has entered a period of profound, fundamental, and unprecedented change. During this time of change, many people will be forced to adopt new modes of thinking, perceiving, and behaving in order to be able to not only endure but, more important, also to assist a world needing to undergo deep transformation. Our planet is experiencing a major *transition stage,* and humanity, both individually and collectively, needs to understand that rapid change is both creative and destructive.

1

Change has always been a cyclic component of nature, an inherent part of our cosmological story. Without change there can be no evolution, no momentum, no forward push or backward decline. As in seasonal transition, there are processes of birth, growth, peak, renewal, and regeneration. Once-great civilizations such as the Roman and Persian empires have also been part of this grand story, with their declines now being eminent features of today's history books. Yet within the grander scheme of things, these cyclic social renewals were of a smaller scale. They were more regional than global, and they were strongly aligned within terrestrial cycles and events. However, the changes confronting global society in the upcoming years will be profound: the upcoming transition is a part of a grander evolutionary cycle, when terrestrial and cosmological cycles coincide. Not only is our global society approaching rapid and accelerating tipping points akin to the turning points of prior civilizations, but these events also are aligned with larger solar and galactic cycles. Such times in evolutionary history are not only profound but also offer vastly increased creative energies for radical transformation.

Yet periods of developmental change often require chaos and upheaval as "evolutionary agents" to trigger rapid growth. In the context of what is occurring in the world today, this book describes how we are currently witnessing the convergence of catalytic events. Further, this series of transformative pulses, including periods of chaos and collapse, will provide opportunities for readaptation and renewal. It is hoped that our social, cultural, and spiritual regeneration will foster a "renewed humanity." It holds the promise for a new period of exterior and interior growth, a time to reconnect our species to a creative universe and once again to our universal story. We are on a mythological journey that requires our collective participation and continuation.

I am not alone in this assertion. For at least two decades now, many of our leading thinkers, futurists, and visionaries have been warning us that the upcoming years will present an evolutionary crisis to our global society. Further, this crisis period will involve great changes, potentially catastrophic, that will shake the foundations of our social systems and invoke great changes in people's personal lives. I consider, as do many others, that this transformative period is a necessary requirement in our evolutionary journey. For most of our recorded human history, we have no precedent for this; very few public records exist to help us understand the situation. We can say that there exists neither map nor guide to assist us at this crucial period. We are, to put it bluntly, asleep to the influences that direct our lives, and this makes us vulnerable to the situation. Quite literally, we are in dire need of waking up.

The philosopher-mystic G. I. Gurdjieff repeatedly stated that humankind required a "shock" in order to wake itself up to the "terror of the situation" (whatever that "terror" might be). One of his more provocative tales describes what he sees as "a very good illustration of man's position":

> There is an Eastern tale which speaks about a very rich magician who had a great many sheep. But at the same time this magician was very mean. He did not want to hire shepherds, nor did he want to erect a fence about the pasture where his sheep were grazing. The sheep consequently often wandered into the forest, fell into ravines, and so on, and above all they ran away, for they knew that the magician wanted their flesh and skins and this they did not like. At last the magician found a remedy. He hypnotized his sheep and suggested to them first of all that they were immortal and that no harm was being done to them when they were skinned, that, on the contrary, it would be very good for them and even pleasant; secondly he suggested that the magician was a good master who loved his flock so much that he was ready to do anything in the world for them; and in the third place he suggested to them that if anything at all were going to happen to them it was not going to happen just then, at any rate not that day, and therefore they had no need to think about it. Further the magician suggested to his sheep that they were not sheep at all; to some of them he suggested that they were lions, to

others that they were eagles, to others that they were men, and to others that they were magicians.

And after this all his cares and worries about the sheep came to an end. They never ran away again but quietly awaited the time when the magician would require their flesh and skins.[1]

This so-called magician's hypnosis is the collective "hypnotic sleep" that many of us experience as our daily lives. Yet for the majority of us, it is a very meaningful slumber. In fact, many people might be offended to learn that their everyday efforts and struggles are little more than sleep-walking. After all, we put a great deal of effort into what "makes" our lives. We also have a lot of investment in what we have constructed around us, so to dismiss it casually could cause unease. However, our lives—in the context of our everyday physical world—are being challenged now, and in ways that are increasingly difficult to ignore. This is because great change is taking place, and this change will become ever more visible in how it affects our daily lives. Everything around us is in flux, and there are good reasons for this. The Earth is, quite literally, shaking: what have been termed Earth changes are occurring with greater frequency, with ever-increasing destructive consequences, and they are dangerously close to irreversible tipping points. Global human society too has accumulated such complex interdependencies that it has effectively become an integral body, such that a pain in one of the limbs will affect the whole. Further, this whole body of global humanity has reached critical points in its equilibrium. It is at a point of dynamic critical vulnerability, and at such moments the slightest of impacts can set into motion an unpredictable chain of events. However, the opportunity also presents an incredible moment in the capacity for transformation. An intervention at the right time, and in the right manner, can bring forth accelerated change.

We are thus passing through an evolutionary moment of heightened sensitivity—a period of transition—with the possibility for unprecedented, accelerated human and sociological development (breakthrough) or for sudden and cataclysmic collapse (breakdown). How this epoch plays itself out will be a defining moment, either way, for the human species on this planet. It is, in all respects, a "trigger point" within the evolutionary journey of humankind. And the implications go beyond our daily lives as evolutionary cycles manifest within a vast and complex system of impacts that are planetary, solar, galactic, and universal. It is an immeasurable Indra's net.

> Far away in the heavenly abode of the great god Indra, there is a wonderful net that has been hung by some cunning artificer in such a manner that it stretches out infinitely in all directions. In accordance with the extravagant tastes of deities, the artificer has hung a single glittering jewel in each "eye" of the net, and since the net itself is infinite in all dimensions, the jewels are infinite in number. There hang the jewels, glittering like stars of the first magnitude, a wonderful sight to behold. If we now arbitrarily select one of these jewels for inspection and look closely at it, we will discover that in its polished surface there are reflected all the other jewels in the net, infinite in number. Not only that, but each of the jewels reflected in this one jewel is also reflecting all the other jewels, so that there is an infinite reflecting process occurring . . . it symbolizes a cosmos where there is an infinitely repeated interrelationship among all the members of the cosmos. This relationship is said to be one of simultaneous *mutual identity* and *mutual intercausality*.[2]

Within this abode of *mutual intercausality*, all things have their connection. Processes reflect each other, and so a period of development can be, to use a familiar phrase, a rising tide that lifts all boats. Other times there is no trickle-down effect, just a tornado that brings everything into the collective storm.

In these current times of tornados and storms, there can exist immense feelings of fear and insecurity. It is a period where familiar support structures that have existed to keep everything together are now being shaken badly, or for some pulled away. People may experience great financial loss and difficulty, with future securities crushed, stability and order decapitated, and more important, perceptions and beliefs stretched to the limits of credibility. Such a degree of change is both unnerving at best and increasingly fear inducing in its worse moments. It has to be said that many people actually fear change; for them it brings both trouble and the unknown. And what people cannot understand usually becomes a self-created spectre of fear. Politicians often perform the best in this situation, usually because change in the long term is avoided in favor of short-term change that involves immediate repercussions for the people, and not always for the better. So the status quo has been safe for some time, yet now there is little future for the status quo amidst today's global events. Transition is upon us, whether we accept it or not. We need to know for ourselves what is happening, how this will affect us, and what we intend to do about it.

So back to the subtitle of this introduction: "Standing at the Precipice of Change." Just what is meant by this? I am not alone in stating that global society stands at a strategic crossroads in humanity's evolutionary journey. And before this sudden shift occurs, we might have to bear witness to some chaotic upheavals. This is because many of the old structures that society has relied on for so long are finally creaking and collapsing. Yet this is not only supposition; these processes are how evolution functions, as I discuss in chapter 1 of the book. Just like in the life of a human, on a grander scale our species' life has its own particular stages: its childhood, adolescence, adulthood, and elder maturity. And at each stage, as author Ernest Scott notes in *The People of the Secret,* "Man has to abandon the secure, the trusted, and—for his present moment—the ultimate. At each stage he has to struggle with the denying force of inertia. He has to surmount a mental obstacle as once he had to surmount biological obstacles. If he succeeds, he learns more, understands more, gets closer and closer to participating. It may be that he is now required to confront—and accept—the mechanism of his own evolution."[3]

And this is where we now find ourselves, both individually and collectively—confronting a transition stage in our own evolution.

Further, the choice we have to make is whether we accept—and participate—in the mechanism of our own evolution. It has been a long journey, punctuated by starts and stops and by catalysts of numerous kinds, including revolutions, wars and conflicts, science and the arts, and innovations and communications. In other words, for a new global social order to emerge, it is necessary to first go through a series of transformative pulses, including periods of chaos and collapse. Not only is this necessary, but it may also be welcome. After all, you can't fill a bottle with new wine when it is already full: you need to empty it before the new wine can be introduced. And Earth, too, as part of the solar family, has her own cycles that require this periodic cleansing.

So within the long tail of evolutionary time, there are periods of upheaval that serve cosmic purposes (to put it simply). And most of the time, these upheavals create havoc for the creatures resting on the skin of Earth. Only very few are those who have in times past been aware of these cyclic occurrences. To the general masses, these are often seen as times of craziness, when war and strife seem like everyday madness. As P. D. Ouspensky stated, "There are periods in the life of humanity which generally coincide with the beginning of the fall of cultures and civilizations, when the masses irretrievably lose their reason and begin to destroy everything that has been created by centuries and millennia of culture. Such periods of mass madness, often coinciding with geological cataclysms, climatic changes, and similar phenomena of a planetary character, release a very great quantity of the matter of knowledge."[4]

This release of knowledge that comes with upheaval can be used to help civilization push through to a higher level of functioning. Information is itself a catalyst for rapid evolutionary change (as explained in chapter 1). Evolutionary progress appears to operate through various release and gearshift mechanisms, in that physical chaos provides the release of energy and information necessary to fuel a leap, or "phase change," in evolutionary development. The problem in the past has been that these transitions often create disturbances for life on the planet. However, to be forewarned is to be prepared. Such transition stages can be best navigated when people are more aware of the coming changes and can act as conscious participants. The bottom line is that there is never an end; everything is in the process of further transformation. So the world is not coming to an end, despite what some soothsayers and doom mongers predict. What these upcoming times foretell is a period of accelerating evolutionary change. And more important, what the coming transformation requires is that we, as individuals, consciously participate through our own creative and positive energies.

It has been suggested that evolutionary progress on Earth has been a guided operation that has, so far, culminated in humankind. This process, it is conjectured,[5] has been achieved by making available at a planetary level a succession of energies, each higher in frequency than the one before. These conscious and creative energies have been turned on sequentially in order to give rise to the entire evolutionary progression, from molecule to man. The way these energies operate is by each new, higher frequency being applied while planetary life is still struggling to adjust to the existing energetic level. Thus, each new energetic stage is introduced long before living systems (including humankind) are fully deploying the current energy. In this way, evolutionary progression is constantly reaching for the next energetic state.* However, at transition eras between energetic levels, there often manifests disruption, like quantum interference, as differing energetic zones collide. At such times of *interference,* great change is possible.

Through active awareness of these transformative times, humanity is able to process higher and finer forms of the energy streaming into Earth. It can be said that sufficient numbers of receptive individuals are needed to transmute and transmit certain energies, especially during these times, when such energies seem to be increasingly radiating our cosmic sector. A critical mass of humanity is required to start awakening to aid the process of planetary and human evolution. It does not require a majority—for that will never be reached in time—it only requires

---

*A good analogy of how these energetic stages exist alongside each other can be found in Doris Lessing's masterful novel *The Marriages between Zones Three, Four and Five.*

quality. A "sleeping mass" (i.e., an unaware humanity) does not transmit energy well. Such energies are thrown off into physical and emotional attachments and distracted into other social channels. As writer Frank Herbert presciently said in *Dune,* "The sleeper must awaken."

One of the highest forces at our disposal is conscious and unconditional love. It sometimes seems that Earth is degenerating or devolving as a result of human life lacking the reception and transmission of such forces and energies. This capacity needs to be provoked and stimulated within people, and it may be that the coming years will inspire renewed activation and growth, as periods of transition often shock people out of their everyday stupor and into reinvigorated appreciation and gratitude. It is often the case that humanity is coaxed and coerced along its optimal evolutionary line by contrived situations that involve chaos and suffering before renewal can occur. As Duane Elgin writes, "It is the immense suffering of millions—even billions—of precious human beings coupled with the widespread destruction of many other life-forms that will burn through our complacency and isolation. Needless suffering is the psychological and psychic fire that can awaken our compassion and fuse individuals, communities, and nations into a cohesive and consciously organized global civilization."[6]

It is fair to say that Earth is in ecological crisis and humanity is in spiritual crisis, and that a similar response is required for both, as the two crises are fundamentally tied to the same source. Humanity needs to evolve, not just physically but also psychologically and spiritually, as time is both speeding up and running out simultaneously. Our lack of *conscious contribution* may be said to be behind much of our life dissatisfaction and disconnection. Yet we can connect. The cords are in place; we need only to ask, reach out, and sincerely offer our intentions to do so. These unprecedented times that we now find ourselves in are ripe opportunities for personal growth, knowledge, and understanding. Why? Because we are now, as a planetary species, moving through an historic civilizational shift. And during such times, *how we think* is of paramount importance.

In periods of relative stability, the consciousness of individuals does not usually play a critical role in the behavior of society, as there is a generalized level of social consensus. However, when there are signs of cracking and chaotic moments in a society or societies, life becomes more sensitive and responsive to the consciousness of the people. There occur fluctuations in the values, beliefs, worldviews, and aspirations of the people, and as Margaret Mead famously said, "Never doubt that a small group of thoughtful, committed citizens can change the world. Indeed, it is the only thing that ever has." It is the mind-set—the consciousness—of people during transition times that will be challenged and, it is hoped, found responsive to the challenge. Human consciousness—how one perceives the world and our part in the world—needs to evolve in order to better adapt to the requirements of a changing world (see chapter 4). In what may be deemed a remarkable coincidence (or agreement), the emerging planetary change seems to be in fortuitous alignment with the date predicted by the Mayan civilization for epochal change. The Mayan calendar indicates that our current epoch—the Age of Jaguar, the thirteenth *baktun* (a period of 144,000 days)—will come to an end on December 21, 2012. That date, according to the Mayan system, will mark the switch to a new era of planetary evolution, one that requires a radically different kind of consciousness. Although I find it difficult to prescribe an exact date for such a radical shift, I do agree that these indications portray an upcoming—and necessary—period of transformation for all life on Planet Earth.

It is important to remember that this is not the end. There never is an end; there is always transition and transformation. And the transformation requires that we, collectively and individually, participate through our own creative and positive energies.

This book is divided into three parts. Part 1, "Resilience," sets the background for how evolutionary systems operate and includes an examination of contemporary crises and the critical impacts we face as a global society. It ends with a look at how our social lives are being presently affected and some of the responses now being witnessed.

Part 2, "Readaptation," examines how these changes will affect us psychically, mentally, and practically. I first talk about the need to use the physical changes as transitional catalysts toward developing new modes of perception. In short, we need to use them to bring into being new faculties of perception—*a new mind for a new world*. Later chapters in this section discuss some of the findings in the new sciences of quantum mechanics and biophysics and how this information can help us understand our inherent connection to not only the processes unfolding around us but also our relationship to each other in these evolving times. The renewal of our perceptual structures can act as a constructive response to the social dislocation and the social disturbances that will occur as old global structures break up and fail to provide for our comfort.

Part 3, "Renewal," is the final section of the book and discusses how all the aforementioned changes are a lead-up to a spurt in human social and spiritual evolution and renewal. The consequences will be that humankind will have the opportunity to manifest not only new perceptive faculties but also new value systems. The inner health of a person will become more pronounced as more is understood about how the physical and spiritual human operates. It is highly possible that more energy will become available to assist in the growth of new or latent spiritual faculties within each individual. This could spur species development toward what has been long envisioned as the "over-man"—the next stage in evolution that some have termed *homo luminous* or *homo noeticus*. Either way, there is opportunity in these transformative stages for participating in the mechanisms of one's own evolution. If anything, this is the central message of the book you now hold in your hands, that each of us can have a meaningful and conscious participation in the human evolutionary journey now unfolding. It is a very long journey, yet there are times when moments are more crucial, when critical phases become available as trigger points. We are now passing through one of these epochal windows. It may very well be the most significant period our human species will ever experience: *these are, if nothing else, momentous times*. And we need to realize and accept, deep within ourselves, that this change is not a punishment, nor is it something good or bad. It is a natural part of evolutionary change, and with this change comes tremendous potential for a positive shift in species consciousness. It is important to know that by understanding these coming changes as a part of our path, we have a road map for the next beginning phase of the journey. In other words, we can prepare for our conscious participation—without fear. It is my wish—and hope—that this journey be shared together. This book was written to serve that purpose.

A Tale to Finish

It was autumn, and the Indians of a remote reservation asked their new chief if the next winter was going to be cold or mild. Now, he was an Indian chief in a modern society, so he had never learned the old secrets, and as he watched the sky he could not predict what would happen in the near future. Anyway, to be sure, he told his tribe that the winter was going to be cold and that the members of the village would have to collect firewood to be prepared. But being also a practical leader, after a few days he had an idea: he went to the telephone cabin and called to the National Meteorology Service and asked, "Is the next winter going to be very cold?"

"It seems that the next winter will be cold enough," said the meteorologist in charge. So, the chief returned to his people and told them to collect more firewood, to be prepared.

A week later, the chief again called the National Meteorology Service and asked, "Will it be a very cold winter?"

"Yes," said the meteorologist in charge, "it is going to be a very cold winter." The chief returned again to his people and ordered them to collect all the pieces of firewood they could find.

Two weeks later, the chief called the National Meteorology Service once again and asked, "Are you absolutely sure that the next winter will be so cold?"

"Absolutely, without any doubt," the man answered. "It will be one of the coldest winters ever."

"How can you be so sure?" asked the chief.

And the meteorologist said, "All you need is to watch the Indians collecting wood like mad!"

PART ONE

RESILIENCE

INTRODUCTION TO PART ONE

The first section of this book focuses mainly on disruptive events. It is a way of laying the groundwork (the background context) to our narrative and journey. As an overview, chapter 1 examines the nature of evolutionary cycles and describes how evolution is not a gradual affair but rather is a "sleeping giant" for long periods that then wakes up to provide short, sharp shocks in the form of rapid and often radical transformative pulses. In other words, when an evolutionary cycle comes near to its end and a new one is ready to begin, a leap is required in order to achieve the next rung of the ladder. Such a leap often involves a short period of chaotic yet dynamic energy. These periods can cause disruptive events for the life of humanity. Chapter 2 discusses these events in terms of how complex systems operate, and it shows how global society is now entering a period of rapidly converging crises and that these disruptive triggers mark a moment in our history when we are in a need of a global breakthrough in order to continue our survival as a planetary species. Chapter 3 continues this theme by examining the potential social and civil unrest and the likely instability that could affect this planet. Thus, as both individuals and a collective, it is important that we manifest our resilience. We have the capacity for such resilience, and it will be required of us that we prepare ourselves for energetic variations in our everyday lives and in the world around us. These times are critical moments in the human evolutionary journey.

1
EVOLUTIONARY
TURNING POINTS

Critical Moments in the Human Journey

Nothing endures but change.
There is nothing permanent except change.
All is flux, nothing stays still.

SAYINGS OF HERACLITUS

The changes presently taking place in human and earthly affairs are beyond any parallel with historical change or cultural modification as these have occurred in the past. This is not like the transition from the classical period to the medieval period or from the medieval to the modern period. This change reaches far beyond the civilizational process itself, beyond even the human process, into the biosystems and even the geological structures of the Earth itself.

THOMAS BERRY, "THE ECOZOIC ERA"

Everything is in a constant state of change. Physical and social worlds manifest change, movement, paradoxes, ambiguities, and contradictions. This is the normal state of affairs, not the static and stationary state that we sometimes view our lives to be in. Normality—if we can use that word—is not one of stability and balance, rather, it is about the processes of flux and flow.

Historical epochs have been eras of change, yet their change is not always perceptible to those living at the time. The early years of the twenty-first century are no exception: they seem to have been, and continue to be, times of great changes, shifts, developments, and fluctuations. The world seems to be incessantly in flux and susceptible to impacts, whether local, global, or nonterrestrial. We live on a planet that is constantly adapting to social, environmental, solar, and cosmic influences. The past contains its own examples of a world of flows, of dynamic change and processes of noncausality. The Chinese Book of Changes (often referred to as the I Ching) and the works of early Greek thinkers such as Heraclitus show attempts at integrating processes, movement, and unexpected phenomena into accounts of the everyday world.[1]

Today, because of technological advancements, it is possible to learn more about what is happening in the global world while simultaneously knowing less about the unpredictability of global processes of change. It has been an ongoing human project to learn about how the natural and social world operates and to gain mastery, or at least knowledge and control, of these processes. From gods to guardians, the responsibility for and interdependency with our physical world has induced a need to know. Philosophy too has had to deal with the ebb and flow of dynamic processes and energies. Instability and unpredictability are reminiscent of Friedrich Nietzsche's view of the world. As he writes in *The Will to Power*:

> And do you know what "the world" is to me? Shall I show it to you in my mirror? This world: a monster of energy, without beginning, without end; a firm, iron magnitude of force . . . as a play of forces and waves of forces, at the same time one and many, increasing here and at the same time decreasing there; a sea of forces flowing and rushing together, eternally changing, eternally flooding back . . . out of the simplest forms striving toward the most complex, out of the stillest, most rigid, coldest forms toward the hottest, most turbu-

lent, most self-contradictory, and then again returning home to the simple out of this abundance.[2]

The world is, and has always been, a monster of energy, a magnitude of force, as Nietzsche recognized. Yet only relatively recently has mainstream thinking accepted dynamism, unpredictability, and uncertainty into accepted thought. Again, the social consensus of reality limits its own perception toward what it views as the limits of reality. So the world becomes what it has been perceived to be. Social institutions have generally benefited from notions of stability, regularity, and constancy. These terms helped to formulate social cohesion and order, thus strengthening class and religious structures. Science too was mechanical in its Newtonian view of a clockwork universe. Localized living made it almost impossible for people to view their lives as anything but orderly and often monotonous. The ebb and flow of today's global processes were beyond the ken of most people living within their own historical epoch. The only exceptions to this were perhaps the merchants who navigated the early global networks of trade. Yet today's globally connected world, with its instant delivery of news and information through the Internet, brings home the chaos, dynamism, flows, processes, and interrelationships that appear to be in continual phases of negotiation and complexification. The future too appears to be increasingly unpredictable, uncertain, and often on the fringes of instability. So are we heading toward too much complexity? And what happens when things become too complex? This is exactly the point where the jump or the fall often occurs—the "chaos point" for transformation.[3] In other words, the moment for paradigm shift.

The paradigm shift theory proposed by Thomas Kuhn describes how revolutions in thought occur not through a gradual and smooth process but rather when current patterns of thought encounter anomalies that cannot be explained by the present way of thinking. When enough anomalies have emerged to throw accepted ideas into a state of crisis, those amassed anomalies themselves form the core of the new body of accepted knowledge, thus affecting a jump to a new paradigm of thought. In other words, in order to regain stability with the parameters of human thinking, the once-excluded anomalies are welcomed into the house of human knowledge.[4]

Similarly, in biology there are parallel findings. American paleobiologists Stephen Jay Gould and Niles Eldredge, in a theory they term punctuated equilibrium, describe how evolution occurs not as a smooth process but rather when a dominant group within a species is environmentally destabilized and overtaken by a subspecies on the periphery. Again, the dynamic jump manifests here within species evolution.[5] At critical moments in any evolutionary system, there exist opportunities for tremendous change. If this wasn't so, we wouldn't be here. In fact, there would be no oxygen to breath, for one of the earliest recorded jumps in our evolutionary history occurred with the near-death decision of our bacterial ancestors.

The latest species in a long line of human development—*Homo sapiens sapiens*—owes its existence to a great many causal and interdependent events. In particular, a huge debt is owed to the ancient bacteria that first formed on our Earth some two billion years ago.[6] Having blanketed Earth, the bacteria proceeded to use up available resources in such processes as fermentation, photosynthesis, and respiration. Within time (evolutionary time that is), the bacteria changed tactics due to a dwindling of resources and began to invade each other—a phase that has been referred to as bacterial imperialism.[7] This phase led to a renewed crisis in bacterial survival because, like human activity today, their early attempts at globalization, with huge bacterial colonies, were based on competitive exploitation of each other. The solution, after the extinction of great amounts of bacteria, was to evolve a cooperative division of processes in what we now know as the nucleated cell. This formation required each bacterial cell to donate a part of its own DNA to a central, collective DNA storage that became important for the nucleated cell's overall functioning. In other words, the natural survival mechanisms inherent in bacterial growth over Planet Earth evolved the first processes of cooperation and exchange. Competition for resources was an extinction strategy. This new development became the first experiment in DNA exchange and recombination.

This need for cooperation and exchange among bacterial cells spurred a creative emergence in information transfer systems. Evolution biologist Elisabet Sahtouris makes an interesting comparison by saying that "by evolving ways to exchange DNA information among themselves around the world, we can rightly say they invented the first worldwide web of information exchange . . . information exchange gave bacteria close relationships that facilitated both competition and cooperation in communal living."[8]

Microbiology shows us that the human network of information communications and information transfer is as old as life itself. Also, it shows us that there comes a time when a species can be faced with an extinction threat, and in order to evolve further, a leap must be undertaken. This manifests as an evolutionary jump that can usher in accelerated rates of growth and capacity. In terms of our bacterial ancestors, the "decision" to cooperate on dwindling resources resulted in the birth of the nucleated cell and the creation of DNA transfer and recombination. These significant steps became the foundation for later multicellular organisms, and from those steps the human species emerged into physical being.

Microbiology also shows us that bacteria formed what can be called perhaps the earliest global brain, prior to human global communications. Further, we see that information sharing has been a basic property of life, from the time of Earth's earliest life forms to the present day. The sharing of information, then, is nothing less than an evolutionary prerequisite for survival, and information spurts have been instrumental in the sociocultural evolution of human systems. This occurred not as a continual, smooth process, but rather (as in punctuated equilibrium) in sudden bursts of energy and renewal interspersed with long periods of stasis.

HUMAN SOCIAL AND CULTURAL EVOLUTION

Although a sweeping statement, it can be said that some forms of human societal structures developed from a nomadic tribal-based grouping, then to settled communities with husbandry skills, to feudal systems of specialized role positions, and finally to the modern, complex structures of economic and political states. Yet what underlying force provided the impetus and energy for these developments? For any system to develop, it is necessary to harness external energies, much the same as the human body requires an intake of oxygen and minerals (food and water) to fuel the body. In the case of the general development of human societies, it has been argued that technology is the factor that has enabled societies to access and consume increasing amounts of external energy for continual development.[9] Yet technology does not necessarily mean microelectronics or computerized devices; technology can be anything that facilitates greater interaction between humankind and nature. By providing greater access to the resources of nature, technology thus becomes a major agent for stimulating social change.

Again using broad generalizations, it has been recorded that a shift occurred from the Palaeolithic era, with the limited use of kindling and fire along with simple hand tools, to the Neolithic era, where more sophisticated tools such as saws, hammers, and sickles came into use. Thus, some ten thousand years ago, the human community emerged through the introduction of new social structures, craft skills such as weaving and pottery, and the domestication of local food crops and animals. This saw the early development of village life. Out of this village life emerged the early cities of the world along the Tigris, Euphrates, Nile, Indus, Yellow, and Mekong rivers. Later came the civilizations of the Mayas on the Yucatan peninsula, the Toltecs in Mesoamerica, and the Incas on the high plateaus of Peru. Western civilization had its beginnings in Sumer, some five thousand years ago, and from that we eventually derived our European civilization. However, except for the transference from iron to steel, the eight thousand years from the Neolithic era to the Industrial Revolution saw little in the way of dramatic innovations in basic agricultural tools. In one sense, we can say that this was a slower period in human culture in terms of rapid jumps, that is, within the evolutionary scale of things.

Yet the last one thousand years have seen a noticeable change in societal organization as technological innovations have been amplified by the rapid growth in transportation and communication, especially in the service of the rising, dominant economic powers and military conquest. Empires that had sustained themselves for centuries, especially those along fertile river stretches, such as along the Nile, Tigris, and Euphrates rivers, were also sites of tremendous fluctuations, destabilizations, power struggles, and military conquests. Likewise, technological developments in the Middle Ages enabled multiple wars, personal and private conquests, and the repositioning of various belief systems through dominant local social structures. In fact, war can be seen as a trigger influence toward greater exchange of social energy. Roberto Artigiani notes, "War could help produce information structuring societies. War, like trade, is simply a means for exchanging energy, matter, and information between human groups. . . . But war allows us to see the effects of exchanges more clearly."[10]

With the advent of the Industrial Revolution (and the use of steam-powered technology), a radical upheaval was triggered in working, living, and production practices that revolutionized Western societies. With each technological revolution, more energies began to be accessed, stored, and used than had been in the preceding epoch. This helped to fuel the growth of emerging human societies and cultures. Developments were tied to the ever-greater efficiency in the use of energy, materials, and information.[11] Yet technology was not the only factor in creating sociocultural triggers for development: information too is a form of energy. The planetary global brain also requires that perceptual energies develop, with rapid periods of acceleration, in order to produce a finer quality of mental energy.

Human scientific investigation, spurred on by technological innovations, ultimately yielded the Enlightenment. This major cultural shift, and later the use of the printing press, the Reformation, and other major cultural transformations recorded by history, all helped to accelerate human progress.[12]

Cultural information within human societies can be passed down through the generations so that each successive generation can benefit from what has passed before it. The externalization of the inner world of the human can be seen as far back as the period of Cro-Magnon man, who replaced Neanderthal man with a culture that was rich in complex symbols and imagery. Late Palaeolithic man showed the ability, through realistic paintings of animals, to externalize and represent the world around him, in other words, to project information that was in his mind. The Neolithic revolution, which saw the domestication of agriculture, then gave rise to a new stage in the externalization of information.[13] And since the time when the earliest tool technology was used, the possession of such knowledge has acted as a catalyst for the emergence of a language system and a means of culturally preserving such innovative information.

The earliest known examples of recorded writing are called proto-cuneiform, as they precede the use of cuneiform characters (from the Latin *cuneus,* or wedge). The oldest examples are dated between 3200 and 3100 BCE and were found at the site of the great temple in the Sumerian city of Uruk: they mix pictographs, symbols, and emblematic signs and are perhaps the earliest known example of human society storing and coding information.[14] Following on from this, what is sometimes referred to as the Classical Age is said to have begun with the creation of the Greek alphabet, as it constituted one of the earliest forms of writing capable of capturing the nuances of speech. The modern alphabet was undoubtedly a major step in that it allowed for the transmission and reflexivity of human thought. Following on from the Classical Age is what has been termed the Modern Age; this era in human sociocultural development eventually gave us the Renaissance and the rise of printing. The Gutenberg printing press was a dramatic revolution in that it made available, often for the first time, information within the public domain. And this, in turn, affected the physical and physiological condition of those exposed to printed information. Not only did the general masses take up reading on a large scale, but also the very act of reading (which for Latinized Western cultures was done from left to right) stimulated parts of the human brain hitherto underused. Further, the sudden increase in a reading public put emphasis on the need for greater social organization as the written word became responsible for promoting increased individualism and instances of opposition to ruling structures (as is very much the case today).[15]

Around the same time, the acceleration of human knowledge and thinking created a worldview that was mathematical; thus was born the idea of a clockwork universe. It took until the early decades of the twentieth century for this worldview to be challenged sufficiently and for a new, rapid shift in human perceptions to occur.

The rise of quantum physics in the early part of the twentieth century signaled another significant shift in human thinking and perception. In this radical departure from a deterministic and linear world, structures once assumed fixed and orderly were challenged by notions of waves and flow, and uncertainty and indeterminacy. Thus was the shift made into a quantum world, where nothing could ever again be taken for granted about the workings of the universe.

Suddenly, as if overnight, the new physics was telling us that the world, and the universe, was not as we had previously thought; it was a lot more unstable, complex, and inherently unknowable. And with this development came the birth, in the mid-twentieth century, of what has been called the Information Age.[16] Not only did we see the emergence of the computer at this time but also a revolution in how information could be stored, transmitted, and shared—faster, and with more power, than at any other time in known human history.

The latter half of the twentieth century saw most human societies shift toward an increasingly interconnected global world, a world characterized by communications, interconnectedness, and interdependency. The external flow of information has helped to catalyze not only human knowledge but also individual perceptions. The present era, in some ways, is the culmination of the evolution of information. It represents the continuation of the information flow from the genetic to the neural—from the genetic information processes that helped to organize biological life, to the neural and cultural information that assisted in the growth of human societies, to the tool-using tribes, to the present. Yet it is important to understand that external development in the evolution of information is a mirror to the growth in conscious intelligence. In *The Third Millennium: Living in the Posthistoric World,* Ken Carey writes, "Yet new information technology merely reflects the field of intelligence that is growing upon the earth. It does not cause it. The leaves and branches of the vine reflect an inner genetic design, yet they are neither its architect nor its cause. There is no breakthrough in information processing that does not have its corresponding realization in human consciousness."[17]

We have now arrived at a critical moment, not only for the future development of complex human societies but also for the future evolution of our entire species. From the information available to us today (genetic, neural, and cultural), we will be required to make some crucial decisions as to what degree we participate in the mechanisms of our own evolution. For perhaps the first time in recorded human history, we stand at the gateway toward accepting a knowing participation in the conscious evolution of humanity as well as the evolution of human consciousness.

However, the processes of evolution do not play out in a vacuum. The notion of *containment* is a purely human one. For too long, we, as the human species, have viewed ourselves as an evolutionary accident squatting on a rock hurtling through space. Further, many of us have been feeling that what happens to us as a species is between us and our "rock," nothing more. Even today, debates over climatic variations and Earth changes consider them the consequences of human actions alone. Such myopic views are full of hubris over the significance of human life while neglecting the larger arena of life: the cosmos. Conditions on Earth do not occur as events in isolation but rather in relation to a larger context of living systems. In our case, Earth responds, adapts, and reacts to stimuli, impulses, and conditions within our solar system and beyond. Earth has, in the very least, an energetic and gravitational interdependency with other bodies within our solar family. Astrological studies and insights, which have been used for millennia by ruling castes and royal houses for correlating human actions, are not mere whimsical fancies for the fervent few. When the cosmic winds blow, so to speak, Earth shakes and vibrates like a ball floating on the ripples of a lake: it is only that most people have no experience of this.

CYCLES AND GREAT AGES

Cycles are everywhere a part of living systems—universal, solar, planetary, and in nature. As above, so below. Again, most of the time we do not recognize that cycles are occurring around us constantly. We live our lives immersed in daily, weekly, seasonal, and annual rhythmic cycles, as well as biological, tidal, and astrological cycles. Circadian cycles of roughly twenty-four hours govern how our bodies function and are catalyzed by daylight. Menstrual cycles average twenty-eight days, and the ebb and flow of tidal waters reflect the changing positions of the moon and sun relative to Earth.

Solar cycles of solar magnetic activity are characterized by the frequency of sunspots appearing on the sun. The average duration of the sunspot cycle is about eleven years, with the solar maximum and the solar minimum indicating the relative phases of the cycle. These sunspot cycles are what produce variations in our solar weather, sometimes disrupting (or even knocking out) global communications. They are also responsible for the frequency of sun flares and coronal mass ejections and the intensity of solar radiation (see chapter 2). Solar cycles are also known to indirectly adjust the intensity of high-energy galactic cosmic rays entering the solar system. These solar cycles, to a very large degree, affect how life on Earth exists, survives, and develops.

Thus, cycles are significant, and the most significant are the ones that originate off-planet, in other words, the ones that are nonterrestrial. As mentioned, when the cosmic winds blow, Earth shakes and vibrates. And knowing when great cycles are occurring, when their peaks and troughs are, helps in understanding when periods of transition are at hand. Some periods can offer opportunities for accelerated growth, while others can signify a phase of disruption.

It appears that we are now within a part of a cycle where a greater number of events have their impact simultaneously, thus affecting a period for more pronounced physiological change. Such eras have been known to exist as part of what are called great ages. Examples of such great ages include the Great Year (the precession of the equinoxes), measured to last about 25,765 years, and the Yugas of Hindu philosophy (epochs within a cycle of four ages: Satya, Treta, Dvapara, and Kali). Such ages are part of known cycles within celestial motion, and within these macrocycles occur significant periods of planetary change. It is for this reason that many Earth myths contain references to celestial cycles and many great civilizations have made attempts to map these transitions. According to the book *Hamlet's Mill,* a work of comparative mythology, there are more than two hundred myths and folk stories from more than thirty ancient cultures that refer to the Great Year, the precession of the equinoxes.

Celestial calendars have been the central structure for many past civilizations, whose rituals and social lifestyles were arranged in resonance with celestial cycles. Likewise, various cultures would embed this information into their songs, dances, and other audio-visual forms that were used to store and transmit the knowledge pertinent to the survival and growth of their culture. One of the most famous of such calendars is the Tzolk'in calendar, which is the 260-day calendar used by the Mayan civilization. Today this calendar holds great significance for many people, who feel that it signals the end of the present age, to occur on December 21, 2012, which will usher in great transformational change. Although largely unknown at the time, it is likely that much social change has occurred on our Earth in relation to celestial cycles, for their energetic effects on planetary systems have been significant.

Likewise, the cyclic nature of cultural civilizations—the birth, self-expression, decay, and death sequence—has been described by historians such as Arnold Toynbee and Pitirim Sorokin. Toynbee himself said that civilization was a movement and not a condition, a voyage and not a harbor. It has been observed that civilizations display a form of a life cycle in which eight years will be the period of gestation of a culture, eighty years the period of its physical self-expression, and eight hundred years the total of its life. At the end of eight hundred years, it will die.[18] Eighty years is thus viewed as the period of a culture's peak expression, as expressed in its invention and creativity. And similar to other generational cycles, the generations of culture also overlap, with a new culture beginning long before its parent culture has died.

We can see a succession of cultures—a family tree of generational cultures—in the following way. It can be said that Egyptian civilization gave birth to Greek civilization through such intermediaries and influences as Solon, Thales, and Pythagoras. And it is well known that the Greek civilization parented that of Rome through the Epicurean and Stoic influences. From the Roman Empire, we have the birth of the early Christian civilization, which was heavily influenced through the teachings of Jesus Christ and the New Testament gospels. Monastic Christendom, which followed, was represented by such figures as Saint Benedict and the rise in monastic orders. Some see this phase as a stopgap, a dark age, in the transmission of cultures that signified a latent period until arrival of the medieval Christian culture. The medieval Christian culture was marked by the work of the cathedral builders, who constructed, for example, the major European cathedrals at Cluny, Chartres, Rheims, and Mont-Saint-Michel, and of course, by the Crusades. The next cultural epoch to emerge was that of the Renaissance, in Florence circa 1450. This era was populated by such notable figures as Cosimo de' Medici, Leonardo da Vinci, and others of the intelligentsia. This influence spread to Cambridge, Oxford, and many other centers of learning and education. The Renaissance was the precursor to the Western culture of today, which is marked by its high level of development for electronics and technology. In regard to our present civilization, it has been said that its gestation period of roughly eight years lasted from 1859 (from Darwin's *The Origin of Species*) until 1865 (the unification of the United States after the Civil War) and that it reached its peak of development (after approximately eighty years) around 1935, with road and air transportation, radio, and cinema.[19] Now come many decades of decay as evolution is accelerating toward a new culture in gestation, with profound implications for our global societies (and humanity, too).

Turning to a more microscopic level, American historians William Strauss and Neil Howe have done extensive research on sociohistorical cycles (from an American perspective, although the findings can be indicative of social cycles in general). They write in their book *The Fourth Turning* that history is marked by cycles of eighty to one hundred years, which match the lifespan of most human beings. Further, these cycles are marked by four generations of twenty to twenty-five years each that show remarkable consistency throughout history. Each of these four generations is noted to belong to one of four archetypes, which are repeated sequentially. In cyclic patterns, particular generational archetypes emerge to dominate the personality of each particular era. Within these cycles also reoccur patterns of increased spiritual activity and secular crises. Strauss and Howe write:

> Turnings last about 20 years and always arrive in the same order. Four of them make up the cycle of history, which is about the length of a long human life. The first turning is a High, a period of confident expansion as a new order becomes established after the old has been dismantled. Next comes an Awakening, a time of rebellion against the now-established order, when spiritual exploration becomes the norm. Then comes an Unraveling, an increasingly troubled era of strong individualism that surmounts increasingly fragmented institutions. Last comes the Fourth Turning, an era of upheaval, a Crisis in which society redefines its very nature and purpose.[20]

The authors state that U.S. society is now entering a "fourth turning," the winter period of social cycles. Previous crisis periods in American history included the American Revolutionary Era (1773–1794), the Civil War (1860–1865), and the twin crises of the Great

Depression and World War II (1929–1945). All these previous periods were marked by major warfare, which, Strauss and Howe state, is indicative of crisis cycles.

> A CRISIS arises in response to sudden threats that previously would have been ignored or deferred, but which are now perceived as dire. Great worldly perils boil off the clutter and complexity of life, leaving behind one simple imperative: The society must prevail. This requires a solid public consensus, aggressive institutions, and personal sacrifice. People support new efforts to wield public authority, whose perceived successes soon justify more of the same. Government governs, community obstacles are removed, and laws and customs that resisted change for decades are swiftly shunted aside. A grim preoccupation with civic peril causes spiritual curiosity to decline. Public order tightens, private risk-taking abates, and crime and substance abuse decline. Families strengthen, gender distinctions widen, and child-rearing reaches a smothering degree of protection and structure. The young focus their energy on worldly achievements, leaving values in the hands of the old. Wars are fought with fury and for maximum result.[21]

The authors inform us that each crisis era begins with a catalyst, a "startling event (or sequence of events) that produce a sudden shift in mood." Such catalysts are often a "series of sparks" that give rise to "a new sense of urgency about institutional dysfunction and civic vulnerability." The Black Tuesday stock market crash of 1929, which is noted as the catalyst for the Depression and World War II, ushered in the crisis years from 1929 to 1945. That we now live in a global society of increased economic, military, and social interdependency makes it clear that what are crisis periods for U.S. society will now also be critical triggers for the rest of the global community. An economic crash in the U.S. financial system, for example, could herald a global financial meltdown of unprecedented proportions. And we are already experiencing this financial domino effect in world markets today, especially because many emerging financial powers, such as China, hold a large amount of American foreign currency in reserve and serve as creditors on an incredible global U.S. debt. When the trigger comes—when the sparks fly—the global system will manifest a complex set of cumulative effects that will magnify regional crises into total and comprehensive international crises. And as the next chapter will show, global society is currently on the precipice of a range of impacts that are ready to shake the threads of our social web virtually simultaneously.

As a recap, in this chapter, I have argued that historical processes manifest as long periods of little change interspersed with periods of rapid change. Such moments of rapid change, or revolutions, can often be as much disruptive as they are progressive, leading to collapse as well as development. At such times, societies show increased sensitivity to opportunities for growth, when increased energy (often from the disruptions themselves) can be used to catalyze accelerated social evolution. What this shows is that sociocultural evolution on Planet Earth is not smooth, necessarily an improvement, or inevitable. In the words of Nobel Laureate Ilya Prigogine, "In accepting that the future is not determined, we come to the end of certainty."[22]

A Tale to Finish: The High Road

A long time ago in the small town of Hondo, Texas, there used to live a cowboy nicknamed H. R. One day someone asked him, "H. R, why do people call you H. R.?"

He replied, "'H. R.' stands for 'High Road,' but people do not understand."

"They do not understand what?" the other asked.

"Well you see," said H. R., "people want to take the high road because it makes them feel superior. Some people think that the high road is the road less traveled, and they believe it will help them avoid roadblocks, road rage, and low riders. Some even try the middle road. The fact is that there is no such a thing as a high or low road. Actually, there are no roads at all! We are the high road, and the low road, the only road. That is why I call myself H. R.: the High Road."

2
CONVERGING CRISES
Toward Humanity's Tipping Point?

The fatal metaphor of progress, which means leaving things behind us, has utterly obscured the real idea of growth, which means leaving things inside us.

G. K. CHESTERTON,
ENGLISH WRITER, 1874–1936

Our present civilization is based materially on an extraordinarily successful technology and spiritually on practically nothing.

DENNIS GABOR, NOBEL PRIZE PHYSICIST;
INVENTOR OF HOLOGRAPHY

In this chapter, I discuss some of the present and upcoming crises that could, through a combination of complex, interplaying events, create some potentially dangerous shifts, or tipping points, for life as we have come to know it. It is my understanding that global humanity presently stands on the verge of an unprecedented shift toward drastic social change. And this sudden change may come about amid a melting pot of social vulnerabilities and breakdown points. In fact, we only need to look at some of the evidence around us to know that all is not well. On one hand, we are nearing a cusp in how we have abused our natural environment through a combination of deliberate human interventions (e.g., climatic and environmental pollution, depletion of natural resources, unsustainable population growth, accelerated urban expansion). On the other hand, there is a growing feeling within many people that something is seriously out of balance with the present human condition. It may manifest in how people interact within their everyday social life and how their bodies feel drained of energy or increasingly "out of sync," or there may be a rise in instinctual, gut feelings without a clear knowing of why.

In all of these cases, there is a considerable recognition that human progress has become disharmonious. At such moments, we feel our vulnerability more clearly, and when our human, social, and environmental systems are vulnerable, they are wide open to be shifted through even the smallest of impacts. Like a mountain of sand that we used to build as children on the beach, that one final grain placed at the top could be enough to topple the whole mountain. The new sciences of chaos theory and complex systems call such periods moments of self-organized criticality. Such critically self-organized systems might become catastrophically unstable if simultaneous impacts leave them unable to organize and maintain their self-organized state. This has occurred previously in the history of human societies, and the results have shown a trend of resounding collapse.[1]

I contend that our planetary human society, now implicated together through willing and coerced forms of globalization, has entered such a moment of heightened criticality. The future therefore will not be the same as it has been, nor can it continue along current linear trends. As I hope to explain in this chapter, global society now finds itself in new territory and on the verge of major and drastic local and global transformations.

STRESSED TO THE MAX

Increasingly, we are reading headlines about extreme weather and geological events: droughts in China and North America, drastic flooding in Australia, erratic snowfall in Europe, increased cyclone activity, seismic shakes across many regions, increased volcanic activity, and devastating hurricanes hitting tropical coastlines. On top of this, we hear about impending oil shortages and peak-oil arguments, avian flu and novel swine flu cases on the rise, acts of international aggression, domestic security incidents, and the list goes on. It is not surprising, then, that many of us feel instinctively that things are out of control and that our societies are facing a very possible collapse. Our global social systems are stressed to the max already, and what differentiates a minor crisis from a major one is when vulnerable social systems are hit by multiple shocks simultaneously. We are, in two words, *stressed out*. Already, some social commentators are making parallels between ancient Rome and our modern global civilization. And Armageddon scenarios are rife with supporters and missionaries. There is a zeitgeist of change permeating through the climate of our times, and the bandwagon is being seized by activists, moralists, and politicians of all creeds. The danger here is more one of misinformation and manipulation than it is of ignorance. Change can be feared, and fear is the exemplar of political and social control. The climate of change that I wish to highlight throughout this book is one of *positive transformation*. That there will be system collapse is, to some degree, inevitable. As described in chapter 1, this is the nature of evolutionary change. Yet if sufficient numbers of people can awaken to the changes (to wake up from the magician's hypnosis, as in Gurdjieff's tale), then the change need not be so traumatic. It is a question of preparation, adaptation, and resilience. Yet why am I so sure that dramatic change is upon us?

Leading sociologists have shown that societies are far more likely to break down when they're overloaded by converging stresses—for example, rapid population growth, resources depletion, and economic decline.[2] As the quality and quantity of stresses increase, society tends to respond (in the same way as most living systems) by making its internal institutions more complex. As a state, nation, or civilization increases its level of internal complexity, more energy is required to stabilize the system and maintain its working capacity. In other words, the complexity of any system must be regularly fed by an appropriate degree of available energy and resources. Not only does this strategy cause a great strain on resources, but it also makes the efficiency of the system so sensitive that it becomes more vulnerable to shocks. This efficiency not only limits the flexibility of the system but also ensures that the system's high degree of connectedness helps any shock travel farther and faster across the system. The overall net effect is that the system becomes more rigid and frail. In other words, it loses its resilience. Anthropologist and historian Joseph A. Tainter, in his book *The Collapse of Complex Societies*, notes how these very same principles could be seen as triggers for the collapse of the Mayan and Roman civilizations.[3] The significant trigger for societal collapse was not solely environmental mismanagement, but more important, the rate of return of energetic investments required to maintain the level of social complexity. In a worrying comparison, Tainter sees that the energetic returns on our present investments are diminishing, making our modern global world open to the same type of stresses that were responsible for the collapse of prior civilizations.

Canadian sociologist T. Homer-Dixon notes that the rapid growth of the Western globalization project has ensured that humanity now faces a future where disturbances and shocks feed back on a planetary scale.

> In the last half-century, largely because of the enormous growth and relentless integration of the world's economy, humankind and the natural environment it exploits have evolved into a single socioecological system that encompasses the planet. This system has become steadily more connected and economically efficient. Partly as a result, a financial crisis, a terrorist attack, or a disease outbreak can now have almost instantaneous destabilizing effects from one side of the world to the other. The system has also developed increasingly severe internal pressures. . . . Managing these pressures demands steadily more complex institutions and technologies and, in turn, steadily higher inputs of high-quality energy.[4]

The concern here, as can be gleaned from the final sentence in the above quote, is that just when we need a plentiful and cheap supply of energy, the world is entering an energy crisis where the supply of abundant cheap energy (oil and natural gas) is in a critical phase. This helps to explain the recent shifts in the geopolitical "great game" to secure precious energy supplies and routes. Our global predicament is that just when our complex sociopolitical systems need energy the most, we find ourselves entering a period of decline in terms of abundant and cheap high-quality energy. In the second decade of the twenty-first century, most of the world's oil-producing nations have passed their peak. However, the significance of the peak-oil debate is not about running out of oil, rather, it is about the potential collapse of a world economy faced by the prospect of no further oil-fueled growth. The magnitude of this dilemma is beyond the comprehension of many, yet very few people (and certainly not our politicians) are discussing or even acknowledging the significance of this situation—and it is of epochal importance.

To put it simply, just as we are in dire need for more energy to feed our global family, not only does the food supply begin to diminish, but also the quality of that food declines. It's just not sustainable to feed more on less. It will rapidly become increasingly more difficult to sustain our present level of global complexity because our critical fuel supplies (including food and water as well as fossil fuels) will be insufficient for present and future levels. Looking at the situation in this way, it seems inevitable, then, that change will be upon us. And if change is not implemented by ourselves in a way that is manageable and sustainable, then change will be forced upon us in a succession of sharp shocks. We are, it seems, unable to get off this unsustainable spiral. Homer-Dixon says, "We find it impossible to get off this upward escalator because our chronic state of denial about the seriousness of our situation—aided and abetted by powerful special interests that benefit from the status quo—keeps us from really seeing what's happening or really considering other paths our world might follow. Radically different futures are beyond imagining. So we stay trapped on a path that takes us toward major breakdown."[5]

The breakdown, however, may also be the catalyst required in order to make the breakthrough. Often, the shifts between different kinds of epochs require disruptive energy, if only at times to clear away the brushwood, to sweep the house clean for new occupancy. This may, however, sound somewhat flippant when involving the lives of thousands—if not millions—of people. Evolution, though, tends to operate at a much larger macroscale, which we must acknowledge. We do, after all, have our own house to get in order before we can rightly throw stones.

It is likely that the upcoming years will mark the beginning of a shift from our present, modern (largely Western) global industrial project toward another kind of societal model. Just exactly what type of civilization will emerge remains to be seen because it will require that we allow our own new mind to be a part of the process. First, however, we need to discern what are the converging crises on the horizon.

CONVERGING CRISES

Some very powerful forces around the world are beginning to impact simultaneously on environmental, social, and cultural planetary systems. When I say "beginning to," I speak in broader terms, for these forces have been brewing for a number of decades and are, in fact, the culmination of the long, drawn-out process of the history of human progress. The recent complex array of problems have been raised, talked about, alluded to, shouted about, and warned of for the better half of the twentieth century. Yet so few people were actually told of these issues in the mainstream media. One of the active institutions, the Club of Rome (founded in 1968), was established to adopt a global approach to the problems of a world growing into a singular planetary system. Its stated premise was to focus on issues of a "longer-term perspective" than governments and to seek "a deeper understanding of the interactions within the tangle of contemporary problems—political, economic, social, cultural, psychological, technical and environmental," which they termed *world problematique*.*[6] The Club of Rome raised considerable public attention with its controversial report *The Limits to Growth* (1972).

---

*The Club of Rome defines *world problematique* as "the massive and untidy mix of interrelated difficulties and problems that forms the predicament in which humanity finds itself."

This infamous report predicted that economic growth could not continue as it was because it would run into problems of resource scarcity. At the time, this was anathema to the pundits of continued growth and profits. Today, the report's authors have reached a revised conclusion that states, "Human use of many essential resources and generation of many kinds of pollutants have already surpassed rates that are physically sustainable. Without significant reductions in material and energy flows, there will be in the coming decades an uncontrolled decline in per capita food output, energy use, and industrial production."[7]

The problem today, say the authors, requires that we start to transcend our own self-imposed and limiting beliefs and mind-sets. To not do so will result in "not only possible but certain" collapse "within the lifetimes of many who are alive today." This is the science and hard fact behind the almost inevitable change that is upon us. For those people who prefer to assess the data before making their conclusions, the evidence is already out there, and it is culminating faster as each day passes. However, it is the premise of this book that such changes are evolutionary mechanisms for growth. Regardless of whether we agree that the changes have their origins in physical or metaphysical sources (or a combination of both), the outcome is largely shared by both parties. What is of paramount importance is how we, as a collective species, react, respond, and adapt to these changes that are thrust upon us. To react in fear and anxiety will serve to increase the chaos around us, whereas the breakthrough scenario requires us to be positive about using the disruptions as opportunities for growth. For too long, we have allowed our own perceptions, beliefs, and mental patterns to be our greatest enemy. To all effects and purposes, we have long been fighting ourselves. As Alexander King and Bertrand Schneider write in *The First Global Revolution,* "It would seem that humans need a common motivation, namely a common adversary, to organize and act together in the vacuum; such a motivation must be found to bring the divided nations together to face an outside enemy, either a real one or else one invented for the purpose. . . . The common enemy of humanity is man."[8]

The "common motivation" needed to unite us as a species may be said to be the coming Earth changes, for nature's forces are now unraveling at unprecedented speed. Yet even with our meddling in planetary affairs, we need to understand that Earth has changed, does change, and will change, irrespective of our human actions. This does not mean that we do not contribute to some of the factors implicit within these changes; what it does infer is that we are a project within a much grander *evolutionary project,* and as such we are under the influences of forces of that we, to a large part, know nothing or very little about.

Global Climate Change

Let's be honest: despite our scientific advances we still have much to learn about how the Earth's climate and feedback systems operate. And it wouldn't be as bad if some of us, some of the time, could admit to our lack of knowledge. As it is, many of our Western societies are being driven toward uncertain (or undesirable) goals through the coercion of social consent based on the politically accepted crust of "expert" evidence. It is a path built on shaky foundations and unfortunately largely predicated on the greed of the few. In some respects, change may be a blessing—in whatever disguise it appears. And one of these disguises will come through the changing of the Earth's climate and biosphere. Temperatures are fluctuating due to feedbacks creating local warming, such as in the Arctic where recent increases in temperature have been 3–5°C over the past 30 years.[9] To the best of our recorded knowledge, major past disturbances on our planet have largely come about through changes in solar radiation and the occasional asteroid impact. Gerard Bond, a respected geologist, was convinced (before his death in 2005) that most climate change over the past ten thousand years had been driven by solar activity (sunspots and solar radiation emissions) and amplified through feedback mechanisms such as ice formation and the ocean conveyor belt. The ocean conveyor belt, sometimes referred to as the great ocean conveyor, is a large-scale ocean circulation system that conveys temperature gradients through the world's oceans by means of both deep-water and surface currents. The

Gulf Stream, for example, is said to have a considerable influence on the warmer climates of Northern and Western Europe.

What has been the general consensus, so far, is that average global temperatures have risen over the past century (by at least 0.74°C), and this could in part be explained by the higher levels of greenhouse gases in Earth's atmosphere. Greenhouse gases serve to trap the sun's rays, and as a result of this, Earth warms. The effect of this warming will change patterns of temperatures worldwide and result in a greatly increased frequency of extreme weather events.[10] Sudden and unexpected changes in Earth's climate will very likely become the most significant threat to human life and social organization on this planet. Even officials at the U.S. Pentagon announced that climate change will result in a global catastrophe costing millions of lives in wars and natural disasters. And they consider the threat to global stability to be beyond that of global terrorism.[11]

The United Nations–sponsored Intergovernmental Panel on Climate Change[12] (IPCC) 2007 Report declared that the warming of the world's climate is now "unequivocal" (and the panel is generally known to be conservative in its estimates). While this book is not a discussion on the *causes* of global climate change, it is about recognizing the very real and different physical consequences, such as the increase in Arctic temperatures, reduced size of icebergs, melting of icecaps and glaciers, reduced amount of permafrost, changes in rainfall patterns, new wind formations, droughts, heat waves, tropical cyclones, and other extreme weather events. There will be increased risks of flooding for tens of millions of people due to storms and rising sea levels, especially for those who live in the poorer southern and equatorial regions of the world, such as Bangladesh. In addition to an increased scarcity of freshwater, there may also be sudden rises in new vector-borne diseases (e.g., malaria, dengue fever) and water-borne diseases (e.g., cholera). For example, the World Health Organization calculated as early as 2000 that more than 150,000 deaths were caused each year by changes in the world's climate. Yet even these cautious interpretations do not factor in all the uncertain effects that may develop over the next few decades.[13] Today's temperature increases, if they continue, will almost certainly trigger further increases through what are known as positive feedback loops.

For example, it is possible that temperature increases could trigger the melting of Greenland's ice cap, which could result in the alteration of sea and land temperatures worldwide. It could also affect the flow of the Gulf Stream, possibly even turning it off. Such a series of diverse yet interconnected changes within Earth's environmental systems could create a vicious circle of accumulative disruption, as less heat would be reflected back from the surface of Earth. Recent geological studies of ice cores have shown that ice caps during previous glacial and interglacial periods have historically formed and disappeared with "speed and violence" rather than as gradual events.[14] Such rapid changes, which were the norm rather than the exception, have brought about very abrupt changes in Earth's temperature. The average temperatures at the time of the last Ice Age were only 5°C colder than they are today. If the West Antarctic ice sheet were to disintegrate, which is another possibility, then the sea level over this century could rise by meters rather than centimeters.* As a consequence, most human settlements located close to the ocean's edge would be washed away, resulting in massive disruption to populations around the world.[15] As one climate investigator Fred Pearce recently noted, "The big discovery is that planet Earth does not generally engage in gradual change. It is far cruder and nastier."[16]

So what does the picture of future temperature rise look like? The Stern Review† states that there is a 50 percent risk of more than a 5°C increase in temperatures by 2100. This would transform the world's physical and human geography through a 5–20 percent reduction in world consumption levels.[17] Even a global temperature increase of 3°C is completely beyond any recent experience of temperature change and would totally transform animal, plant, and human life as we know it on

---

*The Intergovernmental Panel on Climate Change predicts a sea level increase of eighteen to fifty-nine centimeters over this century.

†The Stern Review on the Economics of Climate Change was an economic report on global warming that was done for the British government.

this planet. Yet this is just one of the major impacts currently affecting our planetary life.

There is the danger that proponents of climate change could neglect other processes affecting our global state of affairs. As well as the levels of carbon dioxide and greenhouse gases, other possible contributors to conditions here on Earth include periodic variations in the sun's radiation and cyclic sunspot activity, variations in Earth's orbit and spin, volcanic geothermal activity, complex changes present within Earth's troposphere and stratosphere, and atmospheric impacts on ocean heating and currents.[18] In the recent words of James Howard Kunstler, "It may not matter anymore whether global warming is or is not a by-product of human activity, or if it just represents the dynamic disequilibrium of what we call 'nature.' But it happens to coincide with our imminent descent down the slippery slope of oil and gas depletion, so that all the potential discontinuities of that epochal circumstance will be amplified, ramified, reinforced, and torqued by climate change."[19]

These "ramified" and "reinforced" changes are global and are likely to substantially reduce the standard of living in the Westernized north and to detrimentally affect the capacity for life in poorer countries, especially as catastrophic impacts begin. The planet will endure, but many forms of human habitation will not if they are subject to abrupt change. Environmentalist and scientist James Lovelock is very clear when he says, "The real Earth does not need saving. It can, will and always has saved itself." He also says, "Our greatest efforts should go to learning how to live as well as is feasible on the soon-to-be-diminished hot Earth."[20]

It is age-old human hubris to think that we are the controllers (and saviors) of Planet Earth, to believe that all change is a consequence of our actions and that life on Earth revolves around our actions and our actions alone. Such hubris is the subject of the finest Greek tragedies, from which no one escapes unscathed. Part of our hubris is also in believing that we have the correct knowledge to assess nature's cycles upon Earth. There are now many valid arguments being put forward to suggest that we are actually heading toward a period of cooling, a new mini ice age. That is, the fluctuating increases in temperature are not permanent but are the signs of instability that occur before ice ages. Recently the support for global warming has dropped among the public as many are beginning to see this as a manipulated agenda for more carbon taxes. Such is the division and uncertainty these days that most "experts" now refer to the climatic debate as "climate change" rather than "global warming." What is certain here is that whichever way the temperature fluctuations waver, there will be change one way or the other.

Climatic tipping points are around the corner, and human activities will be forced into change. This change is likely to be dramatic and, for some, probably catastrophic. The good news is that this change could very well be our saving grace; it could provide both the energy and the stimulus, not only for renewed growth along more harmonious paths, but also for a clearing out of all our rotten inefficiencies, our old ways of thinking and behavior, and the worn-out threads that we have sown into crusty corners. Human civilizations have in the past disappeared, and it now appears that our current patterns of global civilization are arriving at a similar crossroads. This makes our *transition period* highly vulnerable and precarious as well as potentially groundbreaking and liberating.

And our present critical instability is being rocked further by a looming global energy crisis since it seems that oil (and gas) supplies around the world are about to start running down.

Peak Oil

Whether we fully realize it, most of us are reliant on a global economy that is deeply dependent on, and embedded into, the abundance of cheap oil. Most industrial, agricultural, commercial, domestic, and consumer systems are built around, and predicated on, the plentiful supply of what has been called black gold. The decline in oil production and supply, coupled with the problems of securing distribution channels, will strongly affect not only global markets but also the fundamental stability of many developed and developing nations. Already, we are witness to the first resource wars of the twenty-first century, now taking place in Middle East regions, with energy blackmail by nation-states also on the rise. So, is peak oil a reality?

The peak oil hypothesis states that the extraction of oil reserves has a beginning, a middle, and an end. And at some point, it reaches maximum output, with the peak occurring when approximately half the potential oil has been extracted. After this, oil becomes more difficult and expensive to extract as each field ages past the midpoint of its life.*[21] This does not mean that oil suddenly runs out, but the supply of cheap oil drops, and the oil extraction process becomes less profitable. In other words, the energy put into the production of oil will increasingly produce diminishing returns.[†]

Some predictions have suggested that global peak oil occurred as early as the late 1990s, while others estimate that the peak came around 2004 or 2005.[‡] More optimistic predictions, however, locate the peak around the 2020s or 2030s. In terms of new developments, the largest oil fields were discovered more than half a century ago, with the peak of oil discovery being in 1965. New fields are not being found at the same rate as they were, which makes it a fair estimate that oil production worldwide peaked around 2010.[22] And the bad news is that demand for oil is still growing as the world's population continues to rise alongside expanding needs from industrializing nations such as China and India. In fact, the International Energy Agency suggests that global demand for oil has been increasing by two million barrels a day over the last few years. This oil demand could possibly rise from the present level of around eighty million barrels a day to 125 million within the next two decades, that is, if no significant interventions occur to disrupt global

---

*Oil production typically follows a bell-shaped curve when charted on a graph, called the Hubbert curve. In 1956, M. King Hubbert, a geologist for Shell Oil, predicted that the peaking of U.S. oil production would occur around 1965 to 1970. (The actual peak was in 1970.) This became known as the Hubbert curve and Hubbert peak theory (or peak oil).

†This ratio is referred to as the energy return on energy investment.

‡Colin Campbell of the Association for the Study of Peak Oil and Gas believes the peak occurred in 2004. Kenneth S. Deffeyes says the peak came in late 2005, in his book *Beyond Oil: The View from Hubbert's Peak* (New York: Hill & Wang, 2005).

"business as usual." Yet the peak oil story is not so much about the running out of oil as it is about the collapse of social systems—and ways of life—that have been dependent for far too long on the plentiful supply of black gold. It is also about a singular planetary civilization that has no prospect of unity and growth fueled by oil. We are, in all respects, coming closer to the end of an era of life as we know it. Already we are seeing the signs of a desperate world.

Political instabilities in many oil-producing countries are creating increases in fluctuations and uncertainty in the oil supply and future energy security. This was evidenced recently by the protests in Egypt that erupted in late January 2011. Such instabilities are being reflected in the seesawing surges in oil prices that impact almost immediately on global consumers of oil, especially those people whose jobs are dependent on affordable fuel. For example, June 2008 saw tens of thousands of Spanish truckers block roads in Spain as well as on the French border. Fuel protests were also seen in the United Kingdom, Portugal, and France, bringing together different types of workers, including truckers and fishermen.[23] More worrying perhaps are the recent initiatives being taken by nation-states to secure new oil regions, potentially catalyzing new tensions for the twenty-first century.

It appears likely that the Arctic Ocean's seabed, which may hold billions of gallons of oil and natural gas,* will become the next highly contested energy region. In August 2007, Russia planted its flag 2.5 miles (four kilometers) beneath the North Pole on the ocean bed in an attempt to lay claim to an undersea formation called the Lomonosov Ridge (which Russia claims is part of Siberia's shelf).[24] And in March 2009, Russia made public, in a document published on its national security council's website, its plans to set up a military force to protect its interests in the Arctic. Russia says it expects the Arctic to become its main resource base by 2020.[25] Similarly, the United Kingdom is claiming sovereign rights over a vast area of the remote seabed off Antarctica, with an application to the

---

*This includes perhaps as much as 25 percent of the world's undiscovered reserves, according to the U.S. Geological Survey.

United Nations covering more than 386,000 square miles.*[26] It thus seems increasingly likely that climate change and the peaking of oil will provoke major new conflicts worldwide, especially in the thawing Arctic.[27]

It is almost inevitable that future oil scarcity will generate significant economic downturns, civil unrest, and more resource wars. James Howard Kunstler, an American author and social critic of urban development, considers the system's effects to be dire. He states, "At peak and just beyond, there is massive potential for system failures of all kinds, social, economic, and political. Peak is quite literally a tipping point. Beyond peak, things unravel and the center does not hold. Beyond peak, all bets are off about civilization's future."[28]

With "all bets off," the future becomes a place where uncertaintity and unpredictability can become creative forces to catalyze new and unprecedented opportunities. First, however, it appears that such interventions will be disruptive (as will be discussed in chapter 3). And when "the center does not hold," in the words of Kunstler, the urban epicenters just may be the hot spots waiting to ignite.

Urban Growth

The twenty-first century has already become the century of urbanization. In the late 1990s, the world's population was growing by about nine hundred million per decade, the largest absolute increases in human history.[29] This is equivalent to a new London every month. By the end of the twentieth century, the world population passed six billion, and it is expected to reach 9.1 billion by 2050. In 2005, urban dwellers already numbered 3.2 billion, about half of the world's population.[30] More than half the world's population now lives in urban areas, with the United Nations forecasting that 60 percent of the global population will live in cities by 2030.[31] It seems that we now inhabit an urban planet.

Already, modern cities are the largest structures ever created. There

---

*The United Kingdom's claim is in defiance of the 1959 Antarctic Treaty (of which the United Kingdom is a signatory), which states that no new claims shall be declared on the continent.

are megacities such as Tokyo, with around thirteen million residents (thirty-five million in the greater Tokyo area), and São Paulo, with around eleven million (with unofficial estimates much higher). These megacities will soon be joined by Mumbai, Delhi, Mexico City, Dhaka, Jakarta, and Lagos, as well as by New York City. This will be accompanied by the rapid growth in the number of cities of between one and ten million people. Dr. Phil Williams, a professor of International Security and strategic analyst, estimates that by 2015 "there will be 23 megacities, 19 of them in the developing world, and 37 cities with populations between 5 and 10 million."[32] Much of the flow of population around cities comes from refugees; in 1978, there were fewer than six million refugees, by 2005, there were twenty-one million, and by 2006, 32.9 million.[33] The numbers will rise further as climatic changes will displace large rural communities in what has been provocatively termed climactic genocide.[34]

Rapid urbanization in developing countries also exposes large populations to many hazards, such as shortages of clean drinking water and sanitation and increases in air pollution and airborne toxins. Most megacities within developing countries fail to meet World Health Organization standards for air quality. Rising populations also add to the global consumption of energy and raw materials and affect the environmental carrying capacity, leading toward further resource depletion. Today's cities consume three-quarters of the world's energy and are responsible for at least three-quarters of global pollution.[35] Overall, where cities were once viewed as cradles of civilization, they now produce disastrous social inequalities, and much of the twenty-first-century urban world (at least one billion people) squats in squalor in what are termed global slums.* Many such conurbations will increasingly pose manageability and security problems.

In extreme cases, some urban centers may degenerate into what have been termed feral cities. A feral city has been described by analyst Richard J. Norton as a metropolis of more than one million people where the rule

---

*For information on how there are probably two hundred thousand contemporary slums, mostly located on the edge of cities, see Davis, *Planet of Slums.*

of law has broken down. In feral cities, according to an article in *Naval War College Review,* "Social services are all but nonexistent, and the vast majority of the city's occupants have no access to even the most basic health or security assistance. There is no social safety net. Human security is for the most part a matter of individual initiative. Yet a feral city does not descend into complete, random chaos. Some elements, be they criminals, armed resistance groups, clans, tribes, or neighborhood associations, exert various degrees of control over portions of the city."[36]

Such descriptions represent the collapse of once-urban centers back into earlier forms of brute tribal law. While this may sound far-fetched for what are considered to be cities in the developed world, we should remember that our civilized concrete worlds increasingly rely on the stability and maintenance of interdependent infrastructures that are vulnerable to crashes and tipping points. After all, what would happen if a city lost its power for a number of days—or even weeks?

Recent events that come to mind include the North American electrical grid failure of 2003, where people all along the East Coast of the United States and in Ontario, Canada, experienced a massive power outage. At the time, it was the most widespread electrical blackout in history, affecting an estimated fifty-five million people. Another infrastructure collapse occurred when the World Trade Center was hit on September 11, 2001. At the time of the attack, Manhattan had, under its streets, more fiber-optic cable than was in all of Africa; also, the two main telephone switches in New York's financial district had more lines than many European nations, and there were more than 1,500 antenna structures on top of the World Trade Center's north tower.[37] The collapse of the buildings delivered a huge blow to the telecommunications infrastructure, resulting in a severe overload and a partial loss of service as well as disruption to financial data networks and storage networks.

With today's massive dependency on global communications and power infrastructures, what would happen if there were severe disruptions and loss of service? A global crash may just be in the cards, waiting to happen, if our solar generator decides to start firing.

Space Weather and Solar Storms

Most people are aware when major natural disasters strike, from hurricanes to tsunamis, yet are unaware of the impacts caused by solar geomagnetic storms. Solar storms are often visible in our night skies as dancing colors and mesmeric light displays, yet looks can easily deceive. Solar storms possess tremendous energy and power and can even travel at speeds up to five million miles per hour. They carry with them highly disruptive and potentially dangerous effects, especially for a world that is so tightly woven together with all of the possible electric connections and webs. They could conceivably knock out virtually every major system of infrastructure that we depend on: transportation, security and emergency response systems, electricity grids, financial data systems, telecommunications including satellites and other wireless networks, and most household electronic equipment. Homes could be sent into darkened silence, with not even a phone call available. We would, literally, be pushed back into the Stone Age: it would be candles and wood fires all over again. This is not science fiction: it has already happened, but our societies were not so technologically wired at the time. And thus it will happen again, and most probably soon.

The solar storm of 1859, known as the Carrington Event, was the most powerful solar storm in recorded history. On September 1, 1859, the sun expelled huge quantities of high-energy protons in a large sun flare that caused a massive coronal mass ejection that traveled directly toward Earth, taking eighteen hours (whereas usually such a journey would take three to four days). The first and second days of September saw the largest geomagnetic storm, which caused the failure of telegraph systems all over Europe and North America. Fires erupted in telegraph stations due to power surges in the telegraph wires, and in the United States, the northern lights (aurora borealis) were reportedly seen as far south as Florida.[38] This event, according to new scientific research, is said to have ripped Earth's ozone layer to a greater extent than human-made chemicals have in recent decades. If such a solar storm occurred today, it would very likely be even more damaging to the ozone and to human life as well.

And the Earth is undergoing regular yet sporadic solar bombardment.

The solar storm of March 1989 melted the transformers of the Hydro-Québec power grid, causing a blackout in Quebec, Canada, for nine hours, affecting six million customers and costing the power company more than $10 million. Similarly, the solar storms that impacted Earth between October 19 and November 7, 2003, disrupted operations at the International Space Station, as well as satellites and global communication systems, air travel and navigation systems, and power grids. The list of solar storm disruptions is a long one. It includes disruptions to sensitive satellites that cost government militaries millions each year; disruptions to military operations, as in interruptions to high-frequency radio communications during the Gulf War in 1991; disruptions to airline navigation that necessitate flight diversions to lower latitudes in order to avoid human exposure to increased solar radiation; and other related complications. Such flight diversions can cost as much as $100,000 per flight, and this value does not even take into account economic loses to passengers.[39] However, the cost to Earth-bound systems is much more severe. At present our global high-power grids act as efficient antennas, effectively channeling enormous amounts of electricity to distributed transformers. In a solar storm, a high-plasma surge could be sent along these grids, resulting in a meltdown of possibly all transformers. This new threat is now being taken seriously, with Lloyd's of London, a British insurance and reinsurance market, publishing in February 2011 the risk report "Space Weather: Its Impact on Earth and Implications for Business." This report, perhaps the first of its kind, examines the threat for disrupting businesses (energy, food, transport, communications) due to increased magnetic storms hitting Earth as the sun nears its "solar maximum" period. Today's global village, which is increasingly interdependent on technological infrastructures, is now, ironically, more vulnerable to the heightened activity from our massive generator 150 million kilometers away. In 2006 NASA launched its Solar Terrestrial Relations Observatory mission, or STEREO, to provide three-dimensional images of coronal mass ejections from the sun. Space scientists from the UK are now hoping to send a swarm of spacecraft into orbit around the sun to provide an early warning system for the huge solar explosions that are expected to interfere with the electronic equipment now prevalent throughout our technological societies on Earth.

Technological society has made itself open to potentially catastrophic solar storm impacts. A new study from the National Academy of Sciences outlines some of the potentially dire possibilities for a worst-case solar storm scenario. The report states how electrical grids are interdependent with systems that support our lives, such as water and sewage treatment plants, food delivery infrastructures, financial markets, power stations, fuel-pumping stations, and more. To have these systems rendered inoperative would be catastrophic for everyday life in developed nations: it would be a natural disaster of the most sophisticated, technological kind. According to the report, we could expect the following:

First to go—immediately for some people—is drinkable water. Anyone living in a high-rise apartment, where water has to be pumped to reach them, would be cut off straight away. For the rest, drinking water will still come through the taps for maybe half a day. With no electricity to pump water from reservoirs, there is no more after that.

There simply would be no electrically powered transportation, no trains, underground or overground. Our just-in-time culture for delivery networks may represent the pinnacle of efficiency, but it means that supermarket shelves would empty very quickly; delivery trucks could only keep running until their tanks ran out of fuel, and there would be no electricity to pump any more from the underground tanks at filling stations.

Back-up generators would run at pivotal sites, but only until their fuel ran out. For hospitals, that would mean about seventy-two hours of running a bare-bones, essential-care-only service. After that, no more modern health care. With no power for heating, cooling, or refrigeration systems, people could begin to die within days.[40, 41]

On top of this, there would be a breakdown in the distribution of essential medicines and pharmaceuticals. All those people who are weak and infirm would find life close to unbearable. According to the National Academy of Sciences report, the impact of what it terms a severe geomagnetic storm scenario could be as high as $2 trillion, with this accounting for only the first year after the storm. The report goes on to say that the recovery time would be expected to be around four to ten years.

The National Academy of Sciences report concludes that damage to national power grids and global communications systems could be catastrophic, with worse-case effects resulting in a "potential loss of governmental control of the situation."[42] Space weather and solar storms have never been more of a threat to our way of life than now. Our technological means of energy distribution effectively acts as a conduit for channeling incoming energy surges, such as described. Plasma blasts and solar energetic particles could simultaneously knock out virtually all of our modern infrastructures and severely disrupt Earth's radiation belts and all orbital systems. A powerful solar electromagnetic blast could even have the potential to disrupt the electrical management systems now ubiquitous in modern cars, effectively stranding millions of drivers. In short, a modern occurrence like the 1859 solar storm would cause significantly more extensive, and possibly catastrophic, social and economic disorder. On top of this, it now seems that we are also less protected than ever before from such solar activity.

In December 2008, the U.S. National Aeronautics and Space Administration announced that the Themis Project had detected a massive breach in Earth's magnetic field and that in the near future this would allow large amounts of solar plasma to enter Earth's magnetosphere.[43] Similarly, scientists in South Africa have already measured cracks in Earth's magnetic field that are the size of California.[44] In the past, we have always relied on Earth's magnetic field to protect us from solar storms and coronal mass ejections. Yet it now appears that there is evidence to suggest that Earth may be undergoing a magnetic pole reversal. During the course of this reversal, Earth's magnetic field will become weaker, increasing the danger from solar and stellar radiation. And the news is that we are heading for the next solar maximum peak of activity around 2012. What is even more significant is that around the same time our *transition phase* may also be given a vigorous boost of interstellar energy.

Russian geophysicist Alexey Dmitriev and his colleague Vladimir B. Baranov, using data originally gathered by the Voyager spacecraft as well as more recent data, believe that the solar system has entered a more highly energized region of space. And this extra "donation" of energy is creating "excited energy states" in all planets in our solar system as well as the sun. This turbulent region, it appears, is making the sun hotter and stormier and has already caused climate changes on several planets.

> Effects here on Earth are to be found in the acceleration of the magnetic pole shift, in the vertical and horizontal ozone content distribution, and in the increased frequency and magnitude of significant catastrophic climatic events. There is growing probability that we are moving into a rapid temperature instability period similar to the one that took place 10,000 years ago. The adaptive responses of the biosphere, and humanity, to these new conditions may lead to a total global revision of the range of species and life on Earth. It is only through a deep understanding of the fundamental changes taking place in the natural environment surrounding us that politicians, and citizens alike, will be able to achieve balance with the renewing flow of PlanetoPhysical states and processes.[45]

The authors write that the exposure to a stellar region of increased energization will affect our planet's own energetic capacity for growth, as it will result in some of Earth's systems being in a highly charged and excited state. Thus, the present situation now confronts humanity with the need to adapt to this new environment, especially since these new, highly energized conditions are not uniformly spread and often emerge as being chaotic. The capacity for living organisms to adapt and comply with the new biospheric conditions will be instrumental in how each species evolves through the transformation, according to the Russian geophysicists. Further, we are told that these "evolutionary challenges always require effort, or endurance, be it individual organisms, species, or communities." This period is thus significant in our stellar history in that we may very well be experiencing a transition stage, not only in human life but also in the "vital processes of living organisms."[46] It may signify a period for energized evolutionary growth on an individual, species, planetary, and solar scale. In other words, we are well and truly within a *shock period*. We could be quite literally heading for a cosmic-energy thunderstorm of unprecedented proportions.

Planet Earth is rapidly approaching a moment of criticality that could be a trigger for a major pulse of social transformation. According to known history, such pulses have only been experienced by humankind three or four times during the civilization phase of our evolution. These include the transition from hunter-gatherer communities to agricultural settlements, the Industrial Revolution, and the recent global communications revolution. Today, we are on the cusp of another such transformative revolution. At such moments, the chaotic energy released can be both frighteningly destructive and astonishingly creative. The question is, are we ready for it?

Let us remember the *taste* of such moments.

A Tale to Finish: The Sweetest Fruit

A man crossing a field found himself in front of a tiger. He started to run as the tiger chased after him. As the man arrived at a cliff, he stumbled and fell, yet managed to get a hold onto the roots of a wild vine as he hung over the abyss.

The tiger could smell the man, just below him, from the cliff's edge. Shaking, the man looked downward, where another tiger stood waiting to devour his body.

Two mice, a white one and a black one, began to nibble the vine slowly. The man saw a bush of appetizing strawberries. Holding onto the vine with one hand, he took some strawberries with the other.

How sweet was their flavor!

3

MOMENTS OF TURBULENCE

The Expected Disruptions of Transition

But is it possible that all the bad things going on are a reaction, a dragging undertow, to a forward movement in the human social evolution that we can't easily see? Perhaps, looking back, let's say in a century or two centuries, is it possible people will say, "That was a time when extremes battled for supremacy. The human mind was developing very fast in the direction of self-knowledge, self-command, and as always happens, as always has to happen, this thrust forwards aroused its opposite, the forces of stupidity, brutality, mob thinking?" I think it is possible. I think that this is what is happening.

DORIS LESSING,
PRISONS WE CHOOSE TO LIVE INSIDE

This book's hypothesis is that humanity might be involved in a much larger process of change, that is, a course of *grand evolutionary change.* What *is* clear is that there are multiple forces at work in these critical times. As I have so far attempted to show, there are very real physical and astrophysical impacts converging simultaneously at this time in our

Earth history. This suggests that our global Earth culture is at a tipping point, a crossroads where a *shift* is needed in order to break through, or jump, to another (higher) scale of planetary evolutionary growth. To not accomplish this may result in a breakdown scenario, which could well have occurred in the histories of civilizations past (now either forgotten or relegated to the annals of myths and legends).

In the language of complex systems, when multiple interdependent and connected systems reach a peak of maximum complexity, they require extra external energy in order to jump up to a level of increased complexity.[1] This ensures the survival of the system, much like how hunter-gatherers shifted into more organized forms of agricultural settlements. To not do so would result in the overall system collapsing and losing its organizational complexity (as in the infamous case of the Roman Empire). Yet during the transition phase, there is a reorganization of internal linkages and connections. In human social terms, this indicates a revamping of internal institutions, social roles, and behavioral modes. Naturally, the chaotic period causes fear and panic for many as old structures shift to readapt to newly emerging patterns. Common chains of supply and demand (and command) often get disrupted or even halted. For a time, things *come apart* in order to *come together* anew. In a world that has been largely established in modern times to socially nurture consumers, this can be a real invasion of our comfort zones.

So it is expected that there will be moments of protest, civil unrest, and even peril. People will be scared and angry, and they will begin searching for someone to blame. There is the danger that when people find that they have nothing to lose, they may finally *lose it*. This is exactly the range of attitudes that leaders can exploit to build political power and divide social groups. It is also exactly the type of response that will be used by governing powers to strengthen their social control and to establish draconian surveillance policies. When disruptions shake the trees of authority, they dig in their roots to consolidate their power. Those authoritative powers that seek control *fear the change* more than all of us put together. We should not be manipulated into sharing their fear; it only serves to validate their control over us. As the astute thinker Idries Shah once said, "Knowledge is power, they say. But if only power were knowledge, that would be something worth thinking about."[2]

So being ready means preparing today for disruptive change tomorrow, remembering that times of crisis are also times of enormous social fluidity when societies can be pushed into new paths.

REVOLUTIONARY DISRUPTIONS

What will unfold over the upcoming years will not be the outcome of some predetermined set of human-engineered processes. The outcome will be far from linear, yet policy experts continue to insist in seeing the future as a continuation of present trends. It is a recurring weakness to view the world as an extrapolation of known physical forces and coercive human interventions. As an example of this, the U.S. National Intelligence Council initiated the 2000 report *Global Trends 2015: A Dialogue about the Future with Nongovernment Experts.*[3] This piece of shortsighted, linear policy forecasting envisioned the world of 2015 to be much the same as the world was in 2000, with a growing global economy, yet with the exception of some demographic changes. Some of the potential discontinuities, however, were cited to be "violent political upheavals due to a serious deterioration of living standards in the Middle East" and "the collapse of the alliance between the US and Europe." These threats can be said to be horizontal and symmetrical in that they are outcomes from expected factors. What could not have been expected was the asymmetrical nature of the threats that have been rolling in during the early years of the new millennium. The matrix of revolutionary disruptions now at our front door is creating a postmillennium state of insecurity. This state will become the foundation for truly revolutionary transitions, yet initially there may be some uncomfortable physical situations.

Many have argued that the world mind-set changed on September

11, 2001, with the collapse of the twin towers of New York's World Trade Center and that irreversible conditions were set in motion. The events of that fateful day certainly orchestrated a radical shift toward a global state characterized by massive new insecurities. And many powerful forces have sought to determine that the new "global terror" is the most significant of contemporary insecurities. This strategy of overwhelming force has served in part to exacerbate the potential threat of physical terror and violence within the minds of millions, if not billions of people. It is, without exaggeration, an artificially crafted global collective unconscious. Yet the matrix of fear is still found lacking, so the world is being thrust beyond terror, into cascading and colliding multiple threats (as discussed in chapter 2). Some of these threats will be bound with natural forces, yet their impact will be social. Further, it is evident that authoritative powers will seek to harness the upcoming threats as reasons to tighten security measures and strengthen undemocratic policies. These maneuvers toward decreased social liberties will be promoted in the name of transforming conditions for a better, more secure life for us, the global citizens.[4]

A 2008 report by the Oxford Research Group highlighted the expected social impacts from an increasingly insecure world.[5] It noted that the next decades will be crucial for how human life manages to secure the essential resources of food, water, and energy. The impacts of rapid climate change, peak oil, and population growth make all of us less secure and will likely engender extensive civil unrest.[6] Actions by governments to impose heightened forms of security on peoples and regions may generate new forms of social resistance. As the crunch hits the daily lives of everyday, working people, security in large, high-density urban centers could become a problem. Further, increased governmental protective measures would no doubt lead to further resentment against authority, leading to the possible breakdown of social order. This, in turn, would lead to further draconian measures of state security. Already, many cities around the globe are minisurveillance states. An academic paper published in 2002 stated that there were 4.2 million security cameras in the United Kingdom; that's one camera for every fourteen people.[7] It is now 2011, and there are no verifiable updated figures.

As a similar example of the concern toward upcoming uncertainties, the U.K. Ministry of Defence awarded a £12-million contract in 2007 to determine the regions, nationally and internationally, where Earth changes and disruptions will create conflict and security threats.[8] Other governments have instigated similar studies, with the aim of assessing their defense and security capabilities in the face of possible upcoming social crises. A 2007 report in the United States noted, "While both the stability of the civil order and its ability to suddenly collapse are *prima facie* political occurrences, they are almost invariably precipitated by a witches' brew of causal factors, which can include climate or weather stress."[9] Perhaps they should have added to this "financial stress" and "people's anger." Reports such as these, and others, warn of various catastrophic insecurities that are potentially just around the corner for incumbent and future governing bodies, as well as for all people. Yet there is so little public debate or general awareness of these pressing issues; it is as if the public is being deliberately shielded from the real depth of this information. Despite a virtual blackout in the mainstream media concerning these potential, upcoming disruptions, governments around the world are, however, very well informed on such matters. These disruptive matters may well include some of the following examples.

The emergence of oil shortages and extreme weather events such as droughts, heat waves, flooding, and desertification may well lead to an increase in the number of failed states (and failed city-states, such as New Orleans in late 2005). These states would be unable to cope with an increase in internal instabilities, and this instability could then spread across borders, affecting neighboring regimes. For example, various nongovernmental organizations have reported that climate change could, within the next few decades, generate up to two hundred million environmental refugees.[10] This could further exacerbate sociopolitical conflicts within and between states, straining international relations and creating further global resentments and tensions, especially between less-developed and developed regions.

Also, we are already seeing how maritime boundaries are being reevaluated in light of climatic changes, such as the opening up of potential transportation routes through the Northwest Passage.[11] In a similar manner, transportation and energy-supply networks rely on ports that are located on coasts or river deltas; any rise in sea levels could bring huge disruptions to these networks. Small increases in sea levels would seriously affect the transportation and delivery of vital resources and supplies, such as food. The greatest potential impact on transportation systems would be the flooding of roads, railways, transit systems, and airport runways in coastal areas because of rising sea levels.

Perhaps the next greatest security issue in the world will be the access and supply of clean water. The secretary-general of the United Nations, Ban Ki Moon, told delegates at the first Asia-Pacific Water Summit in December 2007 that water scarcity threatens economic and social stability and is a "potent fuel for wars and conflict."[12] It is calculated that a temperature increase of 2.1 degrees Celsius would expose up to three billion people to water shortages.[13] Four-fifths of our planet's surface is covered in water, yet 97.5 percent of this water is saltwater, whereas humans need freshwater; two-thirds of the remaining water is held in polar ice caps and underground. The renewable freshwater that is potentially available for human use—in lakes, rivers, and reservoirs—is no more than 0.007 percent of the water on the surface of Earth. Add to this the fact that modern food production, especially for rich, Western markets, is hugely wasteful of water, and you have the beginnings of global infighting. There will be increasing demands from growing urban populations for water, especially from those living in the megacities of the world.[14]

As well as water-security problems, there are also likely to be more problems of food security as increased flooding, droughts, and erratic weather patterns begin to cause significant disruptions to our global food supplies. Also, the diversion of agricultural land into agro-fuel crops has already resulted in increased food prices.* For example, the price of wheat saw a 130-percent increase in a single year, partly because of land being used for agro-fuel crops, resulting in an increasingly urbanized world and putting more demand for food production onto our decreasing agricultural regions. At the present rate, two to seven million acres of cropland are being lost each year. If this process continues, around 741 million acres will be lost by midcentury; this will leave only 6.67 billion acres to support eight to nine billion people, which comes out at no more than 0.74 acres per person, the area needed for subsistence-level food production.[15] On top of this, we need to be reminded that much of our food production depends on oil (fossil fuels) for the fertilization of crops, to harvest and process them, and then to transport them through the supply chain. Geologist Dale Allen Pfeiffer notes that if oil shortages increase, "Food could be priced out of the reach of the majority of our population. Hunger could become commonplace in every corner of the world, including your own neighborhood."[16] Already, we are hearing reports of poor harvests because of droughts and floods (as in Australia, China, and North America) as well as plummeting stocks in major fishing areas.

It seems crazy, then, that people in developed nations consume what seem to be idiotic "food miles." A Swedish study found that the food miles involved in a typical breakfast (apple, bread, butter, cheese, coffee, cream, orange juice, sugar) equaled the circumference of Earth.[17] It was also noted that by the end of the twentieth century, almost 93 percent of fresh produce in the United States was moved by truck.[18] We may find that the peaking of oil supplies and issues of heightened security over global food distribution will bring about enforced social austerity measures and will likely also lead to increased civil protest and social disruptions.

---

*The U.S. Department of Agriculture claimed that in 2007 the country would use around 18–20 percent of its total corn crop for ethanol production, increasing to 25 percent by 2008. See B. Sauser, "Ethanol Demand Threatens Food Prices."

SOCIAL DISRUPTIONS

We are now seeing clearly that many of the systems we relied on are in fact much more vulnerable and brittle and not as resilient as some had thought. This became apparent as the surprise collapse of Western banking institutions from September 2008 onward brought about a domino effect crash in commercial and manufacturing sectors. It is almost unavoidable that the next systems to be hit will be farming, transportation, and food distribution networks (a combination of the first two). By early February 2009, we had already seen the early warning signs of social unrest in Europe. The global financial crisis was providing the ignition for social anger that was close to combustion. A summary of protests in a number of countries includes the following.

Great Britain: A decision by Total, the French multinational oil company, to bring Italian and Portuguese workers to build a unit at the Lindsey oil refinery triggered a week of protests by thousands of energy workers. In December 2010, violent clashes erupted between students and police in London over plans to increase tuition fees.

Bulgaria: In January 2009, hundreds of protesters clashed with police, smashed windows, and damaged cars in Sofia when a rally against corruption and slow reforms in the face of the economic crisis turned into a riot.

France: Hundreds of thousands of strikers marched in French cities in February 2009 to demand pay raises and job protection. Some protesters clashed with police, but no major violence was reported. In October 2010, French strikers blocked oil refineries, bringing chaos to the French transportation infrastructure, in protest over planned state pension reforms.

Germany: In February 2009, public transportation ground to a halt in ten cities across Bavaria, while schools and hospitals suffered walkouts in northern Germany. Local authorities and schools were also affected in the east of the country.

Greece: Greek farmers put up roadblocks across the country in early 2009 to protest low prices. Most were taken down after the government pledged €500 million in aid. Blockades continued on and off at the border with Bulgaria, and riot police clashed for two days with farmers from Crete. Throughout 2010–2011 major strikes and protests have occurred in Greece as the population reacts angrily to government plans to implement drastic austerity measures.

Iceland: Prime Minister Geir Haarde resigned in early 2009 after a series of protests, some of which had turned violent. He was the first leader to fall as a direct result of the credit crunch.

Ireland: Nearly one hundred thousand people marched through Dublin on February 21, 2009, to protest government cutbacks in the face of a deepening recession and bailouts for the banks. In November 2010, more than one hundred thousand people yet again marched through Dublin's streets in protest over the international bailout and four years of austerity ahead.

Brussels: In September 2010 tens of thousands of people from around Europe marched across Brussels in a protest against spending cuts by some EU governments.

Spain: Spanish workers called for a National Strike Day on September 29, 2010, to protest against the austerity measures in Spain. Hundreds of thousands of people marched in major cities throughout Spain as most businesses and schools closed for the day.

Latvia: A ten-thousand-person-strong protest in Latvia on January 16, 2009, descended into a riot. Government steps to cut wages, as part of an austerity plan to win international aid, had angered people.

Lithuania: Also on January 16, 2009, police fired teargas to disperse demonstrators, who pelted the Lithuanian parliament with stones in protest of government cuts in social spending to offset an economic slowdown. Police said eighty people were detained and twenty injured.

Russia: Thousands of opposition supporters rallied in Moscow and the far-east port of Vladivostok in February 2009 in a national day of protests over hardships caused by the financial crisis. Hundreds of demonstrators in Moscow called for Russia's leaders to resign.[19]

Algeria: In January 2011 a wave of riots erupted all over the country protesting against unemployment, food inflation, corruption, and freedom of speech. The riots were notoriously marked by a series of self-immolations in front of government buildings.

Tunisia: During December 2010–January 2011 what has been termed the Tunisian revolution, or Jasmine Revolution, took place throughout Tunisia in the form of major street demonstrations. The demonstrations and riots were reported to have started over protests against unemployment, food inflation, corruption, and freedom of speech. Nationwide protests succeeded in ousting the incumbent regime.

Egypt: On January 25, 2011, a series of ongoing street demonstrations, marches, rallies, acts of civil disobedience, riots, and violent clashes erupted in Egypt. The protests began with tens of thousands marching in Cairo and a string of other cities in Egypt, demonstrating against a mixture of social, political, legal, and economic injustices.

It appears that 2011 has begun with an explosion of protests and rioting, especially in the Arab nations. While some of this concerns corrupt regimes, it also involves spiraling food costs that are affecting the poorer regions as staple commodities are hit by inflation. Indeed, 2011 may turn out to be a year of unrest in regard to food prices. Many people, who in the past might have had no reason for protest, could suddenly find themselves the new victims of social, political, and economic exclusion and could feel alienated as a result. This could lead to a crisis or collapse of social norms and the emergence of behavior not constrained by the standard notions of what is considered socially acceptable. This change is generally categorized as a form of anomie, or the breakdown of social values, the emergence of which can be rapid and unexpected. Strategic analyst Dr. Phil Williams writes, "Iraq after the United States invasion is a classic case of anomie, beginning with widespread looting, moving into an upsurge of violent and sexual crimes, including a massive increase in kidnapping, and culminating in a process of sectarian cleansing characterized by extreme forms of brutality. Other examples, at least for a short time, include New Orleans after Hurricane Katrina . . . other examples include favala areas of Brazil; drug culture in Mexico & Colombia; also parts of Africa, such as Guinea-Bissau and Nigeria."[20]

Any growth of social anomie in developed societies is likely to be catalyzed by financial, energy, and food shortages. And if this growth of instability spills over into a *global anomie,* then it would most likely reverberate throughout multiple interdependent systems. Such spillovers could escalate into increases in social and political instabilities, strains, and stresses, and ultimately strengthen the energies of disorder and chaos. Security expert Ken Booth recently concluded that we are in for a "great reckoning," a "new twenty years crisis," and a "long hot century."[21]

Initially, global political leaders will likely respond by trying to arrange the world into more regionalized and hierarchical structures, driven by what they will see as manufacturing, commercial, and political power shifting to countries with stronger energy reserves, access, and supply. Changes will come not only in the taken-for-granted way we consume energy but also in our work, entertainment and leisure activities, social travel, finances, how we produce and obtain our food, and more. These issues will strike home with a force unexpected for most people, and the initial reaction will most probably be anger and resentment. National and regional governments may be forced to implement authoritarian controls in order to regulate the needed distribution of essentials as well as to maintain social stability. Or, of course, such bodies and institutions may lose their governing capacity altogether, which will usher in pockets of social anomie. Conditions are likely to become volatile for a while as a world once thought of as stable starts to realize the dawning crises of energy supplies and costs, environmental catastrophes, food and water shortages, and emerging and reemerging diseases. Some nations or societies could begin to shift in specific directions in order to resist, or ride out, the coming shocks. In particular, I feel there are roughly three scenarios that could be played out, in varying degrees, by some regional authorities. I refer to these as: (1) localized scarcity, (2) lockdown, and (3) digital draconianism.*[22]

Localized Scarcity

In general, this scenario describes a shift toward social contraction and localized regions of poverty. It necessitates a return to community-based social structures due to a scarcity of available resources. For most people, the era of high technology will be over. There will be ongoing disruptions in the larger infrastructure, which eventually will foster animosity toward larger or external systems. Welfare and survival will be the highest priorities. Long-distance travel will be either beyond the means of most or undesired. Outside help will be minimal and unexpected. There will be a rise in networks of self-reliant, and sometimes semi-isolated, communities. People will live, work, and spend their time within their community boundaries. A new, sustainable way of living will develop around localism, diversity, and autonomy. This could arise in the short term as an immediate reaction to a rupture in modern institutions and a large-scale breakdown. As such, lifestyles would become more intensely local and centered around the home. New forms of work and education would be sought and taught by skilled local people; this would create new cottage industries around education, agriculture, textiles, and so on.

This localized scarcity could come about as a response to a global

---

*My thanks to Professor John Urry for our earlier discussions on these themes.

economic meltdown, such as was triggered by the collapse of the U.S. economy in late 2008, which, in turn, could trigger civil unrest. This would effectively halt the distribution of plentiful supplies of cheap energy and push communities into a new era of energy sustainability. Initially, this could foster a conflict over resources as competition and individualism manifest as the first signs of fear. Over a short time, however, survival instincts should ensure that community-based values such as cooperation emerge as the new paradigm for sustained living. Increased social contraction might then be a catalyst for emerging, cooperative community-based social relations. Social critic James Howard Kunstler recently predicted, "The twenty-first century will be much more about staying put than about going to other places."[23] Kunstler, who in particular views this scenario as highly likely, believes that we are heading toward a necessary downscaling, downsizing, relocalizing, and radical reorganizing of lifestyles in the civilized countries. In particular, he states that the future "will be characterized by austerity and a return to smaller scales of operation in virtually every respect. . . . It will compel us to make the most of our immediate environments."[24] Such a social scenario entails a radical upheaval in the global economy and major disruptions to our financial and social lives. It would, in general, be a drastic response to a collapse in the supply of essential resources.

Yet if large-scale disruptions occur, such as on an environmental and planetary scale, then the next scenario might be a more probable response than localized scarcity, but a lot less preferable. I refer to what I term the *lockdown* scenario.

Lockdown

This scenario describes a fortress-like world where community enclaves and tribal city-states have emerged in response to global social collapse, increased civil unrest, and the dissolution of order. Long-distance travel is too risky, and fear is a significant lifestyle indicator. This scenario foresees a future age of walled cities, in what is described as a return to a new form of the Dark Ages and a neomedievalism.

In this scenario, catastrophic environmental impacts would lead to fuel, food, and water shortages and a collapse in the global financial and communication infrastructures. Standards of living would plummet worldwide, with only relatively weak national or global forms of governance. This would lead to increased separation between different regions, giving rise to new forms of regionalized tribes. Power would no longer reside solely in the hands of national states, but would be wielded by regional warlords, as in feudal times or present tribal regions. Electrical goods and systems would quickly become either obsolete or prized possessions for the small elite groups who could secure forms of energy. Again, computerized objects, such as cars, phones, and televisions, would be largely replaced by less mechanized forms of technology. Localized systems of repair would become dominant, as most consumables around us would break down and become worthless. Cars and trains would rust away, left where they were last used.

As in medieval times, long-distance travel would be extremely risky and only recommended for those who could protect themselves. Different warlord-dominated regions could potentially be in perpetual warfare with each other for control of water, fuel, and food. There would be a dramatic rise in armed gangs as resources become hotly contested and fought over. A global contraction of resources would probably lead some of the more powerful nations to break away from poorer nations into protected enclaves. The world would see the increasing emergence of wild zones more akin to no-man's-lands, where ethnic, tribal, or religious warlordism would be rife. A 1997 report titled "Branch Points: Global Scenarios and Human Choice" refers to this as the fortress world, where "the elite retreat to protected enclaves, mostly in historically rich nations, but in favoured enclaves in poor nations, as well. . . . Technology is maintained in the fortresses. . . . Local pollution within the fortress is reduced through increased efficiency and recycling. Pollution is also exported outside the enclaves, contributing to the extreme environmental deterioration induced by the unsustainable practices of the desperately poor and by the extraction of resources for the wealthy."[25]

This scenario paints a picture of walled cities similar to those of the medieval period, which were set up in order to provide protection against raiders, invaders, and diseases. Such catastrophic effects across much of the world would be similar to those that devastated societies in the past and that may do so again in the near future, according to various sources.[26]

Already, there are foretastes of this scenario today, including the many gated communities that have appeared around the world. Such fortresses would also guard against the massive influx of immigrants from failed states or regions. The vision of such a fortress world can be seen in Robert Silverberg's 1971 novel *The World Inside,* set in 2381. In that book, people no longer lived in cities, but in massive three-kilometer-high towers called urban monads. These urban monads (or urbmons) were thousand-floor skyscrapers arranged in "constellations," and each urbmon was divided into twenty-five self-contained "cities" of forty floors each, with each building holding approximately eight hundred thousand people. More recently, Hurricane Katrina's devastation of New Orleans in 2005 showed how a once-functional city in a modern nation, could rapidly deteriorate into extreme inequalities, civil unrest, violence, and desperation. Life, too, in some less developed parts of the world, such as Afghanistan, Iraq, and Somalia, already shows signs of the decline into tribal regionalism governed through warlord's brutish power. Life as foretold in the dystopic, "future nightmare" film *Mad Max* may not be complete fantasy.*

Or it could be that nation-states, in a controlled bid to retain power, could opt for a deliberate intervention into social order. In other words, they could foster Orwellian-style networks of control to keep a grip on us as the turbulence hits. I refer to this third scenario as digital draconianism.

---

*This film depicts the future through the story of a bleak, dystopian, impoverished society facing a breakdown of civil order resulting from oil shortages.

Digital Draconianism

This scenario suggests that the more powerful, developed states would shift ever further toward draconian measures of civilian surveillance. A Big Brother–style of governance would be further consolidated in Western societies in an effort to control and contain increased social unrest. There would be increased dependency on "databasing" the individual, with more or less no personal movement without digital tracing and tracking. This scenario relies on the various technologies of closed-circuit TV cameras, data-mining software, biometric security, integrated digital databases, and radio-frequency identity implants to track objects and people. It is also possible that microchipping would be introduced into populations to further track and monitor behavior and movement. This would seriously limit a person's freedom to walk, drive, or move about without being recorded. Such measures would be highly intrusive and dangerously threaten civil liberties. The manufactured fear of the war on terror would be further exploited in order to create the need for individuals to be rendered as "data subjects." The privatization of information, as has already occurred with private credit database companies such as Experian in the United Kingdom, is set to become an area of commercial growth. This is likely to create further social unrest as people resist and protest such intrusions of civil liberty.

In this scenario, the near future of social life would be restricted by a "digitization" of each person amid increased authoritarian censorship (similar to China's current Golden Shield Project). Digitized tracking and tracing would curtail social lives and freedom of movement. Those privileged few who would be fast-tracked through social passage could form a new elitist social class, a kind of "kinetic elite."* Those not privileged, meaning the majority, would be required to undergo prescreening before being granted access to movement within and between regions and countries.

Yet in some ways, we are already close to such a scenario; we are already living in a highly monitored and surveyed world. Under the

---

*This term was coined by Dutch architect Rem Koolhaas.

banner of a post–September 11 world, many intrusive technologies are being (and will continue to be) rapidly introduced. The United Kingdom government's information commissioner has stated that people in Britain already live in a surveillance society.*[27] For example, the United Kingdom government's planned ID card will contain and integrate forty-nine separate pieces of personal information, yet it is unlikely to have any effect in preventing terrorist attacks. Its introduction is a further example of how authorities deem everyone in society a potential terrorist.

However, although this scenario may seem the most likely response to an increasingly turbulent world, it still has a fundamental flaw: it relies on working technology. If during the transition phase we experience planetary disruption from solar storms or catastrophic environmental impacts, then the global power infrastructure is likely to be rendered inoperative. Our highly computerized environments are only as efficient as the power source that flows through them. Without their lifeblood, they are as useful as a dead dodo.

The three scenarios briefly outlined above may, in degree or in part, materialize as state or social responses to the chaos experienced during transition. Yet whatever the response, it is best to remember that it will only serve to be a temporary holding pattern. Grim as they may seem, such scenarios would not be sustained in the long run. However, we do need to prepare ourselves for some degree of unpleasantness. And the horizon of hope may seem, for many, to be too far away and too obscure. Energetic shocks to the grand human system will be virtually inevitable; how far-reaching and how successful these shocks are will remain to be seen. Thus, it is being asked of us to consider what efforts might be taken to think about and anticipate how we can, individually and collectively, respond to these coming shocks. It is my firm understanding that the outcome, once we have ridden out the storm, will be

---

*For a recent dramatic examination of the politics of contemporary surveillance, see the 2008 BBC drama *The Last Enemy*.

positive, not only for the human species but also for Planet Earth and our solar family.

It will be important that people attempt to place themselves as observers to the changes rather than being drawn in and caught up with the details of the physical chaos and disruption occurring around them. This means not attaching emotionally to events as they unfold or taking them personally. This may be extremely difficult for some people, especially if financial worries have been exacerbated or their possessions or home have been taken away. Yet to be able to take a step back and find a degree of comfortable detachment (neither personal oblivion nor radical solitude) will be of immense support to an individual. In fact, to be a balanced observer during these transition times is of the utmost importance. Not only does this help a person to fare better during troubling times, but also, significantly, the vibration or resonance of balance that is emitted will help to bring into balance other people and circumstances around the individual. Like a tuning fork, the vibration helps to bring others into harmony and the correct pitch.

An alternative to this is to cultivate a state of denial, a form of cognitive dissonance (a term from developmental psychology). But there is already much cognitive dissonance pervading our present era: it is a collective mental state that obstructs the comprehension of what is really happening around us. Too many people have been complicit in sleep-walking into the future. And to add injury to insult, it is likely that people and events that highlight the negative will continue to dominate the news, the headlines, and the corridors of power. It is possible that during these disruptive times, there will be some people who find themselves increasingly vulnerable and unstable, both physically and emotionally. There are likely to be sporadic outbursts in social and domestic violence, and from people least expected to be prone to such acts. Part of this volatile energy will be due to increased magnetic fluctuations occurring inside of the human body.

MAGNETIC DISRUPTIONS

As discussed in chapter 2, Earth's magnetic field is showing signs of large cracks (some the size of California), making the planet open to potentially harmful bursts of solar winds and coronal mass ejections. And Earth's magnetic field is not a static shield, but it is rather like a wave that rises and falls, oscillating very quickly. This magnetic behavior is known to affect the lives of living systems on Earth, especially those systems, like the human body, with a central nervous system. Biological bodies, being electrical energy units, are sensitive to external energetic and atmospheric variations, though usually these reactions operate at a subconscious level.[28] Likewise, magnetic variations can have very strange effects on human consciousness. This could explain why it has been reported that many people in recent times have experienced an increase in feelings of exhaustion and weariness. Another supposed symptom of magnetic fluctuations is how they impact the short-term memory; this occurs because memory is tied into the electrical (that is, magnetic) functioning of the human nervous system. What this means, quite simply, is that human life, thought, and behavior are affected directly by fluctuations in Earth's magnetic field, something unbeknown to most people. Now there is a valid excuse for those nagging bad days!

The breach in Earth's magnetosphere, which is its natural protective shield, is allowing, and will continue to allow, large volumes of solar radiation (plasma) to enter into the atmosphere. Not only will this increase the impact of solar storms on global telecommunications and environmental processes (see chapter 2), but it can also significantly interfere with the bioelectric circuitry of the human nervous system. And as was stated previously in chapter 2, scientists are expecting an increase in sun activity in the forms of coronal mass ejections and solar storms—and soon. It is probable, then, that the intervention of magnetic fluctuations will increase over the next several years. Exactly what the implications will be for the human body are unclear (although this subject is discussed in more depth in later chapters). Those people who are more energetically sensitive may experience more intensity during the transition process. And if the magnetic interference becomes markedly increased, as it may well do in the next several years, then many people could become consciously affected by the changes, albeit not fully knowing nor understanding why. It is possible, then, that human emotions may similarly undergo a series of fluctuations in line with Earth's erratic or shifting magnetic fields. Also, there is the potential for human DNA to be affected by increases in solar radiation (see chapter 6). Change, it appears, can have impacts on many levels, and the disruptions may not be only in the physical realm.

TOWARD THE BREAKTHROUGH

These coming years will be unique within humanity's living memory in that our history will witness the transition from the final era of a now fading world paradigm to a new, upgraded one. However, much may be lost in the process, and the survival of our species is not guaranteed. Saying this, if there is a corresponding resilience within the perceptions, mind-sets, and behaviors of people, then our species is fully expected to be along for the ride. And many people have long suspected the coming of such an interval—a phase shift—with the knowledge that things could not possibly continue as they were indefinitely. In the end, they thought, if evolution did not force us into rapid readaptation, then we would probably kill ourselves off through our own means. The present evolutionary intervention, if it may be called that, is indeed timely, as there have been multiple warning bells ringing for some time. The mass of humanity can no longer proceed on the assumption that things are pretty much to remain the same. Whichever way you look at the situation, there can be no more business-as-usual models.

On the other hand, we also have our plentiful supply of doomsday predictions. Such Armageddon predictions have their usefulness, too, as they help to raise people's level of awareness and to motivate a shift in consciousness. In this way, they end up becoming "self-falsifying prophecies." Václav Havel once said, "The tragedy of modern man is not that he knows less and less about the meaning of his own life, but that it bothers him less and less."[29] Apathy is one of our greatest dangers, especially when it comes amid increasing signs of social fatigue and deteriorating energies. We hear reports on increases in divorce rates, suicide, violent crime, and depression; we have big houses yet broken homes; we have large amounts of entertainment and visuals yet diminishing vision; and we have larger communities yet less respect.

In other words, we need an awakening; we need something to shake our foundations before they crumble silently beneath us as we lie unsuspecting in our beds. As social thinker Duane Elgin says, "Despite all our good intentions, without this coming era of collective distress and adversity, the human family is unlikely to awaken to its global identity and evolutionary responsibility."[30] In a similar manner, writer and thinker Peter Russell states, "The set of global problems that humanity is facing presently may turn out to be as important to our continued evolution as 'the oxygen crisis' was. Never in the history of the human race have the dangers been so extreme; yet in their role as evolutionary catalysts, they may be just what is needed to push us to a higher level."[31]

I am in agreement that coming events can be viewed as evolutionary catalysts that are crucial to our continued evolution. Yet I would go further and say that these events are themselves part of an evolutionary pattern of change. In other words, we don't drive evolution, *evolution drives us*. And either we get with the program or we lose our ride. And part of this readaptation (discussed in greater depth in subsequent chapters) involves how we can arrange our social functioning to be more resilient. For example, can we shift from competition to collaboration, from possessiveness to sufficiency and sharing, from outer dependency to inner authority, and from separation to notions of connection? Usually, only the familiar populates our lives, so the notion that "everything might change" is a step too drastic for many people. What, after all, can we do in the face of unprecedented change?

First we can begin to change our thinking, to shift our perceptions about how we see the world. Action must begin from vision and intention. Then there can be some degree of planning for the transition, which involves cooperation in place of desperate competition. After all, what is coming will be for the many, not the one. The transition is as much perceptual as it is physical. Without the capacity to perceive how our understanding of the world is shifting, we will not be equipped to manifest our vision in a practical and functional manner. Much of how we will experience the coming social and cultural changes will depend upon how we develop our perceptual frameworks. It is an ancient axiom that *like attracts like*. If we are fearful, so we attract the negative circumstances, and this "law of attraction" has been misunderstood by humanity for far too long. It is necessary that we take back our thinking for ourselves and move away from the negative influence of too much external intervention. It is no accident that fear-centered social orders will be moving toward their own extinction. And we should also recognize that episodes of crisis or breakdown are not always bad things. Rather, they can create both the motivation and the opportunity for resilience, readaptation, and renewal.

We will fare better if we view the future as a natural gift of change rather than something to be bent into shape for the human preference. Despite the likelihood of increasingly disruptive events, those people with the right attitude and positive hope will find themselves more resilient during the rapid transitions. Mihaly Csikszentmihalyi, in his powerful work *The Evolving Self: A Psychology for the Third Millennium,* writes:

> Even if nothing were to change in our lifetime, even if signs of a new dark age proliferated, if chaos and apathy were on the ascendant, those who cast their lot with the future would not be disappointed. Evolution is not a millenarian creed event, expecting a Second Coming next year, the next century, or the next millennium. Those who have faith in it have literally all the time in the world. The individual life span with all its woes and delusions is only an instant in the awesome cosmic adventure. At the same time, our actions have

a decisive impact on the kind of life that will evolve on this planet, and perhaps on other planets as well.[32]

Perhaps another way of saying this, albeit in less prosaic terms, is that the universe never lets you down—well, not in the long run, anyway.

A Tale to Finish: The Hungry Wolf

A skinny and hungry wolf by chance met a well-nourished dog. After the salutation, the wolf asked, "You look so good, where do you come from? What do you eat to be of such a good spirit? I am stronger than you and I starve."

"You would have the same fortune," the dog responded simply, "if you wanted to serve my master the way I do it."

"What services are these?" the wolf asked.

"To guard the door and at night defend the house against the thieves."

"Good! I'll do it. I bear rain and snow in the forests leading a miserable life. How much easier it would be to live under a roof and calmly satiate my hunger with abundant food!"

"All right," said the dog, "come with me." While they walked, the wolf saw the bare neck of the dog, caused by the chain.

"Tell me, friend," it said, "where does that come from?"

"That's nothing."

"Please, please tell me."

"When I am too unquiet," the dog replied, "they tie me during the day so that I sleep when there is light and I watch when the night arrives. When the twilight comes, I walk wherever I want. They bring the food to me without asking for it, the master gives me the bones from his own table, and the servants give me the rest and the sauces that nobody wants anymore. This way, my belly fills up without having to work."

"But if you wish to leave and go wherever you want, do they allow you to do that?"

"No, not at all," said the dog.

"Well then," said the wolf, "enjoy your goods. I don't want to be king in exchange for my freedom."

READAPTATION

INTRODUCTION TO PART TWO

The first section of the book described how our world—and our universe—is a nonlinear and chaotic system. In chapter 1, I outlined how evolutionary cycles are not gradual processes that progress along a smooth and continuous curve, but are periods of static growth punctuated by moments of rapid and tumultuous change. I applied this also to social and cultural cycles that exhibit their own life cycles of birth, growth, peak, and decay. I then outlined how as a planetary civilization we are heading toward a convergence of tipping points (see chapter 2) that will most likely lead to a period of social turbulence and civil unrest (see chapter 3). Part 1 of this book (titled "Resilience") overall examined the upcoming disruptive times within the context of natural evolutionary patterns of trigger points and how we, as a global humanity, will have to be resilient to face such challenges.

Part 2, "Readaptation," looks at the other side of this pattern, namely, that in nature (and living systems) there exists a tremendous degree of coherence and harmony. Yet our weakness as a species is that we fail to grasp this level of coherence and use it. Everything is fundamentally connected to everything else, be it human, nature, or cosmic. Part 2 begins with a call for a paradigm shift in human thinking, or rather, in human perceptions. I suggest (as do many others) that as a species we are now in need of a "new mind" for a "new world." Our current levels of thinking are not sufficient to take us into a new era of revitalization and renewal. Each new evolutionary leap in human progress has been accompanied by a parallel leap in human thinking. As the evolutionary journey unfolds, the universe opens up to the human mind and expands its perceptual limits. The first perceptual limit was nature, where the Divine resided in the trees, waters, and wind. Then human consciousness expanded upward into the heavens, where the planets became Divinity, and again further out into the solar heavens until the sun became the Absolute Divine. Then science intervened to expand humanity's horizons beyond the solar realm and into galaxies, universes, and multiverses, and into endless creative potentials. Now, again, human consciousness stands at the doorway of another perceptual expansion as it accompanies the grand universal evolutionary story.

We need to understand our positions, our vistas, if we are to be better prepared for our journey. Thus, part 2 examines first our minds and then our new sciences, and then how everything is inextricably bound together.

4
GLOBAL MIND CHANGE
Recognizing That Everything Connects

You never change anything by fighting the existing reality.
To change something, build a new model that makes the
existing model obsolete.

BUCKMINSTER FULLER—ENGINEER,

INVENTOR, AND FUTURIST

Every man who had ever lived became a contributor to the
evolution of the earth, since his observations were a part of
its growth. The world was thus a place entirely constructed
from thought, ever changing, constantly renewing itself
through the process of mankind's pondering its reality for
themselves.

JAMES COWAN, *A MAPMAKER'S DREAM*

Old minds think: How do we stop these bad things from
happening? New minds think: How do we make things the
way we want them to be?

DANIEL QUINN, *BEYOND CIVILIZATION*

This chapter addresses the need for a shift in human thinking. Quite
literally, if there is no mind shift, there will be no difference. At the

end of chapter 3, I wrote that those people with the right attitude and positive hope will find themselves more resilient to the rapid transitions, transitions that involve a *new model* of how we perceive our position in the world. I also discussed how it is necessary that we transform our own thinking in order to *perceive the world differently* and to understand the nature of our integral connectedness as a global species.

The difficulty we find ourselves in at the present time is that parallel to the dramatic physical changes we are currently experiencing, there is also pressure for a simultaneous *mental shift*. This is a shift in thinking at least as significant as was the Enlightenment shift from a heliocentric worldview to a humanistic one. The Cartesian view of a mechanistic universe is outdated and incompatible within an evolutionary paradigm. What is required is a total change in our human perception. For example, new findings in quantum biology inform us that in contrast to stories of evolution through competition and strength, evolution works by symbiotic relationships and cooperation. Intercellular communication and gene transfer are processes that involve cooperation in information sharing. It is necessary that findings in the new sciences must help to push forward thinking that is more in-line with natural, environmental, and universal principles. Ultimately, change begins with one's own mind-set and worldview: as the Delphic inscription instructs us, "Know thyself."

German philosopher Arthur Schopenhauer famously said, "Everyone takes the limits of his own vision for the limits of the world."[1] If we can develop and expand our perception of our own limits, we can go some way toward changing how we view the extraordinary capacity inherent in the world around us. There is an old Chinese proverb that warns us, "If we don't change our direction, we are likely to wind up where we are headed," and where we are headed is as much a collective situation as it is an individual one. Further, it is as much an individual psychological responsibility as it is a collective one. What this suggests is that how we think globally reflects the reality of the world we inhabit. And as our once-familiar world begins to readapt to a new phase, so must our understanding; otherwise, we may find life increasingly difficult, stressful, and not only incomprehensible but also outright hostile. We have to accept that it is our responsibility—our imperative—to make ourselves adaptable to a constantly evolving natural and cosmic environment. Perhaps for the first time in history, conscious evolution has ceased to be a choice open to humanity and has become a necessity upon which our future depends.

Conscious evolution is about acquiring evolutionary consciousness, about thinking in terms of the "macro," and about the direction our species is taking. It is our evolutionary imperative to engage actively in conscious and intentional evolutionary transformation if we are to remain a viable living species on Planet Earth. We need to bring forth a new mind in order to accept a new world.

A NEW MIND FOR A NEW WORLD

We all share a common psychological environment, which many of us, most of the time, take for granted. We have underestimated the impact of human thought worldwide, neglecting to consider the power of destructive thought and "mental pollution" on a sensitive and responsive biosphere. Within an integral world (and also within a total integral universe), everything counts. How we are taught (or conditioned) to think will affect how our species manages cultural development and the culture's subsequent intervention into Earth's living systems. It can be stated that, for the most part, humanity unknowingly participates within a cultural hypnosis. From early childhood, our experiences are established to conform to our specific cultural norm; any anomalies are usually corrected and the corrections then reinforced through various socializing processes, such as family, school, friends, and such. Thus, our "world" is often given to us through the medium of particular cultural filters, and so each of us is literally hypnotized from infancy to perceive the world in the same way that people in our culture perceive it. This is a very powerful behavioral and perceptual socializing mechanism. To break from this indoctrinated perceptual environment is extremely difficult and is often beset with many personal problems arising from peer pressure and ties to friends and family. A shock is often necessary in order to catalyze one's own change of mind. Events such as near-death experiences are often cited as examples that radically change people's worldviews. What we may be experiencing on a collective level during our planetary evolutionary transition is a near-death experience as a species. If this doesn't shock us awake, then we may as well sleep forever.

For a new mind to emerge during the times ahead, it will be necessary for people to take power back into their own perceptual mechanisms, to empower themselves by withholding legitimacy regarding old and outdated modes of thinking. Social philosopher Willis Harman has described this by stating, "By deliberately changing their internal images of reality, people can change the world."[2] This change, then, requires us to take back our rightful legitimacy unto ourselves, to decide carefully what we think, how we think, and which beliefs we choose to adopt. This also concerns our opinions, agreements, and support, which we have previously been all too ready to give away. Our beliefs, perceptions, and state of mind are crucial for how we understand the world around us. Thus, giving away our right over the power to choose how we wish to perceive the world serves to empower others over us. This, in essence, is the crux of social control, and this mechanism belongs to the paradigm of the old world and will have no place in a post-transition world.

Many of us are unsuspecting as to the degree of insecurity that governs our perceptive abilities. We focus on the immediate and seemingly ignore the long term, despite the long term having the greater urgency in scale. Our social institutions and media continue to reinforce the immediate and short term, thus strengthening our social myopia. As a telling example, a report recently published in the United Kingdom, titled "Beyond Terror: The Truth about the Real Threats to Our World," focused on the disproportionate attention given to terrorism in the short term compared with the threats that, although they resulted in more fatalities, were classified as ongoing, long-term problems. The report stated that in 2001 in the United States alone, the following numbers of people were killed from various causes:

Malnutrition: 3,500
HIV/AIDS: 14,000
Pneumonia: 62,000
Heart disease: 700,000+
Suicide: 30,000+
Traffic accidents: 42,000+
Firearms-related incidents: 30,000
Homicides: 20,000+.[3]

International terrorism, however, had a figure of around 3,000. This shows our old mind at work, how it perceives and prioritizes events. It is also a mind that goes very far back into our species evolution, a mind that evolved to deal with a very different world. Our early history equipped us to live in relatively stable environments within small communities; challenges were in the short term and nearby. The human mind thus evolved to deal with low-impact, short-term changes. The world that made our mind is now gone, and the world we have created around us is a new world; paradoxically, it is a world that we have developed limited capacity to comprehend. It is fair to say that we now have a mismatch between the human mind we possess and the world we inhabit. Most of the momentous changes in our cultural history have taken place in the past one hundred years. These days, we don't have that luxury of time, as events (with long-term consequences) are rapidly changing around us, before human cultural evolution has had time to readapt. Cultural evolution has worked more or less well until the present century; now, it finds itself hampered by an outdated human perceptual system. Contemporary society still relies too heavily—and unconsciously— on ancient modes of thought and ancient styles of thinking. This begs the question, can a collective and rapid change of mind occur on this planet? In the words of neurologist Robert Ornstein, "Conscious evolution needs to take the place of unconscious cultural evolution."[4]

Let's be clear about this; we arrived late to the evolutionary party. In a well-known analogy that places the evolution of Earth within a single year, from January 1 to December 31, with each day of the year equal to twelve million years, the first form of life, a simple bacterium, arose sometime in February. More complex life-forms arrived throughout spring and summer, and fishes came to the party around November 20. Then the bouncers—the dinosaurs—finally arrived around December 10, only to disappear drunk on Christmas Day. It wasn't until the afternoon of December 31 that the first of our recognizable human ancestors showed up (typically late). So when did we, *Homo sapiens sapiens,* crash the party? Well, we knocked on the door around 11:45 p.m., which leaves all of recorded history taking place within the final minute of the year.

We are, in all respects, a rapid evolutionary phenomenon. And it's going to get a whole lot more rapid. Which means we need to ditch the old mind as fast as possible before we take too many wrong decisions or succumb to mounting insecurities. Our old mind was set up to be on the lookout for insecurities and fear-inducing situations: it was our survival apparatus. Yet this apparatus has continued to be reinforced through social conditioning, resulting in limited perceptual capacity. What is required now is a *reinvigoration of vision:* everything that we have culturally achieved has been the result of human vision. The human imagination is a primary force; it allows the intervention of energies and guidance. It is both creative and destructive, and through it we are able to manifest the world we envision. We now need to upgrade our visionary capacity, to open up more fully to inspired thoughts and guidance. To fail to do so will be a great loss for our species, as these are critical times for the instinctive perceptual faculties, and we need to bring these new organs of perception into being. In *Masnavi,* a three-volume work of mystical poetry, the revered Persian poet Jalalludin Rumi writes:

> *New organs of perception come into being as a result of necessity.*

Therefore, O man, increase your necessity, so that you may
Increase your perception.[5]

Every change requires a change in consciousness; this has always been the case. Many of us are now slowly beginning to recognize this fact and to cooperate with the upgrade. The transition stage we are to experience in the grander evolutionary cycle will likewise affect the evolution of human consciousness and may result in new capacities being catalyzed into emergence. Yet at the same time, it is important that we ourselves participate in an effort to shift our thinking patterns, to develop a new mind-set. If a person's mind-set is rigidly fixed into the old patterns of thinking, then that person will feel threatened by drastic change. The person may even try to resist strongly, to fight to retain a familiar environment where it is business as usual. Yet the twenty-first century will not be a place for business as usual; it will be a new epoch, and as such, it deserves a corresponding consciousness.

Every epoch has fashioned its corresponding mind-set, some more functional than others. For example, the earlier mythic concepts of a sacred world dominated by unseen forces and humankind's integral relationship with the powerful nature developed into a theistic consciousness. In that case, divine right on Earth developed into a hierarchical system of religious authority. This belief of a divinely ordered cosmos then progressed into the Enlightenment's mechanistic, clockwork view of the universe, in which science sought to prove that natural laws held the world under linear domination. However, this materialistic mind-set that has prevailed more or less intact up until the present moment is no longer of functional use to us. In fact, if we continue with it, we are liable to become its victims. Thus, an upgrade of our perceptive capacities is required in a very real and practical way.

For the past three hundred years, mainstream Western society provided its citizens with a worldview and belief system that has encouraged ideas related to the survival of the fittest, with its sense of competition and conquest. Such ideals are now rapidly contaminating our social and cultural environment and leading us on a path to destruction. The next shift must coincide with the transition phase and involve a conscious decision to develop our understanding, worldview, and wisdom through an intensive "inner evolution." The focus of this shift is to replace such obsolete material beliefs with ones concentrating on connection, communication, and consciousness. Mahatma Gandhi was right when he said, "Be the change you want to see in the world."[6] When you evolve your inner world, you also change the immediate world around you and around those close to you. It is time to release, or abandon, obsolete and superstitious beliefs. Our newly emerging scientific paradigm, with its quantum theories of entanglement, reminds us that we participate within an integrally connected and living universe (see chapters 5 and 6). This understanding of a living universe makes it more imperative that humanity lives in accordance with balanced needs rather than consumptive desires. It is about living simply so that others may simply live. As Harman puts it, "Throughout history, the really fundamental changes in societies have come about not from dictates of governments and the results of battles but through vast numbers of people changing their minds—sometimes only a little bit . . . Perhaps the only limits to the human mind are those we believe in."[7]

Such a macroshift[8] in human thought requires that a critical number of people in society evolve their mind-set. It is a radical, yet necessary, shift from a Cartesian worldview of parts to one encompassing a connected wholeness. By way of paraphrasing what Albert Einstein said, the problems created by the prevalent way of thinking cannot be solved by the same way of thinking. This is a crucial insight. Without renewing our outdated cultural attitudes and thinking, we will be unable to regenerate today's dominant, mechanistic civilization into a rejuvenated and integral global civilization. Thus, the modes of colonization and consumption need to be replaced by *connection, communication, and consciousness.*[9] This entails a behavioral shift from possessiveness to sharing, from separation to wholeness, and from outer authority to inner authority. Humanistic thinker Ervin Laszlo offers the following outline of what he believes to be obsolete thinking:

Order through hierarchy
Individual uniqueness
Everything is reversible
Economic growth is good
New is better/technology is the answer
Our country is right.[10]

The upgrade of our thinking patterns is a beginning step to an upgrade in human consciousness, which is necessary if we are to succeed in adapting to our rapidly and inevitably changing world. In other words, if we don't enact a change or learn to adapt to the incoming energies of change and transformation, our presence is likely to be no longer required, or needed. It is a sobering thought.

The human species has entered a period of profound, fundamental, and unprecedented change. It needs to acquire new skills in order to coexist with an environment that is itself undergoing profound change within the larger fabric of living systems—planetary, solar, and galactic. We need to upgrade our capacities in order to have the internal readiness for an upgrade in energies. To not do so may result, quite literally, in us blowing a fuse as a species! Whichever way we look at it, we are in need of preparation. If we are not prepared, that which manifests as truth may very well seem like science fiction. The question may revolve around how our inner vision can be brought into balance with (and provide support for) the impacts of a changing environment. If there is enough critical mass of *mind change,* then there is a better possibility that shifting energies will be experienced less chaotically. Evolutionary biologist Elisabet Sahtouris expresses the same sentiment when she writes, "While people have always created reality out of their beliefs, until now a handful of powerful people dictated the beliefs of each human culture. The glory of our own time is that the news is finally out that each and every one of us has the authority, even the mandate, to choose the beliefs by which we live and create our individual and communal lives. To create the human future well we need good Vistas—consciously created belief systems comprised of worldviews and the values for negotiating them courageously and lovingly."[11]

Our priority is to first change our perceptions and way of thinking. It is a challenge we face, to adapt our thinking so that we "think in sync" with our changing world.

COLLECTIVE INTELLIGENCE
The Need for Synthesis

All living species are inherently connected in varying degrees of subtlety, and the collective mind of humanity is no exception. Often we discover that our ideas are shared simultaneously with our friends or associates as minds in close contact or proximity entangle together and share thought-forms. The collective mind of humanity is moving ever closer to being more awakened, yet we require triggers, or stimuli, in order to activate latent capacities. Global communications have helped to increase our awareness of distant events and to trigger shared empathy and collective emotionality. This is part of what can be termed collective intelligence; others have named this the global brain[12] or the noosphere.[13] The thought-forms that we emanate go toward the state of our collective mind, and they are functional in that an intentional action carries with it more force, power, and effectiveness than a non-intentional action.

A collective species consciousness can exist without being self-aware because it already exists. A collective consciousness does not require that all of its components be conscious because a conscious entity produces an exponential effect, so only a relatively few conscious nodes or "awake people" can represent the many. This is why human history has progressed from the actions of the few; it is not surprising that many of the agents of human history have been conscious of the collective mind of humanity or have been the agents of conscious entities. As proclaimed inventor Doug Engelbart says, "The key thing about all the world's big problems is that they have to be dealt with collectively. . . . If we don't get collectively smarter, we're doomed."[14] Likewise, well-known thinker Marshall McLuhan, who coined the phrase *the global village,* sees humanity as a total global community. He said that where previously human evolution was about the "outering" of physical tools and technology for progress, human acceleration is now concerned with the intensification of the central nervous system worldwide. He said, "Evolution became not an involuntary response of organisms to new conditions but a part of the consensus of human consciousness. Such a revolution is enormously greater and more confusing to past attitudes than anything that can confront a mere culture or civilization."[15]

The analogy is that of humanity operating as a planetary nervous system, a global brain, with each individual representing a firing neuron and our communications representing conscious informational networks. Systems philosopher Ervin Laszlo defines the global brain as follows:

> The global brain is the quasi-neural energy—and information—processing network created by six and a half billion humans on the planet, interacting in many ways, private as well as public, and on many levels, local as well as global. A quantum shift in the global brain is a sudden and fundamental transformation in the relations of a significant segment of the six and a half billion humans to each other and to nature—a macroshift in society—and a likewise sudden and fundamental transformation in cutting-edge perceptions regarding the nature of reality—a paradigm shift in science. The two shifts together make for a veritable "reality revolution" in society as well as in science.[16]

What Laszlo refers to as the "reality revolution" is simultaneously a quantum shift in the collective species mind alongside a global transformation in perception regarding the nature of reality. For such a revolution to occur during our period of transition on this planet would be of tremendous value in terms of parallel evolutionary shifts. As famed Jesuit priest and "noosphere philosopher" Pierre Teilhard de Chardin wrote, "According to the evolutionary structure of the world, we can only find our person by uniting together. There is no mind without synthesis."[17] It is no coincidence that at the same time that our planet, within its solar family, is experiencing a sudden evolutionary jump point (or phase transition), our species is coming also to a peak in its collective mind. We must remember that throughout human history, the real and fundamental changes have always come about from sufficient numbers of people *changing their minds,* rather than from governments or social decrees. By a deliberate change in the way people perceive reality, and thus the world, great shifts can be brought about. It is a dangerous flaw to take our own limits of perception to be the limits of our world, as Schopenhauer so ably noted.

The quality of our perceptions has perhaps never been more crucial to our cultural and social survival. Historians note that there are particular periods in history when society goes through a more fundamental, marked shift that involves not only the people but also most of a society's basic institutions. According to famed historian Lewis Mumford, there have been no more than four or five such great transformations in the entire history of Western civilization. In his 1956 book *The Transformations of Man,* Mumford writes:

> Every (human) transformation . . . has rested on a new metaphysical and ideological base; or rather, upon deeper stirrings and intuitions whose rationalized expression takes the form of a new picture of the cosmos and the nature of man . . . we stand on the brink of (such) a new age: the age of an open world and of a self capable of playing its part in that larger sphere. An age of renewal, when work and leisure and learning and love will unite to produce a fresh form for every stage of life, and a higher trajectory for life as a whole. . . . In

carrying [human] . . . self-transformation to this further stage, world culture may bring about a fresh release of spiritual energy that will unveil new potentialities, no more visible in the human self today than radium was in the physical world a century ago, though always present.[18]

It was prescient of Mumford to view the next epoch not only in terms of ideological renewal but also as one that brings about "a fresh release of spiritual energy." Likewise, British historian Arnold Toynbee (in his *A Study of History*) referred to the possible "transfiguration" of modern society into some kind of "re-spiritualized" form. Toynbee coined the term *the law of progressive simplification,* in which true growth occurs as civilizations transfer increasing amounts of energy and attention from the material to the nonmaterial side of life, toward increased self-articulation. In other words, the criterion of growth is a progress toward self-determination. Any significant shift in society thus requires a change in the incumbent dominant paradigm: today, this requirement is global—a total global mind change. Our historical record as a species is the story of our movement through a series of perceptual paradigms. This is the hallmark of transformation—a change at the deepest levels within our social structures.

Similarly, our own belief systems are themselves social structures that have been reinforced throughout our lives, beginning in infancy and throughout childhood. We literally have any anomalies ironed out of us so that we agree with a consensus picture of reality. In a sense, we are more than nationalized; we are culturally hypnotized. Such processes are well documented by cultural anthropologists, who have shown how people who grow up in different cultures perceive different realities. Yet now such an ideological base is fundamentally inadequate. One of our greatest inadequacies is that we have agreed to a social reality that all but denies the presence and potential of consciousness. Our social affliction thus stems from an omission of consciousness within our paradigm of reality. We are in effect deceiving ourselves. We have become blind (perhaps deliberately so) to the edict, stated by Willis Harman, that "by deliberately changing their internal images of reality, people can change the world."[19]

A well-known story from the East tells of a fool called Mulla Nasrudin. In the story, someone saw Nasrudin searching for something on the ground.

"What have you lost, Mulla?" he asked.

"My key," said the Mulla. So they both went down on their knees and looked for it. After a time the other man asked, "Where exactly did you drop it?"

"In my own house."

"Then why are you looking here?"

"There is more light here than inside my own house."[20]

Individually and collectively, we often search where there is more light, which often means within the old paradigm, the old way of thinking. We need to start looking in the dark for that which we think is lost, for in truth it has only remained dormant: this is *a way of understanding* that will shift how we perceive life, reality, and ourselves.

IMPROVING THE MEME POOL

Psychologist and social thinker Timothy Leary, in his book *The Intelligence Agents,* discusses this need for a shift in social perceptions and intelligence and offers the following advice on how to develop such a capacity:

1. Continually expand the scope, source, intensity of the information you receive.
2. Constantly revise your reality maps, and seek new metaphors about the future to understand what's happening now.
3. Develop external networks for increasing intelligence. In particular, spend all your time with people who are smart or smarter than you.[21]

Leary, in his characteristic playful manner, is drawing attention to the possibility for *mental mutation*. This refers to the capacity for a mutational process to occur within the neurological dynamics of a given society. Such a process is likely to mark the transition phase from our present species, *Homo sapiens sapiens,* to the next (see chapter 9). Whereas in the past, the evolutionary markers were first biological, then cultural, today's evolutionary acceleration demands that rapid change be neurological and spiritual. In other words, the responsibility is on us to provide some of the participatory energies in the form of revitalized ideologies, understanding, and perceptions if we are to engage successfully in the coming changes. Rather than just a change in the gene pool, we also now need a radical upgrade to our species *meme pool.*

A meme (which can act as an evolutionary agent of change) can be anything from cultural linguistic artifacts, social laws, and shared truths to belief systems, either divine or dogmatic. In other words, a meme pool is a repository of ideas from which any given social collective drinks and refreshes itself—or against which it rebels. At the same time, ideas themselves can behave similar to biological viruses, as this extract from "The Global Brain Group" demonstrates:

> Consider the T-phage virus. A T-phage cannot replicate itself; it reproduces by hijacking the DNA of a bacterium, forcing its host to make millions of copies of the phage. Similarly, an idea can parasitically infect your mind and alter your behavior, causing you to want to tell your friends about the idea, thus exposing them to the idea-virus. Any idea which does this is called a "meme." . . . Unlike a virus, which is encoded in DNA molecules, a meme is nothing more than a pattern of information, one that happens to have evolved a form which induces people to repeat that pattern. Typical memes include individual slogans, ideas, catch-phrases, melodies, icons, inventions, and fashions. It may sound a bit sinister, this idea that people are hosts for mind-altering strings of symbols, but in fact this is what human culture is all about.[22]

The externalization of human thinking, in ideologies as well as in icons, is both a threat to our growth and a means for our empowerment and development. Human language, the expression of our thoughts, can be both a virus and an antidote. Just as RNA protein molecules act as transmitters of information between DNA molecules and carry information to instruct the DNA to develop and act and function, so does language in the human sphere act as the transmitter of our thoughts between "human cells" within the global body. If a bacterial virus spreads, such as cancer, it causes cells to decay, and the infected cells are liable to spread the disease further. Similarly, if a segment of the human population gets a viral idea (such as "kill all those opposed to our beliefs"), then this thought can spread rapidly throughout the language and culture. Thus, people and populations, like cancerous cells, can be infected and destroyed. Cultural critic Morris Berman is reported to have said that an idea is something you have, but an ideology is something that has you.

In brief, biology passes on genes, while human culture passes on memes. And the condition of our memes, our species' mind-set, will determine to a large degree our evolutionary fitness in these transition times. It is thus imperative—crucial—that we establish a healthy, positive, and forward thinking mind-set and perceptual paradigm. As described in chapter 1, we are all open systems that use information as energy, and this energy is precious and required to fuel us as we press ahead as a collective intelligence. Discipline, too, is required to ensure that our mindful (perceptual) energies are not lost and wasted through emotions of fear and anger or other inner disturbances that become enlarged, exaggerated, and then projected externally. It is useful to remember that negativity seeks to impress itself upon us to force us to believe it is more prevalent than it actually is. This is because negativity is always in a minority quantity in comparison with the positive; thus, it needs to pretend it is greater than it actually is if it is to have any chance of influence over us. These are the hallmarks of desperate practices. Our defense is the quality of our own thinking and consciousness—at all times. As Tom Montalk writes:

The surest way to work for the betterment of mankind is to improve yourself, educate yourself, become aware and skilled at delivering that awareness to others who are interested. It's more about building up your potential to serve than just going out there and haphazardly trying to do good. . . . Improving yourself means becoming ever more mentally stable and emotionally balanced, acquiring wisdom from observation and experience, taking great care to deal with people according to their level of understanding. Educating yourself means learning more about what really matters, what is really going on in this world and within yourself, the hidden things that manipulate people that could be stopped if only they knew about it, and the positive principles that if known and applied would allow one to progress more intelligently and powerfully yet compassionately through life.[23]

To engage with the transition times does not require from everyone that they should take the role of direct action. Much can be given through more subtle interactions, by simply being "in presence" with the right intentions and energy. The real evolutionary struggle we are facing now is a battle for our consciousness. The changing times of life on Planet Earth now require that we take more responsibility for ourselves. After all, when we lift ourselves, we also indirectly, yet significantly, lift the world around us.

To summarize, the most pressing problem facing humankind is not only a planet in transformation but also the perceptual and psychological state of our minds. As the transformation occurs and the magnetic frequency of Earth is affected, it is imperative that humanity retains, and focuses on, a balanced state of mind. It may be that we are in as much danger from ourselves as we are from the chaotic environment. We should not allow the quality of our human mental and emotional perceptions to degenerate at a time when they are needed the most. Human psychological pollution can be a very real disturbance and threat to us at this time. After all, the pollution from human thinking and behavior may be far more poisonous than physical pollution.

Disturbances of the human psyche are likely to interfere with (or may well disable) most people's capacity to cope with the challenges facing them during the transitional times. In other words, our way of thinking is a far greater danger to us than we have ever recognized. We seriously need to address this if we are ever to be able to forge a correct balance between our external and internal new worlds.

Humanity is required to undergo a *perceptual evolution* as well as a physical one. As such, a critical mass is required to shift away from old and antiquated paradigm thinking toward a revitalized mental maturity. Without this perceptual shift, rapid and accelerating transitions will appear more chaotic than they need to be. A period of explosive development and change will greatly affect how we think. Likewise, stagnant mind-sets and beliefs may attempt to hold back the floodwaters of transformation and cause unnecessary tensions. As a collective consciousness, we need to be psychically centered, balanced, and aware of potential turbulence. A deep psychological crisis may develop as people feel the guilt and shame of a weakened world that has diminished future opportunities for life. As part of the transition, we may cross the threshold between the paradigm of a stagnant and stillborn species and that of a bruised but still relatively healthy evolutionary species. Our evolutionary growth, as Duane Elgin reminds us, "is not an abstract philosophical concept—it is a reality of the flesh that, at each stage, must be paid for in the blood and lives of countless individuals. There are no free gifts in evolution. We must genuinely earn access to each new stage of development."[24]

Already, we are further along the road of reflexive consciousness than we might think: many of us are now aware of the global ethical issues and injustices. The world has seen the Live Aid concerts for Africa and the many Earth Day groups and Earth Summits that tap into our collective resourcefulness. We have begun to coalesce at ever-more-complex levels and scales of consciousness and to voice our collective concerns when we feel that things are not right. It is important we trust these feelings and give them stronger support. *How* we think affects everything around us, from our environment to our friendships. If we believe ourselves to exist on an unconscious rock within an accidental universe, then desires for material gains and environmental mastery appear logical. Our cultural development mirrors our perceptual capacities, and both influence each other: one cannot evolve without the other. Evolution of species, society, and individuals involves long periods of relative stability punctuated by windows of accelerated transition (often chaotic and turbulent) that create new paradigms of perception. Thus, our thoughts constitute a powerful language, one that will become increasingly more active. With communication comes responsibility as we face what Elgin calls a "crisis of civilizational consciousness and communication that is as critical as any of the material challenges we confront."[25]

In the next chapter, I describe how the new sciences are recognizing the prominent role of consciousness as a participating factor in our lives and how, ultimately, we are all fundamentally connected.

A Tale to Finish: A Change of Mind

God decided to come down to Earth for a quick look at how his creation was coming along. He approached Earth and happened to look at a big tree full of howling monkeys. As He looked down, one of the monkeys happened to look up and saw him. The monkey became excited and started to shout, "I see God. . . . I see God!"

None of the other monkeys paid any attention. Some thought the monkey was crazy or perhaps just a religious fanatic. They went on about their daily lives of collecting food, taking care of their young, fighting with each other, and so on, and so on. Not getting any attention, our monkey decided to try to get attention from God, and said, "God, Almighty, You are the Beneficent, the Merciful, please help me!"

In an instant, the monkey was transformed into a man living in his own human community. Everything changed, except for one thing: the monkey's mind. The monkey immediately realized that could *be a problem.*

"Well, thank you, God, but what about my mind?"

"That," said God, "you will have to change yourself."

5
THE NEW SCIENCES

Coherence, Connectivity, and the Quantum World

We are not just an accidental anomaly, the microscopic caprice of a tiny particle whirling in the endless depths of the universe. Instead, we are mysteriously connected to the universe, we are mirrored in it, just as the entire evolution of the universe is mirrored in us.

VÁCLAV HAVEL, FIRST PRESIDENT
OF THE CZECH REPUBLIC

We no longer live within a mechanical universe, the clockwork machine that was the handiwork of Newtonian science. That was the old paradigm that governed the Western world through much of the scientific age. It may have fared well for us in the past, when humankind's limited horizons needed answers for celestial questions. Yet such a paradigm serves us no longer. It is restrictive and denies us our fundamental connectivity. The old way of thinking about our place in the cosmos was isolationist and provided no means for participating in an energetic universe. Life on Earth has been regarded for too long as an evolutionary accident whirling through space. While we have advanced our scientific knowledge of the universe, it has not provided humanity with a more intimate presence within a meaningful cosmos. Yet science need not be lacking; it can be visionary, too, and provide new models of thought. Science can confirm what many people have always felt but could not rationally describe—the inherent connection between all living things and the cosmos. Many indigenous people have known and have lived with such understanding, yet most of modern civilization has denied and neglected such intuitions. Many indigenous people have lived, and continue to live, within a cosmological order, whereas the industrial world went out of sync and lost that vital connection. We need to return to the understanding that we live not so much in a cosmos as in a *cosmogenesis,* which is, according to Thomas Berry, "a universe ever coming into being through an irreversible sequence of transformations moving, in the larger arc of its development, from a lesser to a great order of complexity and from a lesser to great consciousness."[1]

The new sciences (as opposed to the mechanistic sciences) are now revealing to us that we live in a dynamically evolving universe that is fundamentally interconnected. Ours is an integral reality, a holographic matrix of immense, concentrated energy. Further, it now appears that the presence of our universe is no cosmic accident, rather, it was a carefully arranged birth. There are too many finely tuned, correlated constants for the birth of our universe to be chance. The coherence of the universal constants is staggeringly accurate. For example, as Ervin Laszlo notes, "If the expansion rate of the early universe had been one billionth less than it was, the universe would have recollapsed almost immediately; if it had been one-billionth more, it would have flown apart so fast that it could produce only dilute, cold gases . . . that the large-scale coherence of the universe would be merely a vast series of 'coincidences' is extremely improbable."[2]

We do not live in an "improbable" world; we live in a world that is highly organized, patterned, coherent, geometric, mathematical, dynamic, conscious, and which maintains a non-linear stability. The human body, too, manifests examples of incredible fine-tuning. The human body, for example, consists of ten-to-the-fourteenth-power cells—that's 100,000,000,000,000 cells—and each cell produces ten thousand bioelectrical reactions every second. All these reactions and signals are almost instantly correlated throughout the body's cellular structure. The human body operates as a coherent and integral field, components of which are in constant communication at speeds faster than signals can be conducted through the nervous system (as will be discussed later). It is also an inherent capacity of individuals to be able to achieve a high level of spontaneous synchronization in their cerebral functions. H. J. Eysenck, a renowned psychologist, once said, "Unless there is a gigantic conspiracy involving thirty university departments all over the world, and several hundred highly respected scientists in various fields, many of them originally hostile to the claims of the psychic researchers, the only conclusion the unbiased observer can come to must be that there are people who obtain knowledge existing in other people's minds, or in the outer world, by means yet unknown to science."[3]

Perhaps such abilities were as yet unknown to science when Eysenck was writing, yet now this situation is rapidly changing. The new sciences that are emerging tell us that everything is ultimately interconnected and interdependent—a living field. And this understanding will assist in shifting our present global society into a new era of expanded horizons.

QUANTUM SCIENCE, QUANTUM SOCIETY

The arrival of quantum physics signaled an alternative vision to a linear science that was clearly inadequate for an emerging global world. The mechanistic paradigm was serving a dysfunctional social agenda and failing to serve the spiritual needs of humanity. Quantum science delivered a new crisis to accepted thought, a crisis of perception. Quantum science has forced us to see the universe anew, not as a realm of separate objects but as a woven web of relations that forms a unified whole. These relationships are both physical and mental and are defined by their existence within the whole. Matter, which consists of atoms and subatomic particles, is now understood to be formed from a ceaseless flow of energy that manifests physically as interacting particles. Particle interactions then give rise to the structures of the material world, yet beneath these structures exists an endless dynamic cosmic dance of energy. This view creates a perceptual model that is holistic and ecological, as it expresses the nature of reciprocal maintenance. Individuals, groups, and societies are all embedded within interdependent processes and cannot exist independently. In other words, no man is an island (to quote poet John Donne).

Neils Bohr, a pioneer in quantum theory, once stated, "Those who are not shocked when they first come across quantum theory cannot possibly have understood it."[4] Of course, how can a person brought up on a diet of physical reality readily accept that time and space operate as a simultaneous continuum, as a nonlocal field? The reality of the new quantum paradigm compels us to view the world around us as a continuum of interrelated events. Objects are no longer solid or separate, with definite time-space locations, but are instead morphed into mutually entangled creative energies. The quantum world has provided for us a glimpse of the universe in which we participate as undivided wholeness. Part of this wholeness comes through the understanding of nonlocality, which is often presented in the form of the Einstein, Podolsky, and Rosen paradox (known as the EPR paradox).

Experiments using the EPR paradox have concluded that by the act of measuring the spin of one particle (often referred to as the collapse of the wave function), that action is instantaneously communicated to the other particle emitted from the same source, regardless of the distance that now stands between them. In this sense, the particles react as if they are a continuously connected part of an undivided *fabric,* intimately woven together, wherein a local effect is instantaneously transmitted *universally.* The quantum realm informs us that as soon as particles have "met" and "been acquainted," then they retain an everlasting connectedness. Likewise, the particle-wave duality (the concept that all matter and energy exhibits both wave-like and particle-like properties) reveals to us a reality that is created in relation to observation and perception. This tells us that a fundamental quantum can either be a particle or a wave, depending on how we observe it. In other words, both are facets of the same reality and both understandings are required to understand the bigger picture.

We can wonder whether this behavior could not also refer to human beings. In a sense, we can be metaphorically referred to as operating like both a particle (the individual) and a wave (the collective). In today's contemporary world, this can mean, according to social philosopher Danah Zohar, that we can manifest the behavior of a *quantum self*. Zohar writes, "In its 'particle aspect,' the Quantum Self can be seen to have an important individual integrity and yet, through its 'wave aspect,' to be simultaneously in relation to other selves and to the culture at large. This lays the basis for both personal identity and personal responsibility and at the same time for intimacy and group identity."[5]

This nonseparatist view of universal entanglement holds the potential for deeper relationships that are more dynamic and creative. In recent years, more and more people have begun to sense that the new sciences may have the blueprint for a new worldview, a view that would verify, and give credibility to, a life based on a more holistic, less fragmented understanding. Such a perceptual shift from separation to wholeness and connection could help foster a move from competition to collaboration, from greed to sufficiency, and from outer authority to inner authority and well-being. In this sense, the narratives of our scientific knowledge would have first shifted from the physical sciences to the life sciences, then to the human sciences, and finally, now, to the spiritual sciences. And within the spiritual sciences, the concept of the hologram—our *holographic universe*—has been realized.[6]

The holographic principle largely entered quantum science through the work of David Böhm, whose work on implicate order constituted a universal undivided whole. Within this implicate order, each part simultaneously contained the whole, as is now seen in a holographic pictogram. The characteristics of a holographic universe imply that all information is not located in the individual parts but in their interference pattern. Any one part of a hologram thus contains and resonates information of the whole. The focus here is not on individual bodies within specific time-space locations, but on a simultaneous field of information and connection. Likewise, Bohm helped to establish the theory that the brain, with its wave patterns, operates in a manner similar to a hologram. Such understanding gives further recognition and validity to the notions of wholeness, instantaneity, uncertainty, future possibilities, and interdependency.

The coherence observed in the behavior of energy and matter indicates that there is an underlying field active in our universe, a field that produces quasi-instantaneous connections among all objects, even when they are at opposite ends of the universe. Philosopher Ervin Laszlo, in writing about the electromagnetic and gravitational fields, also described this integral field as the *Akashic field*. He writes, "Electric and magnetic phenomena are now ascribed to the universal EM-field, the mutual attraction of noncontiguous objects is ascribed to the universal G-field, and the presence of mass is ascribed to the universal Higgs field. By the same reasoning it is logical to ascribe the nonlocal coherence observed in nature to an interconnecting field . . . ."[7]

This interconnecting field is for Laszlo the so-called Akashic field that underlies the quantum vacuum. For many, the quantum vacuum is seen as the modern-day equivalent of the ether theory, in which there was said to be a universal background energy or medium in space. That the universe is permeated throughout with a medium that connects all has been one of the areas that physicists have looked at in order to account for a grand unified theory. The concept of a fifth field suggests that there is a more fundamental level of reality that underlies our own mapping of the universe. The universe, in this new paradigm, is merely the waves that roll across an ocean, and the ocean itself is the quantum vacuum. The interacting field between the quantum vacuum and our physical universe (the Akashic field) has also been referred to by some scientists as the *psi field*. It is this psi field that permeates all physical reality and manifests as nonlocal consciousness. That is, if all reality is but the surface of an ocean, then all the drops on this water surface are in reality in connection with one another. Likewise, one's mind and consciousness can resonate with other minds if they are in alignment. If other minds are receptive to this, we can have thought transference.

Therefore, we have the new sciences validating what once was thought of as pure mysticism. In the words of Fritjof Capra, "To paraphrase an old Chinese saying, mystics understand the root of the Tao but not its branches; scientists understand its branches but not its roots. Science does not need mysticism and mysticism does not need science; but man needs both. Mystical experience is necessary to understand the deepest nature of things, and science is essential for modern life. What we need, therefore, is not a Synthesis but a dynamic interplay between mystical intuition and scientific analysis."[8]

It has been suggested that the quantum vacuum also exhibits holographic characteristics, implying that it is capable of retaining all known events, histories, and perhaps even thought-forms. Imagine an ocean that could memorize each ripple and resonance that manifested on its surface. This new understanding is important for human behavior in that it suggests that our behavior and our thoughts could be imprinted on this holographic quantum vacuum. Never before, it seems, has science explained the need for good thoughts and deeds within a cosmological framework!

In a similar manner, legendary inventor and thinker Nikola Tesla spoke of an "original medium" that fills space. In his 1907 unpublished paper titled "Man's Greatest Achievement," Tesla writes that there exists an original medium that acts like a kind of force field. Further, this field manifests as matter when prana, or cosmic energy, acts upon it, and when the action ceases, matter disintegrates back into the energy medium. Tesla writes, "All perceptible matter comes from a primary substance, or a tenuity beyond conception, filling all space, the Akasha or luminiferous ether, which is acted upon by the life-giving Prana or Creative Force, calling into existence, in never ending cycles, all things and phenomena. The primary substance, thrown into infinitesimal whirls of prodigious velocity, becomes gross matter; the force subsiding, the motion ceases and matter disappears, reverting to the primary substance."[9]

Laszlo continues this line of investigation to conclude that the human brain would be sensitive to the psi field (Akashic field), as the neural networks of the human brain would follow dynamics similar to those of the resonating interactions of the holographic universe. This reinforces David Bohm and Karl Pribram's holonomic model of brain processing. As for the use of the psi field for transpersonal recall, Laszlo believes that this explains the following phenomena: telepathic communication between individuals, past-life recollections, natural healing, and simultaneous insights among individuals as well as between cultures.[10]

The emerging paradigm of the new sciences links mind and consciousness with matter, life, and cosmology to form a more whole and integral understanding. It is a case of the separate fields of human knowledge and study reflecting how we perceive the separate nature of our reality. Mainstream knowledge has some catching up to do if it wishes to shift toward the bigger picture that is now emerging, not only in scientific papers, but more important, within people's own inner intuitions. Within the quantum energy field, we find that there exists a tremendous degree of coherence, which is essential for connection and communication.

QUANTUM COHERENCE AND SYNCHRONIZATION

The latest findings in quantum biology and biophysics give further validity to the coherence within all living systems. It has been found through extensive scientific investigation that the model of quantum coherence within living biological systems originates from biological excitations and biophoton emissions. What this means is that metabolic energy is stored as a form of electromechanical and electromagnetic excitations. These coherent excitations are considered responsible for generating and maintaining long-range order via the transformation of energy and very weak electromagnetic signals.

After nearly twenty years of experimental research, Fritz-Albert

Popp put forward the hypothesis that biophotons are emitted from a coherent electrodynamical field within the living system.[11] What this now-recognized theory effectively means is that each living cell is giving off, or resonating, a biophoton field of coherent energy. If each cell is emitting this field, then the whole living system is, in effect, a resonating field, a ubiquitous nonlocal field. And since it is by the means of biophotons that the living system communicates, then there is near-instantaneous intercommunication throughout. And this, claims Popp, is the basis for coherent biological organization, which is referred to as quantum coherence. This discovery led Popp to state that the capacity for evolution rests not on aggressive struggle and rivalry, but on the capacity for communication and cooperation. In this sense, we learn that evolution is not about the individual, but rather about living systems that are interlinked within a coherent whole.

Popp and biophysicist Mae-Wan Ho write, "Living systems are thus neither the subjects alone, nor objects isolated, but both subjects and objects in a mutually communicating universe of meaning. . . . Just as the cells in an organism take on different tasks for the whole, different populations enfold information not only for themselves, but for all other organisms, expanding the consciousness of the whole, while at the same time becoming more and more aware of this collective consciousness. Human consciousness may have its most significant role in the development and creative expression of the collective consciousness of nature."[12]

Ho describes how the living organism, including the human body, is coordinated throughout and is "coherent beyond our wildest dreams." It appears that every part of our body is "in communication with every other part through a dynamic, tuneable, responsive, liquid crystalline medium that pervades the whole body, from organs and tissues to the interior of every cell."[13]

What this means is that the medium of our bodies is a form of liquid crystal, thus an ideal transmitter of communication, resonance, and coherence. These relatively new developments in biophysics have demonstrated that all biological organisms are composed of a liquid crystalline medium. Further, biophysics has shown that DNA consists of a liquid crystal lattice-type structure (which some refer to as a liquid crystal gel), wherein body cells are involved in a *holographic* instantaneous communication via the emitting of biophotons (a source based on light). This implies that all living biological organisms continuously emit radiations of light that form a field of coherence and communication. This will be of importance later in the chapter, when I discuss the influence of vibrations. Moreover, biophysics has shown that living organisms are permeated by quantum waveforms. As Ho informs us, "The visible body just happens to be where the wave function of the organism is most dense. Invisible quantum waves are spreading out from each of us and permeating into all other organisms. At the same time, each of us has the waves of every other organism entangled within our own make-up. . . . We are participants in the creation drama that is constantly unfolding. We are constantly co-creating and re-creating ourselves and other organisms in the universe."[14]

The liquid crystalline structure within living systems is also responsible for the direct current (DC) electrodynamical field that permeates the entire body of all animals. It has also been noted that the DC field has a mode of semiconduction that is much faster than the nervous system.[15] As we shall see, the electrical field of the human body is important when we come to discuss coherence regarding planetary resonance.

If living biological systems are operating within a nonlocal interwoven field of resonating energy excitations, then perhaps it is possible to see this manifesting in physical behavior. Mathematician Steven Strogatz describes a remarkably wide range of cooperative behavior in living and a nonliving matter, at every scale, from the subatomic to the cosmic, using the concept of synchronization (or sync).[16] Strogatz identifies three levels where his notion of synchronicity operates: at the lowest, the microscopic level; at the next level, between the various organs; and at the third level, between our bodies and the world around us. As a way of demonstrating how humans can adjust their behavior to lock in with synchronization, the fiasco concerning the opening of the Millennium

Bridge in London serves as a colorful example. On the occasion of the bridge's momentous opening, a multitude of people all began to walk across the bridge, whereupon the bridge began to sway under the feet of the pedestrians. This shock occurrence caused the authorities to close the bridge until further architectural and engineering investigations could locate the cause of the bridge's unsuspected swaying movement. The source of this mysterious swaying was, according to Strogatz, the result of "people-sync." As he explains it:

> As the bridge swayed, the pedestrians unconsciously adjusted their pace to walk in time with the lateral movement. This exacerbated the vibration, which impelled more people to lose their balance and simultaneously swing to the same side, reinforcing their synchrony and aggravating the vibration still further. It was this chain reaction—the positive feedback between the people and the bridge—that no one had ever anticipated, and that triggered the wobbling of the Millennium Bridge . . . it had never occurred to the architects that a crowd of 2000 civic-minded people could inadvertently synchronise their strolling.[17]

In a similar way, Ho describes how coherent excitations in living systems operate in much the same way as a boat race, where the people on the oars must row in step so as to create a phase transition. This indicates that there is an inherent tendency in nature, and in living systems, to resonate together in sync as a way of maintaining order and coherency. This type of behavior serves to reinforce the relationship between the individual and the collective that before had been thought random. This discovery should be a factor in shifting our perceptions from an individualistic framework toward one that sees our evolution within the tangible and evident design of a deeply integral and woven set of relations.

Our sciences and our intuitions are trying to tell us something that deep inside we probably already know, or at least feel or sense: that we are intimately connected to all life around us. Internal and external systems are in coherence, are interrelated, and are in constant, simultaneous communication. In this way, natural systems and most biological organisms are instinctively oriented toward maintaining or improving this sense of community or species coherence. However, it may be that human beings are the only living beings that are, as Laszlo writes, "consciously and willfully destructive of coherence in their bodies as well as in their communities and environments."[18] Yet perhaps human affairs only appear to be chaotic. Author and philosopher Edward W. Russell writes, "Whether we look at the stars and planets in their courses or examine the miraculous processes of life, we see abundant evidence of faultless organization. Only human affairs seem to be an exception to the general rule."[19]

As a species, we may have alienated ourselves from nature, been the transgressor, and believed ourselves to be autonomous. Yet this has always been a delusion maintained through our sociocultural perceptual myopia. Our norms have in fact become our prisons, and now they are in danger of veiling from us our inherent connection to the cosmos and all vibrant creative energies. Perhaps when enough people evolve their thinking and consciousness, they will become aware of their deep ties to each other and to the universal design. As a result, the renewal that humanity so badly needs will be less painful and more of a transition than a collapse and breakdown. Such a manifestation of an evolved consciousness is crucial for humanity's future. As Václav Havel once declared, "The moment it begins to appear that we are deeply connected to the entire universe, science returns . . . in a roundabout way, to man and offers him his lost integrity. It does so by anchoring him once more in the cosmos."[20]

Without being anchored in the cosmos, we forfeit our inherent right for conscious participation in the grand evolutionary journey.

In the next chapter, I continue the journey of the new sciences and explore the crystalline nature of DNA. In particular, I look at how it holds for us the promise of more dynamic interconnection within our energetic environment, and how this is evolving too. Our evolutionary journey continues.

A Tale to Finish: Written in the Sands

A stream, from its source in far-off mountains, passing through every kind and description of countryside, at last reached the sands of the desert. Just as it had crossed every other barrier, the stream tried to cross this one, but it found that as fast as it ran into the sand, its waters disappeared. It was convinced, however, that its destiny was to cross this desert, and yet there was no way. Now a hidden voice, coming from the desert itself, whispered, "The wind crosses the desert, and so can the stream."

The stream objected that it was dashing itself against the sand, only to get absorbed, that the wind could fly, and that was why it could cross a desert.

"By hurtling in your own accustomed way, you cannot get across," said the voice. "You will either disappear or become a marsh. You must allow the wind to carry you over to your destination."

"But how could this happen?"

"By allowing yourself to be absorbed in the wind," the voice told the stream.

This idea was not acceptable to the stream. After all, it had never been absorbed before. It did not want to lose its individuality. And once having lost it, how was one to know that it could ever be regained?

"The wind," said the sand, "performs this function. It takes up water, carries it over the desert, and then lets it fall again. Falling as rain, the water again becomes a stream."

"How can I know that is true?"

"It is so, and if you do not believe it, you cannot become more than a quagmire, and even that could take many, many years, and it certainly is not the same as a stream."

"But can I not remain the same stream that I am today?"

"You cannot in either case remain so," the whisper said. "Your essential part is carried away and forms a stream again. You are called what you are even today because you do not know which part of you is the essential one."

When the stream heard this, certain echoes began to arise in his thoughts. Dimly, he remembered a state in which he—or some part of him?—had been held in the arms of a wind. He also remembered—or did he?—that this was the real thing, not necessarily the obvious thing to do.

And the stream raised his vapor into the welcoming arms of the wind, which gently and easily bore it upward and along, letting it fall softly as soon as they reached the roof of a mountain, many, many miles away. And because the stream had had his doubts, he was able to remember and record more strongly in his mind the details of the experience. He reflected, "Yes, now I have learned my true identity."

The stream was learning. But the sands whispered, "We know, because we see it happen day after day, and because we, the sands, extend from the riverside all the way to the mountain."

And that is why it is said, "The way in which the Stream of Life is to continue on its journey is written in the Sands."[21]

6

OUR RESONATING WORLD

Living within an Energetic Environment

Our spiritual challenge is not to reach beyond this world but to come into dynamic alignment with it.

DUANE ELGIN, *AWAKENING EARTH:*
EXPLORING THE EVOLUTION OF HUMAN
CULTURE AND CONSCIOUSNESS

In the previous chapter, I discussed how biological organisms exhibit unbelievable levels of coherency that create an electromagnetic field within, around, and between organisms. This nonlocal field resonates and acts as a communication medium, as an informational field. In other words, all biological organisms function as information processors. Not only do they take in information about their environment, process it, and use it for survival, but they also receive and transmit information, as would an antenna. Recent discoveries in biophysics also now recognize that cellular structures, including DNA, are made of liquid crystals, a medium that is the perfect vehicle for coherent oscillations. These oscillations are the product of the cells emitting light pulses, called biophotons. As a whole, what this tells us is that living biological systems are liquid crystalline structures that manifest a nonlocal field by emitting coherent light pulses and that are intertwined within a matrix of quantum wave interferences. This is important information, as it now tells us that we are enmeshed within a continual electrical interplay within ourselves, between living organisms, and with external influences. This is of major importance for a world awash in electrical radiation and pollution as well as cosmic radiations. Literally, there is no inside or outside; there is only a continuous field of creative, oscillating energy.

The human nervous system is a part of our evolutionary apparatus. It, too, functions through electrical impulses, and so is affected by, and influences, other electrical fields. It makes one wonder, with the present generation of humans being born into the information age, which includes an overpolluted electronic environment, what are some of the effects on the human nervous system? And to what degree can the human nervous system mutate under these new environmental impacts, knowing as we do that evolutionary change is dynamic in accordance with such impacts?

According to the research of Robert O. Becker (now a retired professor of medicine), "The human species has changed its electromagnetic background more than any other aspect of its environment . . . the density of radio waves around us now is 100 million or 200 million times the natural level reaching us from the sun."[1] Becker has no doubt that the greatest polluting element in Earth's environment during our present era is the rapid growth in electromagnetic fields. Environmental factors are changing at a pace that may be too fast for us. Our adaptation time is incredibly short; the cyclic nature of civilizations should make us think about where we are heading and the time scale. Industrial nations have an immense need for, and use of, energy that has radically changed the total electromagnetic field of Earth. Most of us are unaware of this change in our environment because we are unable to directly perceive it with our senses. Whereas before the twentieth century Earth's electromagnetic field was composed of natural fields, today we are drowning in a sea of man-made electrical currents and discharges. Biological organisms on Earth have evolved over geological time within the electromagnetic fields that were inherent in the basic magnetic field of

Earth, as influenced by the sun; now all this has suddenly changed.

Earth's magnetic field has been measured at roughly 500 milli-gauss, and it remains fairly steady, only oscillating slightly depending upon the time of day and solar influences. Our global communication frequencies, while being in a lower range, are oscillating at greater rates. Becker's research, and that of others, shows that our human bodies and immune systems are being negatively affected by man-made electromagnetic fields, such as those from power lines, satellites, and cell phones. And those of us who live in the richer nations are especially swamped by a world of electrical appliances. The rapid rise in cell phone usage worldwide has contributed significantly to our exposure to electromagnetic energy above and beyond our normal limits. Some cell phones operate in the megahertz range, others in the gigahertz range, which is billions of cycles per second. This means that the electromagnetic radiation is oscillating at extremely rapid frequencies. And the higher the frequencies, the higher the energy radiation.[2] It is almost impossible these days to go anywhere where there is no electromagnetic pollution from human activities and technologies.

Further, there has been much research (not all of it published due to commercial pressure) that indicates that low-strength oscillating electromagnetic fields have definitive effects on human brain function and DNA. An academic article published in the journal *Bioelectromagnetics,* titled "Do Electromagnetic Fields Interact Directly with DNA?" stated, "Studies on DNA have shown that large electron flows are possible within the stacked base pairs of the double helix. Therefore, gene activation by magnetic fields could be due to direct interaction with moving electrons within DNA. Electric fields as well as magnetic fields stimulate transcription, and both fields could interact with DNA directly."[3]

The question here is whether such electromagnetic field increases will have a detrimental effect on our DNA and human nervous system. Also, what effect will they have on our physical and spiritual well-being if they interfere with the natural biophoton emissions of our human DNA? There is little doubt that social behavior, in the Western nations at least, has become increasingly erratic, with the surprising rise of attention deficit disorder (known as ADD) being just one example of a variety of modern "dis-eases." However, scientists are beginning to understand how the human being is susceptible (and possibly vulnerable) to the influence of varying frequencies, both natural and man-made.

That such "technologies of influence" exist is also given validity by what former U.S. National Security Advisor Zbigniew Brzezinski wrote more than twenty-five years ago: "Political strategists are tempted to exploit research on the brain and human behavior. Geophysicist Gordon J. F. MacDonald, a specialist in problems of warfare, says accurately-timed, artificially-excited electronic strokes could lead to a pattern of oscillations that produce relatively high power levels over certain regions of the earth . . . in this way one could develop a system that would seriously impair the brain performance of very large populations in selected regions over an extended period."[4]

The use of frequencies, whether for medicine or social engineering, is already a known technology. There is well-established scientific and military awareness of the susceptibility of the human body to harmonic interference. However, for our purposes here, I focus on the potential for positive influences of frequency on the human body.

In this chapter, I examine the vibrational nature of DNA, how it can be influenced by words and frequencies, and how living organisms are in a resonating relationship with our planet.

OUR RESONATING WORLD
DNA and Harmonics

DNA has proliferated for millions of years and is practically the oldest thing in Earth's evolution still alive on its surface. DNA has a remarkable history, lifespan, tolerance, and above all, adaptability. In one sense, DNA is our blueprint, our human master plan. It is our past, our present, and our future, simultaneously. DNA has always taken a central role in our evolutionary jumps and spurts. Even today, scientists are discovering hidden qualities and properties in DNA, beyond their earlier mechanistic assumptions. Incredibly, junk DNA, a label colloquially used for the approximately 95 percent of DNA for which no function has been identified, continues to puzzle geneticists. Yet DNA is extraordinarily sensitive and receptive to external signals and resonances. In short, DNA receives, processes, and responds to environmental conditions at an astounding rate of change. Without the participation of DNA and its mutational adaptation for change, we would not have evolution as we know it on this planet. Further, it is my contention that our next stage of species evolutionary growth will involve a change in the vibrational structure of our DNA. After all, DNA directly affects how the human nervous system functions, and the history of life and of humanity is often defined in terms of the evolution of the nervous system. It is important, then, to know that human DNA can be influenced by external words and frequencies.

Various voices have, over time, expressed the notion that DNA can be accessed through deliberate, conscious intention, such as in well-documented shamanistic practices.[5] Investigators such as Timothy Leary have discussed metaprogramming the "human biocomputer" by accessing the DNA through various transpersonal methods.[6] Now, however, we are gaining scientific advances into some of the potential properties of DNA. Research has been conducted into how words and environment influence human DNA.

Russian biophysicist and molecular biologist Pjotr Garjajev, who is a member of the Russian Academy of Sciences, directed a group of researchers in the 1990s in Moscow on the study of DNA and human genetics. They began to focus on the junk DNA and found that this "silent" DNA actually speaks a complex language. Further, the Moscow group proved that these extensive codes in the DNA, which are not used for protein synthesis, are instead actually used for communication, more exactly, for *hypercommunication*. In their terms, hypercommunication refers to a data exchange on the DNA level using genetic code. Garjajev and his group analyzed the vibrational response of DNA and concluded that it functions much like networked intelligence and that it allows for hypercommunication of information among all sentient beings. For example, the Moscow research group proved that damaged chromosomes (such as those damaged by X rays) can be repaired. Their method was to capture the information patterns of particular DNA and then to transmit these patterns, using focused light frequencies, onto another genome as a way of reprogramming the cells. In this way, they successfully transformed frog embryos into salamander embryos simply by transmitting the DNA information patterns.

Researchers Grazyna Fosar and Franz Bludorf (who have written on Garjajev's work) write that DNA can thus be influenced, and even reprogrammed, by words and frequencies. They note how Garjajev's research shows that certain frequency patterns can be "beamed" (such as with a laser) to transfer genetic information. DNA, they conclude, can be modulated through the use of external frequencies, if the proper frequencies are being used. This, they further conclude, can indirectly explain such phenomena as clairvoyance, intuition, remote acts of healing, and other psychic attributes. Also, this research suggests that a new form of vibrational medicine could be possible, as DNA could potentially be healed, or reprogrammed, by the use of frequencies without the need for cutting and splicing genes.

Many esoteric and spiritual traditions have stated in the past that the human body can be programmed by the vibrational frequencies of language, words, and thought. Now, perhaps for the first time, we are getting credible scientific proof of such processes. Of course, this does not mean that all spiritual practitioners will be able to demonstrate such refined abilities. Fosar and Bludorf continue their analysis by saying:

> In nature, hypercommunication has been successfully applied for millions of years. The organized flow of life in insect states proves this dramatically. Modern man knows it only on a much more subtle level as "intuition." But we, too, can regain full use of it. . . . Now that we are fairly stable in our individual consciousness, we can create a new form of group consciousness, namely one, in which we

attain access to all information via our DNA without being forced or remotely controlled about what to do with that information. . . . Hypercommunication in the new millennium means something quite different: Researchers think that if humans with full individuality would regain group consciousness . . . When a great number of people get together very closely, potentials of violence also dissolve. It looks as if here, too, a kind of humanitarian consciousness of all humanity is created.[7]

This conclusion harkens back to what was said in chapter 4 about the global brain and collective consciousness. The latest findings in information transfer via frequencies give further validity to such claims, as does the research into quantum coherence. The findings that frequencies affect DNA and cellular information also provide added weight to the hypothesis that changes and disruptions in Earth's magnetic field, via solar storms, could impact human well-being and possibly evolutionary growth. We can also make a reference back to an earlier suggestion that evolution on Earth has been achieved by making available at a planetary level a succession of energies, each higher in frequency than the one before. Does this imply, then, that DNA is actively targeted for mutation by the higher succession of energies penetrating Earth? If so, it suggests that there are formidable times ahead, as Earth's protective magnetic shield is disappearing at exactly the same time that our solar system is, according to some accounts, moving through a highly energized portion of the galaxy. This highly charged energy will also be flowing into the sun, creating the potential for stronger sun flares. This will add to the solar emissions radiating upon the planets within our system, impacting life on Earth in ways that remain unknown to us. Evolution, it seems, may operate as much upon external cosmic influences as it does domestic ones.

Again referring back to the research in biophysics, if all of our molecular structure is composed of liquid crystal that emits biophotons, then we are susceptible to outside electromagnetic influences. This suggests that our internal resonance, and thus our well-being, can be affected by our own deep thoughts (the electromagnetic impulses from our brains) as much as by electromagnetic pollution (such as from cell phones). This provides a new perspective when considering the power of prayer. It seems that intention, meditation, and contemplation are ways to influence the well-being of our body through harmonizing and balancing our electromagnetic biophoton resonance and frequencies. A stillness of mind creates a harmonious frequency field. One of the primary functions of prayer, in its original intention, was to prepare the mind to become more receptive to particular influences through focused brainwave activity. For example, a prayer in the form of a repeated word, be it a mantra, chant, or *zikr,* is a method to act upon the brain via specific sound wave frequencies. It is, in fact, a science, as all true spirituality is. The cosmos resonates with energy that is conscious, dynamic, and creative.

Bruce Lipton, in his book *The Biology of Belief,* introduces us to the science of epigenetics and shows that, in fact, genes and DNA are not the rigid biological components that we are lead to believe. Instead, he states that DNA can be influenced by signals external to the cell, such as those vibrations that result from positive and negative thinking. In other words, our very genetic blueprint is susceptible, to some degree, to *how we think.* Lipton says there is strong scientific evidence that DNA can be made to mutate by external factors within a person's own lifetime.[8] And our lifetime now is going through an unprecedented shift. Maybe every species goes through a similar process of DNA mutation and an expansion of consciousness when it is its time. Well, is it time to upgrade the human nervous system to incorporate the newly arriving increased energies? After all, our nervous system was created for a world that is now rapidly out of date.

To recap, the human body can be influenced by the resonations of external frequencies, whether from our technologies or from close contact with people around us. Yet this is not something new to many of us: have we not often referred to the sensation of "bad vibes" or of feeling drained when in the presence of particular people? At all times, the human body operates as a receiving and transmitting antenna. This capacity is the basis for a new science of harmonic medicine, or vibrational medicine, using what is known as subtle energy therapies.[9] It is still not widely known by the public that human DNA is composed of liquid crystal and emits biophotons, and that human cells use a form of biophoton emission for the quasi-instantaneous transfer of bioinformation. Thus, vibrational medicine techniques create "informational inputs" that affect the patient's biofield in an attempt to alleviate the disease. Yet not only are cellular biophotons used as a medium for bodily coherence, but the water in the human body is likewise a carrier for harmonic resonance. Water, as a liquid crystal, can act as an information carrier within the human body and can also be affected by external stimuli. That water crystals can be affected by thoughts and words alone is reflected in the work of Masaru Emoto.

Emoto has shown, by using microscopic photographs, how water crystals are affected by words and environment. Emoto's water crystal experiments consist of exposing water in glasses to different stimuli (such as music and either positive or negative words or emotions), freezing the water, and then examining the resulting crystals using microscopic photography. As an example, a sample of water was taken from a natural waterfall, and its crystalline molecular structure was recorded. This same sample was then divided, with half of it placed next to a TV and half placed in a busy office environment. Within a day, both samples were taken for examination, and it was found that their molecular crystalline structure had become slightly deformed. Later, one of these two samples was placed within a church and the other was placed in a meditative environment. Within two days, they were examined and found to have reverted back to their crisp crystalline molecular structure. In other words, Emoto believes that water exposed to positive influences produces beautiful, perfectly formed crystals, while water exposed to negativity produces ugly, malformed crystals. Since our bodies are 70 percent water, the power to change the crystalline coherence of water suggests that humans have the power to create both inner and outer cohesion within an environment of energies by means of the correct language, thoughts, and intentions.

While this research is not conclusive, it does indicate another step on the road of the new sciences to emphasize how much of human behavior and thought is a creative and dynamic part of our energetic environment. And if our energetic environment begins to change, then we are soon likely to follow, as like resonates with like. This is especially important when coming to consider how human beings have the potential to be in resonance with the frequency of our Planet Earth. And Earth has recently been shifting her resonance.

SCHUMANN RESONANCE
Riding Earth's Wave

Recently, there has been a rise of interest in the relationship of brainwave frequencies to Earth's naturally circulating rhythmic signal, known as the Schumann resonance (SR). In the early 1950s, German physicist W. O. Schumann calculated that global electromagnetic resonances were present in the cavity formed by Earth's surface and the ionosphere. Schumann set the lowest-frequency mode (the one with the highest intensity) at a frequency of approximately 7.83 Hz, which is in the alpha brainwave range. This range has also been co-opted by the military to be used for extra-low-frequency signals (known as ELF signals) for submarine and naval and military communications. So, put together, Earth's surface, the ionosphere, and the atmosphere form what could be seen as a complete planetary electrical circuit. This planetary circuit acts as a waveguide that handles the continuous flow of electromagnetic waves. In fact, it was this atmospheric circuit of global electromagnetic resonances that Nikola Tesla speculated, in 1905, could be used for the creation of worldwide wireless energy transmission.

Why these SR frequencies are important is that all living biological systems are known to function within electromagnetic field interactions. In fact, electromagnetic fields are what connect living structures to resonant energy patterns (or morphic fields*). The SR cavity formed between the ionosphere and Earth produces oscillations capable of resonating and "phase locking" with brain waves, since the human brain is also an electromagnetic receiver and transmitter. EEG measurements have found that the brain has the following four frequency bands: delta (up to 4 Hz), theta (4–7 Hz), alpha (8–12 Hz), and beta (12–30 Hz). Earth's SR waves have been observed by experiment to emerge at several frequencies related to brain waves, such as during deep meditation.[10] In particular states, a resonance is possible between the energy field of the human being and the planet. In such a state of resonance, it is speculated that a mutual information-sharing energy field is created. This is hardly surprising, since the human body (both physically and energetically) evolved over eons of geological time as part of Earth's own evolution. The human species is thus a product of Earth's environment and must have built up an energetic relationship to the surrounding atmospheric electromagnetic oscillations. Because Earth is surrounded by an ionosphere (a layer of electrically charged particles), natural fluctuations in frequency thus impact upon the energy field within and around the human body.

It is reasonable to assert that the frequencies of Earth's naturally occurring electromagnetic waves have shaped the development of human brainwave signals. If the frequencies of human brainwaves evolved in response to Earth's own wavelengths, then there is every likelihood that variations in Earth's oscillations will result in reactive changes in the human body and mind. Such changes could be categorized as behavioral and mental changes. For example, it could be that incidences linked to the classic states of lunacy (often accredited to the moon's influence) could arise from a variation in atmospheric electromagnetic frequencies in conjunction with lunar or planetary forces. In fact, there was one study that produced an analysis of the correlation between the incidence of ionospheric disturbance and the rate of patient admission to Heathcote Hospital (in Perth, Western Australia) over a three-year period. The results indicated that when an ionospheric disturbance occurred, the admission rate changed.

---

*See the work of Rupert Sheldrake, especially his book *A New Science of Life*.

The report's authors give the probability factor of the association being random at the order of 2,000 to 1 against.[11]

That the electromagnetic field around Earth impacts, resonates, and influences the human body is not esoteric knowledge. At all times, our physical bodies act in a manner similar to how lightning rods ground (or "Earth") energy. The well-documented human biofield thus binds us closely to the ionospheric and electromagnetic fields of Planet Earth. The human brain likewise is a source of extra-low-frequency signals that communicate with the body via the nervous system. As in a full physical-energetic circuit, the body is closely interwoven with Earth's fluctuating energy fields, which to some degree help to regulate our body's internal clocks and circadian rhythms. We need to bear in mind, then, that the planetary circuitry (which produces the SR) is affected by the activity of the sun; its sunspot cycles, solar flares, and magnetic storms determine how energized Earth's ionosphere is. Thus, the emergence of increased solar flare activity (discussed in chapters 2 and 3) could result in changes in human brainwaves and biofields. This information brings us almost full circle in what was discussed earlier about upcoming solar and planetary influences in the form of energy contributing to a potential change in the human physical and mental body. The question is, will this be a beneficial intervention?

Instabilities in human biorhythms have been known to cause various diseases, including obsessive-compulsive disorder, aggressive behavior, panic attacks, and narcolepsy.[12] However, these have been attributed to abnormal fluctuations. What some sources are now indicating is that for decades the overall measurement for Earth's SR was roughly 7.8 cycles per second (measured in Hertz), but now that is changing. It appears that the SR has been gradually rising and remaining constant at higher rates. This is speculated to be the reason behind the continuous remodification of military and civilian satellites and aviation communication technologies.

Science doesn't yet know why this is the case, what to make of it, or even if these reports are credible. While this speculation is still controversial to many people, it may indicate that a grand evolutionary cycle is indeed winding up and accelerating toward the end of a phase. Even if this is not the case, it still correlates with the hypothesis of this book, that increasing energies are made available to Earth at potential phase changes along its evolutionary trajectory. This, after all, is the basic property of all complex systems, that at particular peak moments (the tipping points of converging cycles), an extra boost of energy is required to *break through* to a higher level of complexity. Without this increased energy, the system is likely to *break down* into its lesser, chaotic constituents.

As discussed in chapter 2, Earth has entered a period of very real, converging physical crises. At the same time, however, it seems our portion of the galaxy is about to enter a period of increased energetic activity. Place this together with the expected peak in sun-storm activity and the disappearance of Earth's magnetic shield, and it could make for some very transformative times indeed. Even if you do not subscribe to the hypothesis being put forward here (even though you have made it this far!), you should be recognizing by now that there are tumultuous times ahead, whatever the source. It is a fair assessment, then, that the next twenty years on Planet Earth will be unlike any previous years. It appears, with little doubt, that as a global species we are heading toward profound change. This seems inevitable, as too many irreversible processes have been running close to their finishing lines. Change will come; the important choice will be how you choose to respond to it.

In conclusion to this chapter, it can be stated that the human body is composed of energy fields. These bioinformation fields are coherent and can be produced by a form of biophoton emission from our cells and DNA. In turn, our DNA may be susceptible to influence and mutation from a variety of outside influences. Our physical bodies are sensitive to natural and artificial electromagnetic fields, and our environment is heavily polluted with electromagnetic radiation from a range of both natural and man-made sources. While there is cause for concern regarding this pollution, we also should consider that positive intentions and words can have a dramatic effect on the harmonic resonance of our well-being, as shown by advances in vibrational medicine. Also, remember that Earth's SR coincides with the frequency of human brain waves. Finally, there is a strong correlation between human behavior and external geomagnetic frequencies.

The forthcoming transitional times are likely to involve decisive fluctuations in energy frequencies upon Earth. It is postulated that these "energy steps" are a part of the grander evolutionary design to provide an energetic boost to biological systems living within Earth's ecosystem. How this pertains to the future evolution of the human species is unclear. In the following chapters, I will address what may be in store for a spiritually rejuvenated humanity.

Finally, it may turn out that evolution is not concerned so much with material development as with a convergence toward consciousness. The growth of physical intelligence may be seen as a precursor toward immateriality rather than toward more evolved technological materiality, perhaps as a spiritual renewal of the human within a cosmological environment.

A Tale to Finish: Nasrudin the Wise Fool

Nasrudin began to chat with some friends. One of them, suddenly, asked him about his wife.

"Oh, my wife!" he said. "She stays at home."

"What is her occupation?" the others asked.

Nasrudin shrugged his shoulders and said, "Insignificant activities, unimportant things, small things without any transcendence. She takes care of the work at home, takes care of our children and helps them with their homework, goes to the market, does repairs when they are needed, like painting the house and fixing whatever is broken. She takes water out of the well and waters the orchard, also takes care of her ill mother and my mother, too; sometimes she visits her sister and helps her out with the children . . . those kind of things, small things of no importance."

"And what do you do?" someone asked.

"Ah, friends, I am truly important, of course. I am the one who investigates if God exists!"[13]

PART THREE

RENEWAL

INTRODUCTION TO PART THREE

This third and final section discusses what is foreseen as a personal, social, and spiritual rebirth and renewal—a possible rejuvenation to emerge from the upheavals and changes that will come to pass. The present era is viewed as being of major significance in that it offers humankind an opportunity to develop consciously in line with the accelerated incoming energies.

Part 2 discussed the shifts already underway in human perceptions and cognition as well as the new sciences of coherent energy fields and vibrational influences. Humanity is already thinking differently, impacted by the dramatic rise in new technologies. Many of us are accessing information at rapidly increasing rates, networking online in ever more complex relationships, and knowing more about the global world at our fingertips. The neural mind is in overload, creating new connections both internally and externally. A new mind for a new world is underway, yet it needs assistance. Cultural forms and perceptions are not changing fast enough; the new paradigm of thought has not penetrated deeply enough into our social communities. For a viable future to unfold amid these transition times, it is imperative that we orientate our thinking to let go of the ways that no longer serve us. Our global future together lies within the hope for a more vibrant, creative, compassionate, and communicative environment.

The basis for this understanding is provided by new insights in the sciences of biophysics and consciousness. We now have validation that a human being is not a separate entity; it is a light-emitting energetic field of creative information that is in perpetual communion with all living energies. We, as a species, are an energetic constituent of the cosmos. Our story is a part of the universal story; our collective myths are the representations of a grander conscious order. As the cosmos writhes in dynamic energy, so do we absorb and react to the ripples that reach us. Quite literally, when the universe sneezes, we catch a cold. And our cosmic neighborhood is experiencing a cleanup and renewal in which we are involved, whether we care for it or not. It would be a shame to let the neighborhood down, would it not?

This third and final section discusses this potential renewal. It posits that a spiritual renaissance for Earth and her living family could be waiting as our next evolutionary stage. Various indigenous wisdom traditions have talked of this epochal shift for centuries, and now the timelines are converging. Humanity has been in preparation (incubation, if you will) for a very long time. There is now, perhaps, the potential for an energetic upgrade, to turn once again toward our physical, mental, and spiritual well-being. It is an opportunity to reawaken our slumbering souls and to put our house in order. The master of the house has been away too long, and the unruly servants need turning out: it is time to clean up and prepare.

7
SPIRITUAL
RENAISSANCE
The Inner Search Comes Home

Man didn't come into this world for nothing. Man is an extraordinary achievement that has required long and difficult preparation. This achievement is not complete. It would be quite a considerable cosmic disaster if this experiment with man on this earth were to fail, and for this reason much is being done to prevent this experiment from failing—not because man deserves to survive, but because he is really needed.

J. G. BENNETT,
NEEDS OF A NEW AGE COMMUNITY

Our perceiving self is nowhere to be found within the world-picture, because it itself is the world-picture.

ERWIN SCHRÖDINGER, NOBEL LAUREATE

This chapter addresses how we, as a global humanity, may very well be undergoing a period of renewal toward retrieving our birthright of inner realization. This is a significant step on the way of evolved consciousness. In this context, I examine how known indigenous wisdom traditions have held these upcoming times to be portals, or cyclic renewals, toward heightened evolutionary growth along the cosmological journey. At present, we title ourselves *Homo sapiens sapiens,* meaning doubly wise or doubly knowing, yet this suggests that we already "know that we know." So what is it that we are supposed to doubly know? Or is it that we lost the capacity to know or just plain forgot what it was that we once knew? If we are undeserving of this title, then this coming period should catalyze us, as a collective species, into regaining our inheritance. One step on the way may involve reevaluating the primary role and capacity of consciousness.

Instead of viewing consciousness as a by-product of biochemical processes in the brain, consciousness needs to be reevaluated in terms of our cultural norms and perceptual paradigms. We need to accept that consciousness is a creative and natural force that infuses the cosmos and interpenetrates the various realms: material, biological, and spiritual. For example, the human nervous system is not the producer of consciousness, as many erroneously believe, but acts more like an antenna that receives consciousness from living energetic fields. It's like the tale of the young fish that goes on a watery pilgrimage to visit the old wise fish of the sea. When the young fish arrives to ask his burning inner question, he says, "What's this thing called water?" It is harder to perceive that in which we are immersed, and thus the secret hides itself through its transparency. We breathe it, yet recognize it not.

As the familiar world around us begins to shake, appearing to come apart at the seams, and generally cause us concern, we need to take this rush of rapid air as a time for cleansing. Many of us, for far too long, have lived unbalanced lives, neglecting the self for the substitution of quick gratifications and commercial painkillers. It is necessary to restore the balance between the inner world and the outer world; we need a respiritualization of society that goes beyond the need for social forms toward a new understanding of our integral relationships within a cosmic context. In other words, we need to establish a healthy and vibrant cosmological unity between our inner and outer environments. Renowned historian Arnold Toynbee once said, "The ultimate work of civilisation is the unfolding of ever-deeper spiritual understanding."[1] For Toynbee, the suffering of civilized man was a reaction to the separation of sentient beings from their timeless reality. Many societies have lagged behind in providing the means for personal and collective self-actualization and self-transcendence. Perhaps what our industrial cultures have denied us for too long is a way of experiencing the world that will open us up to ourselves and to our transcendental truths.

We are anchored on Earth, which we must not forget, yet we simultaneously fail to connect our threads with the universal. Thus, we are all too often denied the awareness that we do not exist alone, but are an integral part of a vast, mysterious order. By submitting to the authority of the universal, we can renew our partnership with the human, earthly, and creative spirit. Václav Havel famously said in a 1991 speech to a joint session of the U.S. Congress, "Without a global revolution in the sphere of human consciousness, nothing will change for the better."[2] Such a revolution is imperative if we are to be worthy of keeping our role as participants within a creative cosmos. More important, each individual needs to become aware that he or she is a part of a grand evolutionary process, a process that informs the very basis of our living, benevolent, and turbulent environment.

Various esoteric traditions have referred to how a certain number of conscious individuals can assist Earth in the progress to the next level of evolutionary growth. A hundred conscious individuals, let us say, who are in conscious contact and communication, can create an exponential level of conscious force that influences the rest of humanity. It seems that such influences, which have been with us for epochs, are now shifting up a gear and raising levels of awareness on this Earth at unparalleled speed. The needed shift in collective and planetary consciousness is unfolding, it appears, according to the law of evolutionary design.

The hypothesis of this book is that evolution is not so much a linear progression of gradual progress, but rather consists of cyclic periods of energetic expansion that incorporate all the lesser cycles within them. It is erroneous to think that by evolving we necessarily leave everything behind; instead, evolution incorporates and expands upon the past, discarding the detritus that is no longer functional. For example, consider how our earliest reptilian brain, at the base, has been added to successively as our species developed. We still have the reptilian brain deep within us, yet we have incorporated it within our expansion. So, too, our awareness of conscious evolution is an integration of the constant evolutionary process that has brought us to this point from our earliest cosmic beginnings.

It is required of us that we traverse two paths simultaneously: one path requires inward travel, while the other requires that we balance our outer lives so that our intellectual, emotional, and physical faculties are in a harmonious relationship. If we cannot balance the inner life with the outer life, then we have lost our efficiency, our functionality. Humankind does not (and cannot) exist within a vacuum. We have evolved as a social species; our energetic connections enable us to operate as individuals while simultaneously having integral connections of meaning and significance. *The Book of Mirdad,* for example, reminds us that each thought and action exists within our energetic environment as if on a billboard or mirror. Author Mikhail Naimy writes, "So think as if your every thought were to be etched in fire upon the sky for all and everything to see. And so, in truth, it is. So do as if your every deed were to recoil upon your heads. And so, in truth, it does."[3]

What we are now being forced to recognize is that humankind has to serve a cosmic purpose and that every individual life, too, has a cosmic function. Human function and capacity depend not only on how we interact with our environment, but also on our energetic—*kinetic*—relationships with others around us and, more important, with ourselves. Such was one of the functions of worship and ritual in the past, to enable a certain state of energy to be created in which the whole process of transformation is positively reinforced. The possibility for humankind to realize latent inner capacities and faculties relies heavily upon making a connection to a higher form of energy. So much depends upon us making contact with those great forces that lie as close, or as far away, as we make them. This is because progress within the self is not automatic; it requires the use of the right intentions and focus alongside stimulated capacity.

Jesuit philosopher Pierre Teilhard de Chardin wrote that entry into the future—into the *superhuman*—was open to everyone, that it was the destiny of humankind to advance together toward a spiritual renovation of Earth. De Chardin believed that our evolutionary future awaits a consciously evolved being, and thus it is our responsibility to work toward a consciously evolved state. De Chardin was adamant in reminding people that "no evolutionary future awaits man except in association with all other men."[4]

Evolution of consciousness and conscious evolution are two distinct concepts: the former deals with the development of consciousness through species evolution, and the latter refers to conscious participation within the evolutionary processes. It is this latter process to which I now turn to discuss.

CONSCIOUS EVOLUTION

Life is an evolutionary journey, and humankind is on an evolutionary path. This journey toward more evolved forms of intellect, understanding, and creativity requires capacities that lie latent within our very selves. To accept conscious evolution, then, is to accept that individually and collectively, we have a responsibility toward our future. This involves purposeful thinking and action, the use of our creative capacities to guide our lives and the communities in which we live. To envision a creative, dynamic, and positive future is a preliminary step on the path of conscious evolution. First we make the choice for ourselves, then we give intention and commitment in order to give life to those choices. At its core, conscious evolution is a spiritual endeavor in that it affirms the potential capacity of each human being to participate within a creative cosmos. It affirms our use of and commitment to powerful physical and spiritual energies. It also gives rise to a new worldview, a new perceptual paradigm that views our evolutionary process as a lesser step within grander processes. The opposite of this (which has been prevalent for far too long) is for unconscious human energies to be used without our knowledge or knowing participation.

Conscious evolution is also part of a very real social movement providing for a higher level of cooperative communication and action. It is a partnership understanding that offers personal development and learning, community building and assistance, and ways toward practical, positive social change.[5]

Conscious evolution also implies that each human being, each part, is an integral and interrelated part of the whole. The following personal experience of author Steven McFadden highlights this interconnectedness:

> In 1983, after three days and nights of praying and fasting on a mountain top, I snapped a twig with my fingers and had a revelation. I saw that this simple action had changed the world, and that it would never be the same again. I could never put that twig back together the way it had been. This was a small change, but an important change nonetheless. As the sound of the snap reverberated within my mind, I understood how everything I said and did changed the world. What came with the snapping twig was not an abstract idea or a philosophical insight, but a living experience of how all my actions influence creation.[6]

The new sciences have revealed that the concept of integral relationships is now a reality, that we understand that all living organisms are energetically integrated within a shared informational and creative field. As an evolving species, we are encouraged to work together toward this synergy, or gestalt, in which the whole is greater than its sum and thus leads to the emerging properties of the collective. However, we can only function in accordance with our level of knowledge and our capacity to act. We cannot be told what is or what needs to be done; we can only be guided until that understanding becomes an inherent part of ourselves. Then we have an organic sense of how we should act to fit in with the dynamic whole. Yet we can modify our thoughts, actions, and behaviors through self-observation. We can learn to clear our minds of antiquated belief systems and accumulated junk in order to allow these new thoughts to penetrate. We may think we learn, yet often we learn by rote, without the thinking. We should aim toward a conscious digestion of information: to *learn how to learn* and to *know how to know.*[7]

In a similar way, de Chardin talks about the collective, unified soul of humankind as a "conspiracy" of individuals who conspire together to evolve to a new stage of life. De Chardin wrote tirelessly of how continued evolution toward a cosmic spirit was a conscious duty that was hidden, sometimes forgotten, within humankind. He writes, "In us the world's evolution towards spirit has become conscious. Our perfection, our interest, our salvation as elements can depend therefore on nothing less than pushing this evolution forward with all our strength. We may not yet understand exactly where it is taking us, but it is absurd for us to doubt that it is leading as towards some end of supreme value."[8]

The overarching question for de Chardin was how modern humanity could best organize, maintain, and distribute the vital energies required for this process. In this, there are precise conditions necessary for the storage and use of energies. Referring back to what was said in chapter 2 concerning living complex systems, in order to defy entropy, living organisms are required to absorb, store, use, and distribute energy. The human being and the cosmos are both examples of creative, dynamic, living complex systems; hence, the rules still apply. How we store and use our personal energies is of paramount importance and should become central to our lives.

The twenty-first century is the meeting point where the wisdom of ancient traditions shall find a synthesis with modern science. Our knowledge systems are converging now to help us synthesize and make use of our resources, to help us advance and continue forward. It is a reciprocal process, wherein in assisting the cosmos with its evolutionary design, we are given the opportunity to bring ourselves up, as a sentient species, toward greater knowledge and growth. Humans are a required resource within the greater evolutionary design. Several sources on esoteric matters, such as Ernest Scott[9] and Rodney Collin,[10] have indicated the time lengths involved with the inception of cultures by conscious minds. They further explain how there is a set time designated for our present global civilization to evolve enough conscious minds in order to assist with and provide enough energies for the next planetary phase. This notion, while obscure and abstract to some, is not without its active adherents. One term that has come into context for this situation is *reciprocal maintenance.*

The term *reciprocal maintenance* was used in the writings of philosopher-mystic G. I. Gurdjieff to denote humanity's relationship with the cosmos. This relationship is one in which all beings exist to support each other as well as the larger whole. In other words, everything exists to "feed" something else. This term also explains how everything exists for a purpose, how each living organism can transform and supply energy for the whole. In this respect, the function of humankind is to transform energy while it is alive. And naturally, the best quality of energy is that which is provided consciously rather than extracted unconsciously. For example, algae functions to transform sunlight into more complex molecules, plants function to transform sunlight and raw matter into organic compounds, and bees function not only for themselves but also to pollinate flowers and thus catalyze food chains. In the scheme of things, we can say that humanity functions as a transformer of energy—for ourselves, the community, Earth, and the cosmos. Our possibilities and capacities as human beings may in some way be dependent on the degree to which we are able to fulfill this function. We can say that this is one of our primary functions as sentient biological organisms.

In an old Vedic allegory, there is the story of the Horse (feeling), the Carriage (instinct), and the Driver (thinking), who are at the service of the Passenger or the Owner. However, the problem is that the

Passenger has fallen asleep within the carriage, so the Horse and Driver go where they please, and often at a speedy pace! Thus, the purpose and destination of the Owner is being ignored. This allegory informs us that humankind is asleep at the wheel and has failed to wake up and take control of the situation, namely, to steer oneself to one's correct destination. By waking up, an individual can learn to contribute conscious energy, in greater or lesser amounts, through conscious, creative living and purposeful participation in life. On the other hand, if not enough individuals are contributing such energies, other means may be employed to extract the necessary fuel from us.

It was Gurdjieff's stated belief that the overall quality of humanity's conscious energies has been deteriorating over several millennia, especially in so-called civilized societies. Whereas we had been prodigious energy transformers, we now offer only pale reflections of our former capacities. This suggests that humankind has been forsaking its ecological function in the world, has been reneging on its obligation of reciprocal maintenance. Many people have speculated on these "other means" that are employed to extract the energies from humanity, usually focusing on events that release extreme emotions, such as warfare and natural disasters. This view offers a radical, and unpleasant, reworking of human history. It suggests that warfare, disasters, and calamities are not the result of accidental, sociological, or political causes, but may be interventions created to fulfill the needs of a cosmic evolutionary ecosystem.

While this may be true, it is not my intention to speculate on these matters, but rather to focus on the positive aspects of how humanity may relate to conscious evolution. In this respect, evolutionary design does obligate human beings to function as good energy transformers (as is true in all living systems). In our own ways, we can all return some energies if we act according to the right kind of perceptions and behaviors. It would assist us, also, if we took to reminding ourselves that we are not alone, nor separate in our lives, but instead are interrelated to all processes—social, terrestrial, and cosmic. We are, in all senses, a part of the unfathomable, creative, universal fabric of life.

There is far more depth and wisdom to our lives than is taught in our educational establishments, mainstream media, or institutional religions. Yet this tyranny of perception is entering a transition period, also, as increased amounts of information flood our physical and nonphysical channels. The world of the glittery and gritty consumerist struggle is being invaded by change from all angles. Nothing is immune to these changing times, not even our own immune systems. Many of us have immune systems that have been conditioned and strengthened from birth to accept the perceived sociocultural paradigm of our circumstances. Now, along with many other systems and institutions, our own inner systems are beginning to desire alternative food and more nutritious energies. We know something is amiss when there is an inner urge to start looking for pieces of a different puzzle, when external experiences increasingly fail to sit right with us. In some sense, these stirrings indicate a struggle between powers, between your own inherent power of self-determination and the power from consensus social forces. Everywhere and in everything, power is prevalent in society. It thrives on the material energies produced. Yet there are degrees of power, and genuine power is the power to empower others. And above all, subtle energy is powerful, and powerful energy is subtle. Let us remember that *energy goes where attention flows.* So, what's your attention focused on?

It is now becoming well understood that *like attracts like* is a universal axiom. This relates with what the new sciences are telling us about the power of intention to affect bioinformation fields. We need to exercise our intentions, to ask the right questions. As Grandmother Twylah of the Seneca Indian tradition has stated, "Each person should ask themselves four questions: i) Am I happy in what I'm doing?; ii) Is what I'm doing going to add to the confusion in the world?; iii) What am I doing to bring about peace and contentment?; iv) How will I be remembered when I'm gone?"[11]

Our world, then, as material and physical as it is, is nevertheless malleable. It can be affected by the strength of one's own presence, intentions, questions, and thoughts. Our cosmos is creative, endlessly renewing and replenishing itself. Within this energetic ebb and flow, we can fix ourselves (become the attractor for the flux around us) by focusing our presence within each moment. Much of how we experience the future, specifically the coming Earth changes, will rest upon how we perceive those changes. The members of our present generation are now required to direct themselves in accordance with their thoughts. A visionary impulse is necessary if we are to rise beyond these turbulent transition times toward a more constructive future. In other words, *if we believe that the future changes will usher in a disruptive, apocalyptic scenario, then this will be exactly how it plays out for us.*

This is the "fear equation": if we are fearful, we are likely to attract negative circumstances (again, *like attracts like*). And this fear equation has been holding back humanity from developing for far too long. If we perceive the world as life threatening rather than life promoting, then this will influence how we interpret the changing times. Yet the fear equation is a mask: as an acronym, FEAR stands for *false evidence appearing real.* To be prepared for the upcoming Earth changes, we are being asked, as sovereign individuals, which future we wish to embrace. Austrian philosopher Rudolf Steiner writes, "An additional way of training our thinking and feeling is by acquiring a quality we can call 'positivity.' There is a beautiful legend that tells of Christ Jesus and several other people walking past a dead dog. The others all turned away from the ugly sight, but Christ Jesus spoke admiringly of the animal's beautiful teeth. We can practice maintaining the soul-attitude toward the world that this legend exemplifies. The erroneous, the bad, and the ugly must not prevent the soul from finding the true, the good, and the beautiful wherever they are present."[12]

Another maxim in the general literature says, *"Pigs grunt, dogs bark, penguins waddle, what do human beings do?"* It is amusing, perhaps, and poignant too, yet upon deeper consideration, the answer is that human beings do a lot, or rather have the inherent potentiality to do a lot. One of these potentialities is the power of focused and directed consciousness. Humans, *Homo sapiens sapiens,* have the capacity to act as bridges between spirit and matter, between creative impulse and physical manifestation, between the angelic and the elemental. Again, to reiterate, we can function as transformers, as facilitators of energy.

Human beings can act as transmitters (like energy batteries), directing incoming energy across, into, and through Earth, in a sense grounding the energies. Like a ground wire in electrical plugs, humans are able to ground energy that radiates from nonterrestrial sources into our earthly, planetary bodies. We serve as mobile transducers while the more static energy nodes are the ancient sacred sites, stone circles, and megalith sites that can be found dotted all over our planet. Life, including human life, is a membrane layer of transmuting energy. The power of human thought and intention can play a great part in the process of energy transference. The function of the human facilitator is thus one of the reasons behind the concept of the human pilgrimage.

There has been much research on how the world's many megalith sites were used for solar cults, religious worship, or similar activities. However, it is hard to find one overall, unifying theory that relates to the exact, specific function of these various sites. In general, it can be said that the primary role of such sites is an energetic one. Stonehenge, in the United Kingdom, for example, had a function to channel energy that was made available according to specific times and events of cosmic phenomena. Thus, the site had to be correctly aligned for those precise energy emissions. Various sites over the world show signs of their function as energy channels, be they stone circles, standing stones, dolmens, sacred groves, hills, or shrines. Together, they constitute an Earth grid that operates to receive and distribute cosmic energies along, and into, Earth. Many Christian churches, once considered pagan sites, are built on these energy lines; the sites were part of a functioning knowledge system, now largely forgotten. Larger structures, such as cathedrals like those at Notre Dame and Chartres, were constructed to function as energy accumulators (like batteries), which is often indicated by the symbolic use of spirals or labyrinths in their construction.

An important element for energy storage and transmission is correct timing, knowing when specific cosmic energy is flowing. Thus, at particular times of the year, certain areas are targeted by energy currents entering Earth. Those with ancient knowledge made use of this in the original Christian calendars; this was reflected in the names of the saints to which different churches are dedicated (although the system has undergone some degree of corruption). For example, in some cultures, there is a specific day of the year that is attached to a particular saint, so the original purpose was for the entire community to gather at the church for their saint's day, a day that represented the exact time during the year when the maximum energy was available in that area. Likewise, festivals in specific places in the countryside, along with established pilgrimage routes, enabled a line of transmission wherein people would act as the channel, or conduit, for passing along the energy, thus maintaining the energy flow within the earth grid.

This system is still in place, although the functional use of many sites and events has been weakened. However, the earth grid is still an operative system and is pulsed regularly with cosmic energies, both according to natural cosmic alignments and through specific and deliberate energy feeding from external interventions. So the question of what human beings do is partly answered by the concept of being energy transmitters. And the more focused and balanced the transmitter, the finer and more effective the energies. Of course, we can also waddle, too, and grunt occasionally!

In a similar manner, human beings are energy nodes within the "human grid." We receive, store, and distribute energy among ourselves. As open systems, our energy is information, and vice versa. In this context, it is important to realize that this energy can be used to fuel individual self-development. The more focused a person's thoughts, emotions, and behavior, the finer the quality of energy. Much of our energy is lost daily through wasted emotions when anger, fear, and other corruptive manifestations become assertive and exaggerated. At all times, the negative energy seeks to embolden itself, to present itself as being greater than it is. Again, this is because there is always less negative energy inside us at all times in comparison with the positive, even if we do not recognize this as being so. Thus, the negative energy needs to pretend that it is worse than it actually is if it is to have any chance of great influence over the person. This is something to make ourselves constantly aware of: we can be food for the negative energy as well as the positive. As in ecology, everything is someone else's food!

When confronted with an unpleasant event or issue, we can ask ourselves, is this a problem or a situation? It may help to remember that every problem is also a situation, but not every situation is a problem. By finding out which is which, we will have a better basis from which to act. With an increase in information and awareness comes a parallel increase in responsibility. We have a responsibility to ourselves, to others, and to our earthly and cosmic environment. As each of us develops according to our own capacity, we may feel a strong desire to pass this on to others. Yet it is important that we talk to others in accordance with *their levels* of understanding. There are likely to be times when we feel frustrated that other people are not seeing things correctly, that they are not understanding the evident truths. In periods of chaotic change, people often search for the tried and tested, the trusted and secure. For many people, notions of evolutionary transformation and energetic change will seem nothing more than abstract fantasy, the hallucinations of a mind losing its grip on reality. That's fine: all things come to those in *their own time*. What is important is that necessary energy is not needlessly wasted through vain or egoistic efforts. Frustration and haste can easily eat away at one's own energy reserves, resulting in the person becoming less effective and functional. This is of no benefit to anyone. As in all endeavors, preparation and timing are essential factors. As Ali (fourth caliph of Islam) is credited as saying, "Three things once gone are gone forever: the word spoken in haste; the arrow once sped from the bow; the missed opportunity."

The increased acceleration of events is upon us, yet haste will be against us. A spiritual renaissance in the minds and hearts of more and more people will spread as physical events unfold to reveal their dual positive-negative impacts. In this awakening, let us be assured that when we strive to develop and lift ourselves, we indirectly yet significantly also lift our world and the world of those around us. In essence, spiritual realization is about realizing the spirit of others.

SPIRITUAL RENAISSANCE

Everything will change. Yet humanity will continue, albeit in a different way. Our material structures will change and be transformed, and from this we will have the opportunity to become more human. These are the words of Mayan indigenous elders who have anticipated these changes for a long time. It is time for a renewal of the spirit. By this, it is not meant that people should flock to spiritual doctrines. The true spirit is within the heart of each person, and it is the responsibility of each person to find his or her own contact. Each pathway of experience is unique to every person, for there are as many ways to the spiritual center as there are people's hearts. Nor is the true spirit one of contemplation alone, for the spiritual ideal of our era now is one of considerate action. And through this action, things will change. How difficult or easy these changes will be depends much on the response of each person. What is important is not the event itself, but rather how each person deals with it. The changes we face may be out of our hands, yet each of us has the power to choose how we respond to them.

Willaru Huayta, a spiritual messenger in the Incan tradition, has been traveling the globe telling people, "The world is at a critical point of transition, which is highlighted by the crisis in spiritual and moral principles. Nationality is no longer important. . . . Human truth is one. The most important thing now is to awaken the consciousness in a positive form."[13]

Many of the material structures around us have now become a transparent fiction, including our financial systems, job securities, pensions, educational systems, and others. It is becoming increasingly difficult to believe that these structures will continue to provide for our needs. As we search for land from our rafts, our paddles are being taken away from us. So when we eventually find fertile land, it will be from our own efforts, and the cultivation will be that much more rewarding. As personal circumstances become more affected by the changes occurring in the world, it will become necessary that people wake up to new responsibilities and decisions. After all, the upcoming years will be different from what has gone before. This is inevitable, even on a physical level, as structures once seen as strong begin to lose their source of strength (literally, their fuel). And as these physical changes begin to impact and encroach on each person's well-being, new voices will be rising and asking for assistance, both tangible and internal. There is always help for humanity; assistance is available to those who ask with genuine need. However, we need to remember that help often does not appear in the way that most people expect it. It is definitely present and available—only don't expect a rescue!

It is not the premise of this book to debate the dominant Western thoughts and paradigms of Darwinian survivalist evolution and religious creationism. What this book does suggest, however, is that there is an evolutionary design that allows for the *creative development* of living systems as well as planetary, solar, and galactic systems—the micro and the macro. And humanity is very much a part of this wider developmental design, whether consciously or unconsciously. Yet as the changes in social and cultural systems increasingly manifest, it is hoped that more people will awaken to the understanding of their responsible participation. It is with conscious minds that creative action can have a more powerful effect. Especially amid disruptive circumstances, it will be paramount that individuals respond with balanced minds and thoughtful actions. This is no time for superheroes or martyrs: it is a time to act within the human capacity, away from gratifications of recognition and attention. Diligent work with oneself, with others, and within the community is the action that guarantees a response.

There is no avoiding the fact that negative influences operate within our world and have done so for a very long time. Such forces resist change; they resist anything that is a threat to their power. It may seem that during the times of transition, the negative influences are at their peak. Hunbatz Men, teacher of Mayan science and spirituality, acknowledges these negative forces and contends that it is time to raise the frequency of the global mind. He says, "Now the world has a dark civilization, a dark culture. We need to re-establish a high culture . . . by raising the frequency of brain waves . . . the frequency of the modern mind is going to change in a positive way."[14] Men claims that the Mayans have known for a very long time of the big, sweeping changes that are to come. These changes, he says, are part of cyclic patterns that help to renew and revitalize Earth and her living systems.

The upcoming changes, to some degree, are unstoppable, yet they function to sweep the house clean rather than to reinforce the negative presence. This is important to remember so that we do not mistakenly feel overpowered by the disruptions coming with the change. Such disturbances, however distasteful, are necessary: just as the odor of bleach is distasteful and dangerous, so its function is to clean and purify. As the world struggles to accommodate more and different energies, there will be many ripples spreading out and into the homes of many. And while meditation is important as a means of practicing inner balance and focusing intentions, there will also be a need for disciplined action. Just as there is a discipline that holds the energies of the universe in their creative pattern, so too must human activities be focused with disciplined energy. Part of this can be fulfilled by shifting our patterns away from a self-centered, materialistic, consumerist agenda to a more Earth-centered set of values. As Doris Lessing wrote in her *Canopus in Argos* series, the "broken" Earth needs to regain the energies of SOWF (which stands for "substance of we feeling"). In the end, real knowledge is available and free, and it lives within each one of us.

Our behaviors and actions within our communities will be better served if we can realize that Earth is a biospiritual planet. Further, we need to understand that the cosmos of which Earth is a part is also the context and environment for our enduring reality. Thomas Berry writes, "The archetypal journey of the universe can now be experienced as the journey of each individual, since the entire universe has been involved in shaping our individual psychic as well as our physical being from that first awesome moment when the universe emerged."[15]

We are now living through unprecedented times. Yet this is not a time for fear, as with preparation and certitude the times ahead can be navigated. The keys to growth and renewal have been planted within each person. Much will be expected from people in the coming years as they face more fears and challenges, challenges for which history holds few guidelines. Such challenges, while resonating within the heart of each person, will be aligned also within an earthly context. The spirit does not live in isolation, but walks in life. A Native American Grandfather says:

> Trying to live a spiritual life in modern society is the most difficult path one can walk. It is a path of pain, of isolation and of shaken faith, but that is the only way that our Vision can become reality. Thus the true Quest in life is to live the philosophy of the Earth within the confines of man . . . we must walk within society or our Vision dies, for a man not living his Vision is living death. . . . It is very easy to live a spiritual life away from man, but the truth of Vision in spiritual life can only be tested and become a reality when lived near society.[16]

The human species is, after all, a social species (as anthropologists keenly like to remind us). It is easy to behave spiritually when one is confined to the hermit's cave; then our only struggles are with our ceaseless thoughts. While the realm of the spirit may appear to exist as "not of this world," it very definitely is an important component "of this world." Again, it is the significant play of polarity that brings matter into contact with the nonmaterial. Without the material playground, the spirit becomes ephemeral to us, unable to manifest tangibly within our everyday lives. So the life of the spirit needs to become very real for us—and well-lived. By living that life, the presence of the spirit can have greater effect. As the Grandfather again reminds us, "If a man could make the right choices, then he could significantly alter the course of the possible future. No man, then, should feel insignificant, for it only takes one man to alter the consciousness of mankind through the spirit-that-moves-in-all-things. In essence, one thought influences another, then another, until the thought is made manifest throughout all of creation."[17]

Any spiritual revitalization requires that each individual feel the worth of his or her participation and presence with friends and family and within the community. As there is likely to be a forced social contraction, the transition times will usher in the need for more integral communities (as I discuss in the next chapter). Progress will come through action, knowledge, and understanding, and growth can also be achieved through right actions and intentions. The window of opportunity being presented to humanity through the evolutionary trigger point will provide the energies for growth along with new values, emotions, and ways of intellectual reasoning. To miss this opportunity and crave for the security of old perceptions and the status quo of material gains will be a sore transitory pleasure. This is neither a conspiracy nor a fairytale; it is a narrative of resilience, readaptation, and renewal. This is a cyclic process that occurs at all levels in some form. However, at this present juncture, there is much necessary change required: call it an evolutionary imperative. Really, it's quite serious this time around.

SOWF is needed like wine grapes need good soil. As a global community of individuals, we are being pushed toward developing and supporting a creative collective consciousness. This is our new mind for a new world (as discussed in chapter 4). This, in turn, is a reflection of our inherent connectivity within a species energy field of information and communion, as verified by the new sciences. Yet this call for a new way of thinking is neither new nor unique. Each generation has supplied its spokespeople who have argued for a more elevated and illuminated way of thought and life. In recent decades, this call has come increasingly from tribal elders and followers of indigenous traditions. In 1977, the Haudenosaunee (Iroquois Indians) penned a paper to an agency of the United Nations titled "Basic Call to Consciousness" in which they stated, "Today the species of Man is facing a question of the very survival of the species. The way of life known as Western Civilization is on a death path. . . . Our essential message to the world is a basic call to consciousness. . . . The technologies and social systems which have destroyed the animal and plant life are also destroying the native people."[18]

As an intelligent species, we are being called *into consciousness,* as a necessity rather than a luxury of choice. So will there be a spiritual renaissance in which the *inner search* comes home? What will it be like; will it hit home like a sudden bang on the head or like an inner explosion, shaking the body to pieces? Well, it may not be quite like that (but then again, nobody really knows!). Personally, I am not one of those people who propose that the physical body will be shed like dead skin and that the etheric body will jump into fifth-dimensional vibrations. If it happens, I will be pleasantly surprised and will no doubt welcome the humming sensations. However, my understanding is that the way forward will involve harmonizing our inner realizations and sense of knowing with our physical well-being and humanistic development. By humanistic, I mean a conception of the human being within community, ecological, and cosmic contexts, as a functioning part within grander (and lesser) systems. So part of the coming home is likely to be the dawning awareness that we are currently living out of sync with our natural functioning and that we, as a species, are letting the side down.

As living, sentient beings, we are veiled from the truths of our own energetic potentials. Some individuals may get the "wow" factor one day when they realize that their lives have been spent ignoring these truths for so long. Other realizations will come as material systems increasingly reveal the transparency of their corrupt and inept natures. Through a combination of physical changes on the social, cultural, and political levels, people worldwide will begin to awaken to the audacity of our situation. From this, there may be further awakenings as the ironic, incredible, and absurd factors of many of our lifestyles are brazenly shown in the shocking light they deserve. It is my suggestion that these physically coerced changes will coincide with increased cosmic activity (meaning energetic radiations) that are set to impact our Earth and solar region. These radiations may likely stimulate neurological and physiological activity that, while unbeknown to the person, will force in that person new feelings, intuitions, and perceptions, and a new conscience. Taken in combination, it can be foreseen that the coming transition times will catalyze change on many levels.

However, there is great need to work. We will be required to renew ourselves and our communities and to regenerate our relationship with the world we live in. This is not a time to fear for loss, but rather a time to aspire to new possibilities. A readaptation and renewal brings in new air, new potentialities, and new gains. There is no clinging to the old when there exists much vigorous work to be done. Any spiritual endeavor cannot—or should not—be separated from the physical domain. The human being is a physical creature that is nourished from a physical world. While we sojourn on this planet and while our home remains physical, we have a responsibility to manifest our spirit within the physical domain. This is what is required of us, and deep within, we all inherently know this. We are here to work together, as I discuss in the next chapter.

A Tale to Finish: The Grateful Slave

One day, a good-natured king gave a rare and beautiful fruit to a slave, who tasted it and thereupon said that never in his life had he eaten anything so delicious. This made the king desire to try it for himself, and he asked the slave for a piece. But when the king put it into his mouth, he found it very bitter, and he raised his eyebrows in astonishment.

The slave said, "Sire, since I have received so many gifts at your hand, how can I complain of one bitter fruit? Seeing that you have showered benefits on me, why should one bitterness estrange me from you?"

So, if you experience suffering in your striving, be persuaded that it can be a treasure for you. The thing seems topsy-turvy, but . . . remember the slave.[19]

8

NEW CIVIC ORDER

Rebirthing the Social System

The very aim of our society seems to be to remove from people responsibility for their lives and acts. The way of transformation must be the exact opposite of this. Whatever else it may lead to, it must make us into free, responsible individuals, able to direct our own lives in accordance with the greatest objective good.

J. G. BENNETT, *TRANSFORMATION*

Those of you who make the choice to become part of the holistic transformation of this planet and its inhabitants will lead the way through the transformation of yourselves. Mankind is inspired by example not by words. . . . Your example will be one of living the life of purposeful focus. Each day your intent is to be human becoming for the purpose of mankind becoming and the planet becoming. . . . Take your power and use it with intentional focus to bring balance.

GEORGE GREEN, *HANDBOOK FOR THE NEW PARADIGM*

Man has in him two distinct master impulses, the individualistic and the communal, a personal life and a social life,

a personal motive of conduct and a social motive of conduct.
The possibility of their opposition and the attempt to find
their equation lie at the very roots of human civilisation.

SRI AUROBINDO,
THE FUTURE EVOLUTION OF MAN

The upcoming decades will be different from what has gone before. I say this with strong conviction after what has already been said prior to this chapter. Our global society is in the midst of a great transition that will usher in new social and cultural formations. Many nations have been living the high life as a result of the prosperity afforded by rapid industrial, technological, and material growth. The long tail of this—the technological revolution—has been fundamental in stretching tentacles of dependency far and wide. Complex structures of supply, demand, and energy are now near to their breaking points. In chapter 2, I discussed some of the converging crises now facing us; they range from changes in the global climate and declines in energy resources to urban population growth, geopolitical insecurities, and solar storms. Having the potential for a range of critical impacts to converge simultaneously on our social systems offers the possibility for a major revolution on a worldwide scale. Some of the consequences of these unstable systems are already beginning to play out on the global stage. If, on top of these crises, we witness the reality of political mismanagement, then the ensuing fallout may be exacerbated.

The new century for humankind begins as the traditional structures provided by governments and social and political institutions are overwhelmed and no longer capable of serving humankind in its best interests. Problems and difficulties are likely to rise up, like a tsunami, and manifest in our immediate social environments. Yet unlike a natural tsunami, this one will serve also to clean the slate and clear the brushwood. It will provide the opportunity for individuals and communities to reevaluate their life priorities. It will be a time for reconstruction based on newly emerging perceptions of how better to lead a fulfilling life. Yet this outcome, perhaps, will not be for everyone: there will still be many who choose to return to the old, familiar, tried-and-tested ways, especially if they wielded power in those systems. However, this will prove difficult, as some of the old systems will no longer be functional.

New forms of social innovation will have the energetic support needed to emerge from the chrysalis of the fossilized structures. By this it is meant that more appropriate and creative social, economic, techno-logical, cultural, and political edifices will emerge. New skill sets will be required for the new social and community roles. This may force many people to shift from office and administration jobs, from the service and manufacturing sectors, toward functions that serve a regional and localized need. These may include community teaching (in both theory and practical skills), maintenance and construction, localized econo-mies (both currency and barter), permaculture, farming, creative inven-tions, security management, community committees, and more. Many farms will return to organic forms of agriculture and crop growth in order to combat the rise in soil depletion. According to philosopher Meishu Sama, petrochemicals and synthetic fertilizers negatively polar-ize the soil. While they may produce apparently abundant growth in the short term, in the long term, they deplete the soil and exhaust its natural growing capability. The food produced is thus often lacking in nutrients and minerals. In short, many methods now employed will be forced—or catalyzed—into change.

Never doubt that individuals have the necessary skills to respond to critical needs. As the expression goes, necessity is the mother of inven-tion. New knowledge sets can be learned and passed on; apprenticeships may become widespread once again as sustainable skill sets become more valuable and appreciated than institutional and service-sector jobs. Never doubt that communities can find the resources to reshape local cohesion and growth. Creativity and inventiveness are central to the human talent for tinkering. Innovation is the prerogative of people, not the governments. Again, as Sama reminds us, transformation comes from the tiniest changes. Sama notes, "The fruit is the world and the seed becomes the center . . . and at the center of the seed itself is its essence. Because of this, in order to change the world the smallest seed only need be changed. It is just like throwing a rock into a pond—it creates ripples. In this way, making this world into heaven, the very center of the center, the tiniest point—that's where the various changes are made. Make these changes and you create a paradise on Earth."[1]

As events begin to unfold and social changes become more manifest, it is likely that more and more people will feel the "pull-and-push" toward downsizing and reevaluating their life principles and needs. The old thinking and energies of self-survival and material gain will need to be replaced with a new paradigm of *creation, communication,* and *collaboration.* The new imperatives and opportunities now arising will require us to embark on a path toward revitalized partnership relations of community. The era of global excess and greed, which filtered down to the masses as consumer excess and credit greed, is no longer a viable future path. We have now been getting a wake-up call we cannot ignore. As one-time business advisor David Korten now explains, "Rather than to give in to despair in this often frightening time, let us rejoice in the privilege of being alive at a moment of creative opportunity unprecedented in the human experience. . . . Let our descendants look back on this time as the time of the Great Turning, when humanity made a bold choice to birth a new era devoted to actualizing the higher potentials of our human nature—We are the ones we have been waiting for."[2]

We have been waiting for the opportunity and challenge to adjust to new changes. In this respect, we have been waiting long enough for what will be an epochal transition. The challenges facing us are not so much about a "once change," which will happen and then leave us to sit comfortably in our newly adapted state. Rather, we are encouraged to shift into a permanent state of adaptation so as to be better placed to face uncertainty. Such uncertainties may push social affairs toward reorganization at more contracted levels and scales of activity. In the face of these contractions, individuals need to start thinking soon about what courses of action to take. We can walk into the future willingly, or we can be back-flipped kicking and screaming like children. Either way, it seems highly likely that novel social transitions are coming down the line.

SOCIAL TRANSITIONS

According to social commentator James Howard Kunstler, those of us who presently live in the comfortable Western countries are facing "the comprehensive downscaling, rescaling, downsizing, and relocalizing of all our activities, a radical reorganization of the way we live in the most fundamental particulars."[3] This may come as a shock to the many people who are constantly connected into a networked global world. Does this mean we are to be transported back into the Dark Ages? In chapter 3, I made mention of an almost–Dark Ages scenario that I termed lockdown. This was suggested as a possibility should tumultuous events play out over a prolonged period of time. However, once the turbulence has passed (which I feel will be a relatively short-lived situation rather than a protracted one), there will be a different kind of age. It will be a return to values and relationships no longer obscured by unbalance and folly. The twenty-first century should be the age where we recover many of the valuable insights and skills in the art of living. Our efforts and skills—the very basis of our human activities and our spiritual and moral values—need to be redirected toward creating a more integral relationship between human living and our earthly environment. In other words, we need to discover a way back to an Earth that has been forgotten.

We, as individuals, need to develop our critical, reflexive faculties and to find a balance between our inner and outer needs. We require food, clothing, shelter, and community; we also require a sense of worth and belonging, of communion with our environment. In giving shape to ourselves, radical new social and cultural forms are needed. These new forms should serve to place humankind within the dynamics of a living, cosmic, creative, and intelligent universe. After all, the universe of which we form a part is a fundamental, sacred reality. By losing our connection with the sacrosanct, we create a bubble of alienation between our species and our planetary and cosmic home. These are not esoteric concepts; these are natural laws.

For many of us, the context for our existence has become mechanical and often unfulfilling. We have lost touch with the organic, with the alive and the renewing, and exist in material cocoons that are drip-fed. Within this barren context, we obscure our natural capacity for intimacy and cohesion with the living sea of energy that surrounds us. We have so far lacked the epiphany (or the revelatory experience) needed to shock human consciousness awake and make it aware of its sacred communion with living processes. Perhaps that shocking epiphany will come in the form of crisis transitions. In this sense, we "need to reinvent the human *within the community of life systems*."[4] Instead of being a pivotal force, humankind has become an addendum or intrusion into the organic, living processes because of a lack of spiritual insight and understanding. Cultural historian Thomas Berry reinforces this predicament when he says, "The proposal has been made that no effective restoration of a viable mode of human presence on the planet will take place until such intimate human rapport with the Earth community and the entire functioning of the universe is reestablished on an extensive scale."[5]

This point emphasizes that all things exist in differing degrees within all levels: this is our integrative, creative, and ecological matrix. It is another name for LIFE (which in this case stands for "living an integrated fulfilling existence").

Just as humanity is a social species, individuals are the building blocks of society. The worth of any society is the sum of the citizens who comprise it. Unfortunately, most political systems dumbfound and dumb down the masses and castrate the power of the people. Yet this form of social castration has been increasingly contested over recent years by the welcome emergence and rise of some powerful and potent civil movements and nongovernmental organizations. A part of the upcoming social transitions will be the need for increased social agency. The social community should once again become an empowering body, a collective that invests diverse individuals to work together for the common good. In this way, people would be encouraged to become more creative, constructive, and influential within collective life. This can work as an encouragement for each person to develop to the best of his or her capacity, to be a functional human being, able to transform dynamic inner power into a productive and useful force. Repeating what was said before, the renowned metaphysical poet John Donne once wrote, "No man is an island."*

Social scientist and futurist Duane Elgin has done research and written extensively on the subject of social consciousness and evolving societies. In this respect, he writes:

> When we communicate and reflect among ourselves as citizens—publicly learning about and affirming our shared sentiments as an extended community—then we "know that we know." In our dangerous and difficult time of global transition, it is not sufficient for civilizations to be wise; we must become "doubly wise" through social communication that clearly reveals our collective knowing to ourselves. Once there is a capacity for sustained and authentic social reflection, we will then have the means to achieve a shared understanding and a working consensus regarding appropriate actions for a positive future. Actions can then come quickly and voluntarily. We can mobilize ourselves purposefully, and each person can contribute his or her unique talents to building a life-affirming future.[6]

Elgin goes on to state that for a sustainable future to be viable, there are six requirements: (1) to dismantle consumerism, (2) to return

---

*The original text, from 1624, read, "No man is an Iland, intire of it selfe; every man is a peece of the Continent, a part of the maine; if a Clod bee washed away by the Sea, Europe is the lesse, as well as if a Promontorie were, as well as if a Mannor of thy friends or of thine owne were; any mans death diminishes me, because I am involved in Mankinde; And therefore never send to know for whom the bell tolls; It tolls for thee."

to ecological living, (3) to engage with sustainable futures, (4) to create a conscious democracy, (5) to embrace a reflective paradigm, and (6) to work toward reconciliation. All these features support a communal immersion, the very opposite of what has been occurring within the Western urban landscape. To a large degree, modern urban living has contributed to isolating individuals from their wider social community and from the influence of their peers. Many people have been starved of the developmental input that comes from dynamic social intercourse. Progress cannot be achieved through extremes: neither through total individualism (anarchy) nor through an absolute collective (totalitarianism). As in quantum physics, each living organism has the capacity to function both as a sentient individual (a particle) and as a part of the unified collective field (a wave).

In fact, the concept of the organic collective has been a central theme running through many science fiction stories. As just one obscure example, a 1966 sci-fi pulp paperback book from Norman Spinrad called *The Solarians* contains the following discussion between two characters:

"As the human race evolves, the differences among its individual members become greater, not less. Specialization becomes more and more pronounced. And if the race continued to be organized on the basis of nations, clans, families of like clustering together . . ."

"The human race would explode!"

"Exactly," said Lingo. "The Organic Group is a new basic unit, based not on the similarity of its members, but on their differences. It's not merely a good idea—it's an evolutionary necessity. . . . And of course, with the basic unit built upon this kind of functional cooperation, the whole civilization is stable and unified."[7]

So the growth and development of the individual within a diverse yet coherent collective might be, using the words of Lingo above, not merely a "good idea" but an "evolutionary necessity." To accomplish this may require new forms of social community: emerging microcommunities, transit-orientated communities, garden cities, ecocities, and others. This could foster a new sense of contracted and coherent communities to replace the alienation of large urbanized areas and suburban sprawl.

REVITALIZING SOCIAL COMMUNITIES

Urban life is increasingly out of balance with the needs of the people. This situation will be exacerbated when disruptive events impact the daily life of the urbanite. This is especially so if the individual is dependent on supermarket food supplies, gas station fuel, and other necessary external amenities. In short, the average urbanite is partly (and sometimes wholly) dependent on the plentiful supply of "always-available" goods, such as food and energy. As Western societies, and their cities, have become increasingly complex, their supply infrastructures have likewise become increasingly complex, interdependent, and fragile. As was noted in chapters 2 and 3, a disruption to a part of the infrastructures, such as the power grid, can cause various domino effects, creating havoc. In these modern times, no event occurs in isolation, as everything is connected to everything else; thus, everything matters. As most major cities go, life is comfortable within the home, yet moving around within the city offers less and less pleasure, safety, and comfort. When civil unrest manifests, as it already has in various cities as people protest against food inflation, austerity measures, and political corruption, many more major European and American cities will see bouts of violence, disorder, and potentially, chaos. Perhaps some areas will even become "no-go" zones (which already exist in some U.S. and South American cities). It is necessary, then, to address the issue of creating more sustainable social living zones. Until now, too much effort has been placed into creating suburban sprawls that alienate the community; families are either boxed into their homes or boxed into the iron cage of the car. The rise of suburban living has been described as "best understood as the greatest misallocation of resources in the history of the world."[8]

It is important, then, that creative individuals view the upcoming years (or even decades) as opportunities to transform these dense urban zones into more compact, sustainable living centers. For example, instead of segregated areas, the city could be functionally integrated between living, working, and leisure areas; mixed-income communities would be integrated, as having different skill sets is likely to be important rather than traditional income status. Also, public spaces could be transformed into well-integrated, interconnected, and walkable networks and easy-access corridors. A sense of community needs to be revitalized through the use of open spaces, parks, and community landscaping projects, such as communal gardens and food gardens. Superstores and large shopping complexes should be replaced with local shopping areas and farmer's markets. While this may sound the death knell for many corporate giants, their presence will be replaced by something more beneficial to the community. The large supermarkets have exploited and manipulated consumer demand for too long, and many smaller retailers and farmers have suffered greatly over their monopoly. There are already positive signs that groups of individuals are recognizing the urgent need to transform urban living centers.

A movement called *New Urbanism* was established online in 1998 and has grown to promote "good urbanism, smart transportation, transit oriented development and sustainability."[9] The organization promotes policies for national and local governments to revitalize many existing cities and towns into walkable, car-free, mixed-use communities. This influenced the creation, in 2001, of the Charter of the New Urbanism, which states, "We advocate the restructuring of public policy and development practices to support the following principles: neighborhoods should be diverse in use and population; communities should be designed for the pedestrian and transit as well as the car; cities and towns should be shaped by physically defined and universally accessible public spaces and community institutions; urban places should be framed by architecture and landscape design that celebrate local history, climate, ecology, and building practice."[10]

Out of this new urbanism movement has also emerged a trend in urban development called *transit-oriented development*. For example, in the town of Orenco Station (fifteen miles west of Portland, Oregon) transit-oriented development has been successfully implemented. The development was designed as a neighborhood community and organized around a pedestrian spine that extends out toward a grid of walkable, tree-lined streets and parks. The town promotes itself as a walkable, pedestrian-friendly community and discourages the use of cars and other modes of fossil-fuel transit.

Likewise, the *principles of intelligent urbanism* involve a theory of urban planning that aims to integrate various environmental, technological, sociocultural, and mobility needs into urban design. As put forward by architect Christopher Charles Benninger in 2001, the principles of intelligent urbanism work toward maximizing human interaction, the use of public spaces and movement within them, and environmental sustainability.

A similar movement, which has been gaining momentum within the United Kingdom, specifically aims to transform smaller towns into sustainable communities. The movement, called transition towns, was established as a means to design a strategy for helping small towns move away from fossil-fuel dependency. It also promotes public participation and citizen action within the context of a sustainable and self-sufficient community. The first U.K. transition town was Totnes in Devon, where local town forums were created for citizens to come together and decide on ways to develop low-carbon energy resources, in other words, how better to survive in a post–peak oil world. The Transition Network, in its mission statement, aims to "inspire, inform, support and train communities as they consider, adopt and implement a Transition Initiative. We're building a range of materials, training courses, events, tools and techniques, resources and a general support capability to help these communities. . . . We're hoping that through this work, communities across the UK will unleash their own collective genius and embark on an imaginative and practical range of connected initiatives, leading to a way of life that is more resilient, more fulfilling and more equitable, and that has dramatically lower levels of carbon emissions."[11]

The transition towns movement aims to raise awareness by giving talks and screening films in various towns and villages. One of the creative projects has been the introduction of a local currency (such as the "Totnes pounds") that can only be spent in local shops. The move to local currencies is also on the increase in various towns across the United States as a way to revitalize local businesses in the wake of the global financial crisis. Representatives of the transition town movement have also conducted oil-vulnerability auditing workshops with local businesses to see how they can reduce their reliance on oil. Other local projects set up under the scheme include running workshops on growing fruit and vegetables, baking bread, and darning socks.[12] So far, there are over three hundred towns and cities worldwide that are now recognized as official transition towns, with many as far afield as Australia, New Zealand, Canada, Chile, and the United States.[13]

Schemes such as the transition town movement are on the increase in communities all over the world. People are reading the signs and becoming motivated and inspired. The writing is, as they say, already on the wall, and as more people get this gut feeling, there will be more and more alternative community projects arising. It is essential that in these times people—individually and collectively—start to take power back into their own hands. The creative energies residing within the human network have been either ignored or underused for far too long. People need to take the initiative as familiar structures around them begin to fail and dissolve. The opposite, doing nothing and weeping for sorrow or in despair, will do nobody any good. We are being encouraged (or pushed) to show ourselves how wonderfully resilient, resourceful, and creative we can really be. Many of us may be surprised at what can be achieved when a group of motivated people join together. To quote again the words of anthropologist Margaret Mead, "Never doubt that a small group of thoughtful, committed citizens can change the world. Indeed, it is the only thing that ever has."

For now, the transition town initiative has been largely restricted to smaller towns, where civic engagement and localized sustainability practices from the bottom up have some chance of success. However, the same model could work in larger cities if they split into smaller-scale, sustainable neighborhoods.

A prescient report from 1997 forecasted a possible future social scenario that was termed the *Great Transition,* which involved a social shift toward new paradigms of sustainability in the form of *ecocommunalism.* The report envisioned a network of self-reliant communities, stating, "Eco-communalism could emerge from a New Sustainability Paradigm world if a powerful consensus arose for localism, diversity, and autonomy. . . . Eco-communalism might emerge in the recovery from 'breakdown.' Under conditions of reduced population and a rupture in modern institutions, a network of societies, guided by a 'small-is-beautiful' philosophy conceivably could arise."[14]

Physical social networks modeled on self-reliant communities could be established that are based around ecological practices. Already, some urban design groups are using industrial ecology techniques, as in the integrated resource management system.[15] In this way, there has been a shift that sees urban centers becoming closer to becoming "living centers" that encourage closer physical proximity and interaction between citizens.

Another example of creative architectural thinking is that of the compact city proposal from celebrity architect Richard Rogers. Rogers proposes the creation of the modern compact city, which would reject the dominance of the car and instead favor a design wherein "communities thrive" and the streets are rebalanced "in favour of the pedestrian and the community."[16] Further, Rogers's compact city design proposes that home, work, and leisure districts, regions, and zones become more densely interrelated and overlapped, rather than existing as separated areas. On page 164 is a diagrammatic representation of how Rogers sees the transition toward a compact city design:

The compact city idea is to increase the density of shared spaces so that there are increased opportunities for social connection and

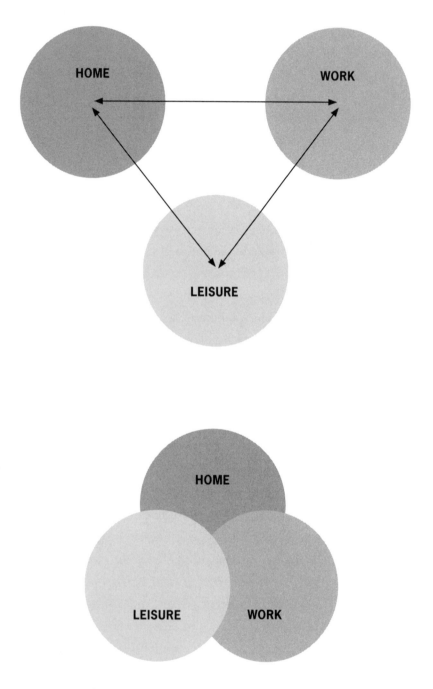

Rogers's compact city design versus the typical urban layout

interaction. There is a rise worldwide in urban innovation that seeks to move toward constructing more compact, sustainable communities. This will become more of an imperative, rather than a luxury, in the ensuing years. Such changes will need to be implemented if our social systems are to be resilient enough to adapt to the coming global changes. The emphasis needs to be on the recycling of goods and waste, efficient alternative energy production, localized distribution systems, and changes in such social drivers as consumerism, economics, and general well-being. Already, several precedents exist, one of these being the concept of garden cities and the garden city movement.

The garden city movement was founded in 1898 by Ebenezer Howard in England as an alternative to existing urban schemes. Garden cities involved the merging of town and country, of rural partnerships with urban dynamics. They were designed as self-contained communities with areas for living, working, and agriculture surrounded by green belts and public spaces.[17] In this respect, Howard's thinking was ahead of its time in seeing the need for both rural and urban improvement as a single process. The garden city movement was inspired by Howard's first book, titled *To-morrow: A Peaceful Path to Real Reform* (1898; reissued in 1902 in a more well-known format as *Garden Cities of To-morrow*). The Garden City Association was founded in 1899, which led to two new cities in England being constructed around this design: Letchworth Garden City in 1903 and Welwyn Garden City in 1920.

Howard planned his garden cities to be located on roughly six thousand acres of land, with one thousand acres set aside for accommodating up to thirty-two thousand residents and an additional two thousand people on the surrounding agricultural estate. The circular garden city town plan had 120-foot-wide, radiating, tree-lined boulevards, and each city would be linked to other, larger cities via railways. The design for such garden cities even today seems remarkably environmentally aware. As noted in *CitiesPeoplePlanet* by Herbert Girardet, "Howard meticulously separated pedestrian streets and vehicle traffic, and residential and industrial areas. When a garden city had reached its optimal population of 32,000, its growth would be halted and another town of similar size would be built within its own zone of land. But the inhabitants of the one could very quickly reach the other by a rapid transit system, and thus the people of the two towns would really be part of one community."[18]

The concept of the garden city was also especially influential in the United States, with the creation of Pittsburgh's Chatham Village, Sunnyside and Jackson Heights in Queens, Radburn in New Jersey, the Woodbourne neighborhood of Boston, Garden City in New York, and Baldwin Hills Village in Los Angeles. In Canada, there is the garden city of Walkerville in Ontario, and the first German garden city, Hellerau, a suburb of Dresden, was founded in 1909.

Howard also believed in citizen participation, whereby the town residents could own a share of the city's assets. Even today, a foundation jointly owned by the citizens of Letchworth controls 5,300 acres of land, including two farms and 118 shops. All the money earned from these ventures stays in the community, and in the period from 1997 to 2003, the community's assets trebled to £160 million.[19] This shows that with the correct organization, intention, and dynamic motivation, communities can be created for the better well-being of their citizens. Also, such living centers can become more self-sustainable and environmentally connected to Earth. The garden city concept can be an inspiration for those communities wishing to accommodate increased agricultural spaces for growing vegetables. Over recent years, there has been a vigorous interest in using the practice of permaculture as a way of combining living centers with agricultural systems.

Permaculture is a way of integrating the ecology of natural agricultural practices with the needs of the community. The word *permaculture,* as a combination of permanent agriculture and permanent culture, reflects the social aspects of the system. Permaculture encourages the construction of self-sufficient communities that work with nature's cycles within the surrounding ecosystem.[20] Permaculture is often seen as a more holistic system, as it looks at both the natural (agricultural) and human systems as a whole, rather than as separate systems. In this way, localized communities could benefit tremendously from incorporating permaculture practices into their way of life. Not only would such practices provide a means for self-sufficiency, but they would also help to sustain the local ecosystems at a time of increased strain.

The future years will demand that we change many of our current practices. It is imperative that creative individuals begin to think out of the box. Civic renewal requires right-hemispheric thinking as well as left, and lateral thinking as well as rational. The good news is that the world is already awash with impressive grassroots social innovations. It seems that our future will be steered more from the bottom up than from the top down.

SOCIAL INNOVATIONS

Frustration and despair can soon shift toward resilience, readaptation, and renewal. When the ground beneath the feet becomes loose, the human capacity to furrow anew comes into play. What is being proposed within this framework of a new civil order is that as people are forced to learn new skills, they will take more and more responsibility for themselves. This will manifest also in revitalized concerns for one's family, friends, and community. A shift of dependency is likely to occur that will take back power that many people had previously given away to external sociopolitical institutions (and commercial dependencies), and they will use this to empower themselves. People's relationship with technology is also likely to undergo a reevaluation. Instead of being wholly dependent on complex, unknowable technologies, people will learn to redesign tools to aid and empower rather than pacify themselves. The view taken in this book is that future years will see not the coming of a supertechnological singularity (as envisioned by inventor and futurist Ray Kurzweil),[21] but a reconfiguring of our technologies. By this, it is meant that instead of technology working *beyond us* and out of our reach, it will be working for us, and sometimes in more simplified forms.

One of the immediate concerns regarding coming technological changes will be energy requirements. Given that a true free-energy revolution is still an uncertainty, alternative energy will need to be harnessed from solar, wind, water, and other natural sources. The corporate red herring of agro-fuels (mass-produced biofuels) is likely to be rejected by local communities that are seeking to shift to low-carbon alternatives using real biofuels. True biofuels are produced from waste such as waste vegetable oil or biogas from manure or landfills.* Their development, however, is so far limited. This situation is likely to change once necessity becomes a key factor. Already, some local communities are developing their own low-key diesel manufacturing through the recycling of waste vegetable oil. These do-it-yourself projects can be developed further by well-organized communities using agricultural processes.

There are a range of oilseed crops, such as sunflowers, rape seeds, soy, palm, and jatropha, that can be converted into biodiesel, to be used on its own or blended with conventional diesel. A range of cellulosic materials, such as various waste products from crops (including grasses, trees, and wood) can be broken down with enzymes and turned into bioethanol.[22] Bioethanol can also be produced from a number of crops, including sugarcane, sugar beets, barley, corn, maize, grain, and cotton. Using cellulosic biomass to produce ethanol would lessen the strain placed on standard agricultural land needed for growing crops.[23] Butanol is currently a potential second-generation biofuel produced by fermentation from a range of organic materials, such as molasses left behind by sugar production or whey from cheese production. Butanol has several advantages over ethanol in terms of higher energy output and being easily blended with diesel.

In the future, we may see regional areas and localized communities adopting a bottom-up biofuels market that would serve to create

---

*It is interesting to note that Rudolph Diesel originally designed his engine to be powered by peanut oil. Another recent project has seen a car powered by modified chocolate.

energy-sufficient lifestyles. This can be achieved not only through tapping a supply of recyclable waste but also through citizen-managed low-scale farming. Genuine biofuel schemes could be located within sustainable programs based within active communities and separate from corporate, top-down energy suppliers. This would involve a move from mass production to localized production and distribution schemes that would aid many communities.[24] It is foreseeable that these, and other, energy innovations will begin to manifest through grassroots pioneering efforts and newly emerging citizen information networks. The corporate control and monopoly on such natural resources and primary human needs will be rejected for local empowerment projects. Part of the civil revolution will occur when people, desperate in terms of supplying basic needs, will be forced to create these supplies for themselves. Then there will be no going back, no return to former dependencies.

Projects and schemes already underway around the world include gardening workshops for growing your own food. Information made available for self-farmers will encourage food production to be once again a prime aspect of family and civic life.[25] There is currently a growth in the number of urban gardens and communal composting. Neighborhoods are sourcing water supplies and introducing local permaculture schemes. Social networks are already established that seek to bring home gardeners together to share tips, advice, and friendship. One such social network, Freedom Gardens, describes itself as "a food security movement person to person. . . . A modern gardening era/movement for the 21st century resulting in efforts to become free of foreign oil, corporate controls, contamination and food miles while creating a sustainable future by promoting local food production."[26] Inspired innovators are currently developing new sustainable alternatives to industrial agriculture that push toward forming a postindustrial food system that is less resource intensive and more locally based and managed. An array of such start-ups includes BrightFarm Systems, SPIN-Farming, Virtually Green, Aquacopia, and NewSeed Advisors. Similarly, new networks are emerging of investors, donors, entrepreneurs, farmers, and activists who are committed to building local food systems and local economies (such as the Slow Money network).[27]

In a similar manner, the Haudenosaunee (Iroquois Indian) elders suggest a revitalizing of sustainable, locally orientated cultures; they suggest the creation of "liberation technologies." By this, they mean technologies that can be created and used by people in a specific locality to enhance self-sufficiency and respect for the natural world. Wind turbines, solar power, biomass plants, and organic agriculture are all examples of liberation technologies. Likewise, Dhyani, who puts forth Cherokee teachings, states, "This age ending has been a time when people have gathered information about building and about inventions to make life better. Now it's time for people to recognize that the inventions are a creation of mind, to put aside such inventions as cause harm, and to bring forth and further develop those activities that benefit all beings and the future generations."[28]

Alternative technologies are arising that seek to bypass traditional dependencies as the civil movement grows in power and determination. There are now markets for rocket stoves, vegetable-oil generators, solar refrigerators, cheap wind generators, and reusable water bottles used as solar lamps. Innovations are also turning shipping containers into virtually cost-free homes. Social information networks are advising people on how to make their own soap, toothpaste, clothes, and much more. Instead of recycling, there is now a movement toward "precycling," that is, training people on how to exist not only on what they have, but also to transform their conception of necessity so that nonprimary needs are taken out of the equation. Individuals and communities are learning how to live more on less. Part of this reeducation is a perceptual paradigm (a new mind for a new world). For many of us, if we don't choose to think and behave differently in the upcoming years, then we may be forced into change—perhaps brutally.

Also on the increase are localized microfinances, wherein communities are issuing their own, specific, local currencies as a means of promoting local business growth. This is a Depression-era idea and helps to tie in local consumers with their neighborhood suppliers. It works by local businesses printing money and then consumers exchanging national currencies for the locally issued ones, which they then redeem in participating stores. Members of communities throughout Europe, North America, and Asia are buying food and fuel with such currencies as the Detroit Cheers and the Bia Kut Chum. Exchange and credit or barter systems have also been running successfully, such as local exchange trading systems, which are local exchange networks that trade goods and services without using a currency. Instead, a credit system is in operation wherein individuals can earn credits by performing services, which can then be swapped for the services of others. At present, it is estimated that more than four hundred such schemes operate in the United Kingdom alone, with others in France, Australia, Switzerland, and the United States.

Such schemes also encourage interactions and a sense of proximity between people and neighborhoods. We are seeing a shift that uses small-scale innovations to replace broader, top-heavy dependencies. As elitist Henry Kissinger once famously remarked, "Control oil and you control nations; control food and you control the people." Such monopolies of control belong to the old paradigm and will find no welcome as people collectively shift toward self-determination. It is predicted that these agents of self-determination will emerge as a new social generation of *disruptive innovators*. A recent report titled "The Disrupters: Lessons for Low-carbon Innovation from the New Wave of Environmental Pioneers" described this "new wave of environmental pioneers" as bringing in new and unexpected forms of "disruptive innovation."[29] Disruptive innovation is that which is unexpected and arrives, usually from the periphery or the bottom up, to provide services that have previously been monopolized. Such disruptions are highly threatening to the hierarchical status quo, yet often empowering to civil society. The report states, "In short, we need disruptive forms of innovation—cheaper, easier-to-use alternatives to existing products or services often produced by non-traditional players." It further notes that this is not only a question of "new technologies" but also of "wider forms of innovation."

There is much disruptive innovation taking place around the world, with many tinkerers searching for solutions that are beneficial for people rather than for profit. And this shall be the new paradigm, the new civic order: a reorganizing of the social sphere away from consumerist dependency and exploitation and toward self-empowerment and community sustainability. People shall be motivated for their families and for other people rather than for profit and those binary digits in a virtual bank somewhere. The fallacy of the old world with its delusional constraints will become transparent and will anger a lot of people. The veil will begin to fall, the curtain will pull back, and Dorothy will see the Wizard as the bald, bumbling man and not as the powerful maestro. We have been fooled for far too long, and it is time to wake up, to engage with the program of evolutionary change, and to move on. As Doris Lessing writes, "There is no epoch in history that seems to us as it must have to the people who lived through it. What we live through, in any age, is the effect on us of mass emotions and of social conditions from which it is almost impossible to detach ourselves. Often the mass emotions are those which seem the noblest, best and most beautiful. And yet, inside a year, five years, a decade, five decades, people will be asking, 'How could they have believed that?'"[30]

The time is ripe for a new kind of emergent innovation, one that comes from high energies of experimentation and enthusiasm. Whatever the disastrous social consequences that the world may be forced to live through in the early twenty-first century, the renewal will be worth it. Evolution is moving up a spiral and needs to shed some dirty, unclean energies. In short, it needs to get its house in order for the move. And so do we, for we shall be moving, too.

A revolution can exist at many levels. It can manifest in physical, emotional, and spiritual change. When that change arrives, it is important to accept the uncertain, the unknown. Many people may be forced into action, even if this seems distasteful and unwanted at first. People are often initially afraid of change, afraid of leaving secure territory. Yet we need to change. And when many things are not understandable, the worth of a person will be found not through his or her wasted thought, but through constructive actions. The next, and final, chapter will discuss some of these evolutionary and potentially radical changes for humankind.

A Tale to Finish: The Melon

While traveling, a teacher and his disciple were having a rest. At a certain moment, the teacher took a melon from his saddlebag; he divided it in two, and both began to eat it.

While eating, the disciple said, "My wise teacher, I know that everything you do has a reason. Sharing this melon with me perhaps is a signal that you have something to teach me."

The teacher continued eating in silence.

"By your silence, I understand the hidden question," the disciple insisted, "and it must be the following one: the taste that I am experiencing when eating this delicious fruit, where is it: in the melon or my tongue?"

The teacher didn't say anything. The disciple, excited, continued. "And as everything in life has a sense, I think I am close to the answer of this question: the taste is an act of love and interdependence between both, because without the melon there would be no object of pleasure and without the tongue . . ."

"Stop it!" said the teacher. "The biggest idiots are those who think they are more intelligent than others and search for an interpretation for everything! The melon tastes good, this is more than enough. Let me eat it in peace!"

9
A NEW HUMANITY
Human Being Is Human Becoming

*An individual person has an integrity, a quality, a being
and an existence; two people acting in a harmonious and
complementary fashion produce an extra factor and a
number of people working and thinking and feeling and
offering themselves together, and each consciously involving their essential being, are capable of producing a thing
of amazing beauty.*

OMAR ALI SHAH

Human history is set within recurring myths of cultural renewal.
Instinctively, we know deep within ourselves that we move between
periods of change, renewal, and regeneration. Many of us have been
conditioned to think in terms of science's Darwinian evolution or a
form of religious creationism. We often forget that we are a part of the
process, yet just as evolution acts on the human species, so, too, do we
respond to these larger processes. This forms part of what was earlier
described as reciprocal maintenance. Yet if we fail to play our part correctly, then by necessity we must be pushed, shoved, encouraged, or
coerced along the way. It may well be that humanity, unbeknown to its
thinking members, has been coerced along an evolutionary trajectory by
means of contrived events of an indefinite scale.

We can surmise that over the preceding millennia there has been a gradual increase in the quality and refinement of human consciousness. Further, we can also surmise that within our most recent epoch, this accretion of consciousness has undergone an accelerating process, as if in preparation for some great shift. For the majority of people, this process would have gone on unnoticed, with little conscious cooperation. The daily affairs of humankind have thus gone by with seemingly no coherent pattern, as if the erratic ebb and flow of events defined their own mad logic of chaos and rebalance. Likewise, a human lifetime of around seventy to eighty years would seem the result of chance and accident, meaningful only within the context of individual fantasies, desires, and satisfactions. However, it just may be that history is not the manifestation of uncertainty and inconsistency, not hazard but purposeful direction. It has been noted by Ernest Scott that

> the universe is a gradient of consciousness and on this gradient the Earth occupies a low level. Its highest raw material is mankind. Mankind is collectively unconscious of the evolutionary process of which he is a part and he is subject therefore to determinism approaching a hundred per cent. Even so, the direction imposed on mankind is only relatively coercive. Because of the high energies which are potential in him, man may not be compulsively directed. Means have to be employed which do not outrage the integrity of his potential nature. This is achieved by arranging a bias in favour of those situations which contain developmental possibilities and by limiting man's opportunities for making involuntary choices. About this line there may be marginal interplay of determinism and free will. On the "present moment" of a man or a generation of men these pressures may appear both random and hostile.[1]

Whether random or hostile, there is a sense that greater forces are involved in the long-term success of humanity's development. This, as has been stated throughout the book, is within the context of a grander developmental scale and necessity. It may be that an event is on the near horizon that acts as a mutation catalyst within our species evolutionary nature. By this are implied novel physiological and neurological capacities of perception and cognition.

By a simple comparison with the pace of geological time, it is clear from the accelerated nature of our social and cultural systems that something unprecedented within human history is on the verge of occurring. At the very least, if we are not heading for a global breakthrough, we are heading for a worldwide breakdown. Yet however close we swing to the cliff edge, it will be this energy of dynamic chaos that will fuel our leap when the jump comes. In other words, humanity is not an end project; it is an evolving one. And the time is near when we shall witness profound changes occurring within all of our global social systems and within the very core of humankind itself. Such changes will radically alter the sense of human identity, meaning, and purpose. These shifts will in themselves be enough to trigger the transition to a new historical epoch within the human journey. And if I am wrong, will it really matter? Yet what if only a part of what I am saying has a grain of truth? What if . . .

One of the points repeatedly stressed throughout this book is that I am not alone in these ideas. Many other like-minded people have expressed the same concerns, in different ways, through a variety of channels. Many sources exist that testify to the emergence of these and similar thoughts. What I have attempted to do in this book is to collect the arguments together into one complete narrative, joining together some of the dots. All of the information is already out there; it is scattered, lying around, secreted within a vast array of books, documents, files, web pages, folktales, myths, and even our thoughts. The recognition of these transitory, transformative times is seeping through humanity's collective consciousness. It is seeping into our inexpressible knowing; it is tapping on the door of our conscience and rubbing against the instinct. There is a heightened sense that many people are attempting to express and unravel these feelings. These times are not for nothing. There have always been indications of the evolutionary role of humankind and its targeted destination, usually semi-veiled through allegory, cryptic tales, and prophecies. Yet they have always been lying within the kernel of the human being.

Kenneth Ring, a professor of psychology, has made extensive study of people's prophetic visions during near-death experiences. In a 1982 article titled "Precognitive and Prophetic Visions in Near-Death Experiences," he describes how there was a strong correspondence in people's visions while in this state:

> The future scenario, however, is usually of short duration, seldom extending much beyond the beginning of the twenty-first century. The individual reports that in this decade there will be an increasing incidence of earthquakes, volcanic activity and generally massive geophysical changes. There will be resultant disturbances in weather patterns and food supplies. The world economic system will collapse, and the possibility of nuclear war or accident is very great. . . . All of these events are transitional rather than ultimate, however, and they will be followed by a new era in human history, marked by human brotherhood, universal love and world peace. Though many will die, the earth will live.[2]

Considering that these studies were performed prior to 1982, they contain elements immediately recognizable and relevant to events transpiring today; in fact, they are eerily so, and perhaps prescient. However, Ring is quick to point out that such prophetic visions should not be taken so quickly at face value, but rather that they bring a message that reinforces the myth of cultural renewal. They foreshadow the collective knowing for transformative change that arrives through disruptive cleansing. Further, Ring believes that the visions are reflections of our collective psyche, for which some sensitive souls serve as channels. This reinforces the notion that the state of human consciousness will have some bearing on how this transition period unfolds, again, reiterating the need for a new mind to manifest and take precedence.

Prophetic traditions have historically described disruptive Earth changes as occurring prior to some major event, as if foreshadowing the interference that precedes a grand shift. Among these disruptions are increased earthquakes and volcanic eruptions, erratic weather and climatic patterns, and societal instability (political, military, and economic) that leads to civil unrest and possible social breakdown. However, the role of prophecy is not always as a harbinger of doom; sometimes, it serves to prepare people and to be a catalyst for behavior change. And just sometimes, if sufficient behavior change manages to avert the worst of the prophecy and to prove it wrong, then ironically, the prophecy has served its purpose. In this manner, prophecies can serve humanity by proving themselves wrong in the end.

In this world of ours, those elements that seem opposed are often working together. And right now, many elements are working to shift humanity from its competitive, exploitative, and selfish phase toward a more conscious stage. What is required is a trigger (or series of triggers) that will catalyze a psychological transformation process within humankind. Such triggers may be wholly unpredictable and come when least expected, and they can be almost anything. It is very likely that such triggers have been in operation for some geological time already. By this, I refer to the cosmic radiation that is a constant, yet unseen, influence on our world. Vital energies continuously bombard our planetary atmosphere and surface and penetrate the human body and nervous system. Such vital energies are a combination of various galactic, solar, and planetary forces, which for most of us pass unseen and unnoticed. Yet in each moment, with each breath, we absorb these radiations and are affected by them in ways beyond our knowing.

The human evolutionary project is thus far an ongoing affair. Yet its movement has been suspected by those sensitive to its workings. The emergence of a higher humanity is a recurrent theme in world myths and philosophical and esoteric treatises. Examples are to be found in Richard Bucke's book *Cosmic Consciousness,*[3] Friedrich Nietzsche's concept of the Übermensch (over-man),[4] and the writings of Sri Aurobindo, G. I. Gurdjieff, John G. Bennett, and various other esoteric sources. Nietzsche in particular understood the evolutionary journey of humankind. His philosophical treatises urged the individuals of present humankind to focus on where evolution could take them and to help advance this agenda. He argued that the significance of humanity was not its present form, but its potential to transcend to something greater. For Nietzsche, the Übermensch was the next great step in evolution for the human. He wrote, "Man is a rope stretched between the animal and the Übermensch—a rope over an abyss. A dangerous crossing, a dangerous wayfaring, a dangerous looking-back, a dangerous trembling and halting. What is great in man is that he is a bridge and not a goal."[5]

The theme of a higher humanity also provides the framework for the alchemical transformation into the "golden human," and it fed the Aryan fantasies of Adolf Hitler. From these works and many more throughout the ages, from personal visions, allegorical texts, and established transcendental teachings, it appears that an evolution of human consciousness is the central driving force behind our terrestrial existence. Moving along increasing gradients of consciousness, from an unconscious (or lesser conscious) to a more conscious state, occupies the central tenet of all celestial bodies. Our next evolutionary transformation, then, as occurs physically on our planet, is expected to also involve a change in the nature of human consciousness. Further, that this consciousness change will also trigger physiological changes within the human body. This will occur most likely within the human nervous system and the body's distribution of vital energies. That such changes can occur is not disputed, for they have been the realm of disciplined teachings for centuries. One example here is in the teachings of yoga (hatha yoga in particular), which aims at releasing a vital pranic energy that creates a physiological change in the practitioner's biology.

Hatha yoga teaches that there is a subtle life force called prana, which permeates the human body through every cell like a field of energy. It is recognized as both a cosmic energy force and as a biological conductor of energy within the human body.[6] A greatly enhanced and concentrated form of pranic energy is released into the body when the yoga practitioner awakens the latent force known as kundalini. This powerful unleashing has the effect of altering the nervous system through increased nerve center activity. This, in turn, makes the human body operate in an altered form, making it more responsive to heightened states of consciousness. It has been noted by those who have experienced this phenomenon that the release of this vital energy, and its corresponding adjustments to the brain and nervous system, is similar to a more powerful electric current passing through finely tuned filaments. According to one recipient of this pranic energy, Gopi Krishna, "I did not know at the time that I was witnessing in my own body the immensely accelerated activity of an energy not yet known to science, which is carrying all mankind towards the heights of superconsciousness, provided that by its thought and deed it allows this evolutionary force full opportunity to perform unhindered the work of transformation."[7]

It is significant that the energy experienced is interpreted as an evolutionary force central to the transformation of the human being. Further, the vital energy of prana is considered within the hatha yoga tradition (and others) to pervade every molecule and atom of matter. Earth flows with prana, the sun is a vast generator of vital pranic force, and all celestial bodies radiate differing gradients of pranic energy. For some, this vital radiating force is the very medium of evolutionary transformation. It is an unseen driver of inner physiological change, affecting the nervous system, cells, and the very core of biological organisms as well as every atom of matter. And as the philosopher Aurobindo noted, "If humanity is to survive, a radical transformation of human nature is indispensable."[8]

This book suggests that humanity is passing through a period of change that will affect the parameters of human consciousness and perception. It is also a time that will facilitate (or force) many people to work through their issues and life stories in order to address some fundamental personal changes. For some, this may involve a change in relationships, jobs, location, or maybe just basic attitudes and beliefs. This is all a part of the experiential learning curve of the developmental process. In each given moment, we are making a decision, no matter how small or grand the gesture. Life is less an accident than most realize; this should be an encouraging sign, as it implies that there are guiding forces that intend success and progress, despite what outward signs portray. What may be in store for humanity is a mutation that informs the next evolutionary stage, a mutation that has been hinted at and suggested in countless scattered documents, treatises, prophecies, visions, and esoteric teachings. Many people have been conscious of this journey, of humanity's design, for a long time; many more, though, have not. Yet the stirrings are growing within the very being of more and more people. There is the feeling, a sense that some form of metamorphosis is occurring to some degree, in some subtle and at times imperceptible manner. Those who feel this are increasing in numbers now. The notion of a change of consciousness, leading to a change within the human species that is our human potential, is no longer an idea of crazy mystics. The truth often hides within open spaces, as the secret knows how to protect itself through the ignorance of others. The forerunners of a heightened, sensitized, conscious humanity are making their presence felt.

HUMAN BEING IS HUMAN BECOMING

It is a great mistake to consider the human being a completed project. As a species, we are unfinished, still on the assembly line of modification and upgrade. There is the outside chance that a newer model will be introduced and we will find ourselves as end-of-line stock, but I don't think so. And neither should you. There is too much at stake to throw the baby out with the bathwater now. Saying this, it is time the baby stopped crying and splashing water all over the bathroom floor and started to learn how to wash itself. Already, I feel that some of this self-cleansing has begun. People's hunger for more meaning and significance within life has been increasing over this century. It rose rapidly during the 1960s as spiritual influences (many from the East) found fertile soil in Western lands. Also, a receptive consciousness began to emerge in the postwar years that seemed to yearn for an alternative to the brutality and foolishness of conflict. In many ways now, amid the cacophony of human cruelty, there are widespread signs of humanity's physical, mental, and spiritual growth. There is also a widespread public recognition of the psychic potential of people, with many alternative health practices finding adherents. The human species is beginning to show its motivation to push against existing limits. These are all signs that a species is coming to the end of one era and is nearing the jump time to another spiral on the evolutionary journey.

Significant numbers of individuals and groups are now consciously working to raise the level of our collective human consciousness. All that is needed, from our end, is enough critical mass. When the right balance of quantity and quality of catalytic consciousness is reached, the effect will spread like an electrical charge boosted through the grid. The present recognition of our emergent collective consciousness represents a dynamic transformation in human evolution. Philosopher John White recently described the newly emerging, hyperconscious human being as *Homo noeticus*. "*Homo noeticus* is the term I use to designate what I see as a higher form of humanity emerging on the planet now, characterized not by genetic changes but by *noetic* changes. In other words, *consciousness* is the guiding principle by which to define *Homo noeticus*. There's a radical transformation of consciousness that characterizes *Homo noeticus*, a movement from self-centeredness to God-centeredness."[9]

Yet the mind is not alone, for as the aphorism states, "Body follows where consciousness goes." While there will definitely be change characterized by a shift in perceptual thought—noetic change—there will also be external vital forces impacting on the human biological organism. On the one hand, human consciousness will affect the body as it responds to a heightened sensitivity of thought and perception, while on the other hand, the human nervous system will be responding to increased amounts of cosmic radiation reaching our planet. These processes occurring simultaneously are the combination of factors usually present when evolutionary shifts occur. In other words, the cerebral functioning of a biological organism extends itself as a response to rapidly changing environmental conditions, combined with increased amounts of energized forces reaching the organism and affecting its cellular resonance and structure.

A range of these ideas has been expressed through various philosophical works, such as those by Pierre Teilhard de Chardin, as well as science fiction novels. For example, Olaf Stapledon's novel *Last and First Men* tackles the subject of successive human evolution over eighteen distinct human species, while its successor, *Star Maker*, examines how different collective cosmic intelligences evolve. Another worthy depiction is seen in Theodore Sturgeon's sci-fi novel *More Than Human*, which describes how a collection of gifted and paranormal individuals form a collective gestalt consciousness. Sturgeon writes, "Multiplicity is our first characteristic; unity our second. As your parts know they are parts of you, so must you know that we are parts of humanity."[10] The novel suggests that the next stage of human evolution shall be a mutation in consciousness toward *Homo gestalt*.

In a similar vein, Charles Laughlin and Sheila Richardson published a scholarly paper titled "The Future of Human Consciousness" that examines the possible evolution of human cognition and perception.[11] They suggest that during our present epoch, "Our species seems on the verge of a revolutionary shift in consciousness that will virtually define a new form of human." Their hypothesis refers to the next stage of human evolution as *Homo gestalt*. They write, "*Homo gestalt*'s development will proceed with knowledge based on direct experience of the implicate order of self and world, not merely on the explicate order of experiences." By this, they mean that the perceptual faculties of heightened human consciousness will sense the essential nature of an experience rather than first filtering the experience externally through a set of conditioned filters. This suggests that there will be a decisive break from the levels of social conditioning and socialized realities that have for so long limited our perceptual capacities. Laughlin and Richardson continue their exploration by stating, "We suspect that communication will be direct from cognized reality to cognized reality (i.e., telepathic) without the necessity of relying on technology to establish 'mind-to-mind' linkage. . . . *Homo gestalt* will exist in a perpetual process of *communitas* with his/her fellows. . . . *Homo gestalt* will have full access to the intuitive knowledge (more accurately, gnosis) inherent in the structure of his/her nervous system."[12]

This thesis describes how *Homo gestalt* will seek novelty at all times and will have developed beyond automated emotional responses. Already, the authors state, various cultures are witnessing an awakening to this future form of consciousness. They conclude their brave academic investigation by asking the reader to consider "transcendence" and "evolution" not as some "vague and alien vestige of eastern mysticism" but rather as a "naturally occurring, biologically teleological process." In the end, they say, "Evolution and the anticipation of the future of human consciousness is the optimal you."

The human becoming that is the subject of this book refers to an internal biological mutation (as in the nervous system) as well as a conscious one. After all, our biological apparatus is a vital part of our existence, and no true spiritual teaching should be neglectful of the physical aspect. While I have emphasized the inner changes necessary during these transition times, the physical changes also are crucial if there is to be any harmony between ourselves as a species and ourselves as a species consciousness. As mentioned previously, the awakening of the kundalini (vital life force) within the human body has been likened to a forerunner of the human mutational process. In other words, there has existed for centuries (if not millennia) a shortcut toward the next stage of human evolution that has been available for those individuals with the capacity for rigorous mental and physical preparation. Those few individuals who have activated the latent evolutionary triggers within the human organism are the forerunners to the next stage awaiting collective humanity. Further, these few awakened individuals, through their presence among us, have assisted to radiate a higher quality of energies into the species biological field. The human body has within it built-in safety devices to guard against accidental or premature activation of the latent capacities. Although in geological time, the jump appears suddenly at the end of a cycle, the human nervous system has been prepared over time for this accelerating phase. This is apparent when one considers the pace of change in the amount of information the human mind-body receives.

Today's world is in information overload, with tremendous multiple impacts on the nervous system, from information communications to entertainment and multitasking devices. Most of our present technologies, from virtual worlds to cell phones, function to externalize our nervous system, to increase our range of sense perceptions and involvement. However, rather than extending our external physical technologies, evolution seeks to extend the range and functionality of the human nervous system, and thus our conscious awareness. Many of us do not realize how vital energies animate the cells and organs of living bodies, how the body could be rebuilt from within by a recombination of nerves and energetic forces. Such a task of transformation must surely appear beyond the bounds of possibility. Perhaps, as some adepts have suggested, the gradual change within the cells and tissues of the body has been underway for a long period, maybe even since early childhood, without the individuals ever knowing of this. Gopi Krishna, for whom the vital force has been awakened, describes the process, stating, "By virtue of the evolutionary processes still going on in the human body, a high-powered conscious centre is being evolved by nature in the human brain at a place near the crown of the head built of exceptionally sensitive brain tissue. . . . Biologically, a healthy human organism with an intelligent brain should provide at its present stage of evolution a fit abode for the manifestation of a higher form of consciousness than that which is the normal endowment of mankind in the present age."[13]

What is being said here (and in various mystical treatises over the ages) is that humankind has the capacity for the next evolutionary stage and that we are at present preparing for the endowment. When this endowment is received—or activated—Krishna expects that a revolutionary and radical change will be enacted in all spheres of human life. The final message that Krishna leaves us with through his own personal journey is that "a marvellous transformation of the nervous system and the brain" will occur, resulting in the "manifestation of a superior type of consciousness, which will be the common inheritance of man in the distant future."

And now this future may not be so distant. Other voices, too, are indicating that we are at a transition shift in human history and that this period of turbulence will birth a new human becoming. According to the prophecies of various South American indigenous wisdom traditions, the human species is going to take a quantum leap from *Homo sapiens sapiens* to *Homo luminous*. That is, the human becoming will be endowed with the ability to perceive the finer vibrations and light that constitute the physical world at a higher level. The changing human becoming will be receptive and perceptive to an increased gradient of vital energies.

Mayan daykeeper and authority Hunbatz Men has openly discussed some of the sacred Mayan ceremonies and how they have been working toward opening up human potential. He states, "The ceremonies that culminated at Chichen Itza were intended to help reprogram human DNA so that we humans can learn to exist on Earth in symbiosis with our light bodies—Sun bodies. Our DNA during the Mayan cycles of the last twenty-six thousand years has been encoded with a flaw that can, ultimately, become a source of deevolution. This flaw causes us to believe that we are separate from the Divine Source. For us to evolve identity, this flaw was required. But now it is time for us to move into communion with the Divine."[14]

These incoming energies and capacities that are hinted at suggest that for the first known time, the human species will be able to evolve not *between* generations but *within* a generation, which contradicts our beliefs about how evolution works. It may be possible for humanity to take a biological quantum leap within our own lifetimes, and the physical, emotional, and spiritual traits we acquire will be passed on to our children and our children's children. Just as our body's cellular structure replaces itself approximately every eight months, it is possible for internal modifications (resonances) to affect the body each time it regenerates itself. As discussed in chapter 6, the science of epigenetics (the biology of belief) has ascertained how an individual's thoughts (external environment) can influence the behavior and physiology of the cell, turning genes on and off.[15] This suggests that powerful external stimuli (thought-forms and cosmic radiation) have a much greater influence on the development of our physical cellular structure than previously thought. This fits in exactly with some of the information filtering through from the new sciences (see chapters 5 and 6) about our inherent energetic interconnections as a collective humanity.

As biological organisms, we are, in essence, configurations of densely packed energy patterns (light). This luminous nature of the human being has been known for millennia in esoteric traditions (as has been depicted in the halo of saints). As an example, the shamans of South America known as laikas have an ancient body of teaching that tells how vibration and light can be organized into countless physical shapes and forms. They consider the human body to have a luminous matrix, a luminous energy field (LEF) that manifests the form, structure, and health of the body.

In his book *The Four Insights,* Alberto Villoldo writes, "The LEF organizes the body in the same way that the energy fields of a magnet arrange iron filings on top of a piece of glass . . . a new kind of human has to come from a new luminous matrix. Over millennia, the Laika learned to access the biological blueprint of light and assist Spirit in the unfolding of creation. They also learned how to heal disease and create extraordinary states of health, as well as to craft and shape their personal destinies, by changing the LEF."[16]

In this way, the LEF is considered to act as a kind of software that supplies instructions for the DNA. If specific data impacts on the luminous matrix, it is possible for the DNA to undergo mutation within a single generation. Without speculating as to future specifics, there is a lot of information currently being made public, especially by indigenous elders, that refers to a shift within the human energetic matrix.

The upcoming transition times will be neither accidental nor unremarkable. There are too many converging impacts occurring within a shared time frame for these events to be casual. Discussions from part 1 have indicated how physical disruptions are coinciding with increased turbulence from cosmic and solar emissions. Both at the present time and within our immediate future, we are to be exposed to radiations and external stimuli beyond our knowing. In line with prophecies of indigenous peoples, we may see an *energetically mutated* human biological organism manifest as a result of these converging factors. This will most likely result in a shift that is cognitive as well as emotional, with a heightened sensitivity of consciousness. However, I am not suggesting that there will be a sudden and dramatic metamorphosis, like a flash of lightening or something equally fantastically transfiguring. Changes will indeed be accelerating as different human capacities are awakened or stimulated, yet the process of change will still be on a physical level, and thus will occur over time. Mutational change within a generation is exceptionally rapid for evolutionary time, yet it still means a human lifetime is required for an individual to absorb the adjustments. Any genetic or cellular change will then be passed on to the offspring, as in the usual way of inheritance. This rapid form of human metamorphosis is similar to the actions of the imaginal cells that transform the caterpillar to the butterfly.

Within the human body, it is said that we possess cells that vibrate at a different frequency from our regular cells. At first, these cells are destroyed by the immune system, which considers them foreign cells. However, by resonating together at the same frequency and thus passing

on information, they are able to multiply sufficiently to enable a transformation to occur in the physical body. These different cells, called
imaginal cells, are considered to have an encoding program lying dormant within them. When it is time for them to awaken, they reproduce
until they begin to resonate en mass. It is cells of this type that are sup-
posedly responsible for the caterpillar's metamorphosis into a butterfly.

In a similar manner, Krishna witnessed his own awakening as a
vortex of energetic light. He writes, "'I distinctly saw my body as a col-
umn of living fire from the tips of my toes to the head in which innu-
merable currents circled and eddied, causing at places whirlpools and
vortices, all forming part of a vast heaving sea of light, perpetually in
motion."[17] Krishna explains how he views this pranic vital force as a
latent energy within all humanity, simply awaiting activation. It may be
that the coming stresses on Earth will provide the necessary triggers for
such activation. According to many different teachings—indigenous,
esoteric, channeled, and visionary—this may well be the case. The bigger picture of humanity's evolution is beginning to unfold as more and
more information is being made public concerning changes in Earth's
energy grid, shifts in electromagnetism around the globe, changes in
the Schumann resonance (the SR), the light activation and vibratory
properties of human DNA, and the ancient indigenous teachings about
the human LEF.

During such transitions, we have the energy and opportunity to reinvent ourselves mentally, emotionally, spiritually, and physically. Instead
of being disempowered by transition phases, we can become inspired by
them to learn to grow and develop. Part of this learning involves being
in a right relationship with ourselves, our social environment, and our
energetic universe. When you are in a balanced relationship, the universe
conspires to work with you, and sometimes the most unlikely possibilities line up to favor you. To be out of sync with our energetic surround-
ings often produces an adversarial environment. Coming into a proper
relationship is an energetic process. As shamanic teacher Don Juan
reminded us through the writings of Carlos Castaneda, "Everything we

do, everything we are, rests on our personal power. If we have enough of it, one word uttered to us might be sufficient to change the course of our lives. But if we don't have enough personal power, the most magnificent piece of wisdom can be revealed to us and that revelation won't make a damn bit of difference."[18]

Castaneda also informs us that it is the duty of the human "warrior" to be aware of the unfathomable mystery that surrounds everything and to try to unravel it. Further, he reminds us that there is no end to the mystery of being, yet it is the true warrior's humbleness to engage with the mystery without ever hoping to solve it. For humanity, our gift is our inherent capacity to participate with the evolutionary program. Whether we participate knowingly or not, the unfolding will still go ahead, with an increasing number of interventions and coercions.

INTERVENTIONS

It has been proposed that humanity must achieve specific goals within the time frame of particular evolutionary cycles. To not achieve them would, it is said, damage the integrity and goals of larger cosmic cycles. Regardless of whether we care for this responsibility, it appears that humanity has a duty for reciprocal maintenance within an environment that is larger than our planetary home. We are thus compelled to respect universal laws, patterns, and processes. According to information presented in *The People of the Secret,* "Certain gains and goals for mankind—and for the biosphere of Earth—must be attained within certain intervals of Earth time. These gains are essential for the balance and growth of the solar system of which the Earth is a part. The solar system may itself be subject to a similar pressure in the interest of the galaxy of which it is a part."[19]

Within the affairs of humankind, there are influences and interventions beyond the scope of what most people wish to consider or comprehend. This is natural and should not be unnerving; we have been living under the mythology of divine intelligences in various guises for millennia. Humanity has never been without its gods; it is only that now the sanctity of religious enterprise is being replaced by pragmatic universal processes. The signs have been with us for a long time, veiled and scattered, with clues hidden under almost every rock. They not only appear in the visions and insights of alert minds, but they also appear tucked away within literary works, films, music, and pop culture. For the attentive collector, attempting to find the scattered seeds of these signs can be an exhilarating process.

Some of these signs indicate that humanity is being coerced into various situations that are required for developmental purposes. While such situations appear to be unhelpful on the surface, we are unable to evaluate them. Yet the energetic potential of humankind is such that total coercion is not possible: our integrity cannot be violated. In this sense, it is similar to the chauffeuring of a person in a direction that is more appropriate for that person's capacity, despite this potential being largely unrecognized. It is hoped that certain conscious interventions into the evolutionary life of humanity will stimulate the growth and flowering of humankind's latent potentiality. In this way, humanity will then be able to participate more fully within the process, which is more or less the case of getting your friends onboard. The human race is required within the larger scheme of things, yet we've been pretty slow so far in getting our act together. This may not be entirely our fault, but rather the consequences of certain historical and cosmic events; however, such past matters do not concern us here.

It appears, then, that there have been, and continue to be, higher influences concerned with the evolutionary impulse in humanity. That these influences be called interventions may seem rather strong for some, as if indicating some forceful intrusion or interference into the affairs of humankind. It is as if humans prefer to consider themselves masters of their own lives and kings of their terrain. Yet, truth be told, the members of the species *Homo sapiens sapiens* do not exist within a vacuum, and they are not free to spread their cacophonous unbalance on their terrestrial and solar environment. That our planet is part of an evolutionary program should not be startling news, as it is how we have arrived where we are. And if this is our present stage, then it should be logical to reason that there is further to go. And should we be in need of correctional guidance and developmental pressures along the way, then such interventions are to be recognized rather than disbelieved and shunted. Such higher influences are likely to have been with us for a very, very long time, and now events are accelerating.

The clues and signposts to this developmental path, as previously mentioned, have been scattered among our various sources and within our mystical traditions over the centuries, and even millennia. A very recent source, known only as A. J. Peterson (who had direct contact with a teaching master), outlined a series of revelations. One extract describes, "There seems to be a framework—a structure . . . a whole new design for life and inner development . . . moving into manifestation immediately ahead of us in time. . . . Every detail pre-planned; originating from above to below. . . . And absolutely nothing can stop it . . . it's already there, out of range of our vision, but as real and solid as life itself. . . . A new force, or influence, is reaching us—coded to produce precise results that will supersede the old modes of development—almost a forced process which will have effects unique in world history as we know it."[20]

Peterson continues by saying that this planned development includes a "stepping-up" of "transformative force" that by its very nature must cause resistance. Such resistance may well manifest physically as some of what we are currently witnessing, with institutions of the old paradigm collapsing and the geophysical world burning, shaking, and erupting. Interestingly, the source says that the animal kingdom and all "natural life" will fare much better than humanity, as they have been following their own "instinctive laws" without deviation, whereas humanity has gone off balance. It is important, we are told, to harmonize and balance ourselves in order to "burn up" or transmute some of the morass of obstructive energies created by the mass of humankind. Such a stimulus, when applied, acts as a form of quickening for individuals and for our species. Humankind is described as a chrysalis in which the evolutionary potential exists, yet lies in an embryonic state. Peterson continues the revelation, stating, "In this state I perceived a vast act of direct intervention in the life of mankind, like a realignment with the source of all manifestation, which necessitated the prior removal of an obstruction to its correct development. This occurrence coincided with the release of a fresh inflow of magnetic influences, also a stepping-up of vibrationary pressure, like entering a more powerful force-field, or submission to a forced process of growth—designed to produce an evolutionary 'leap.' But it all happened in the dimension of the higher Self, and has not yet externalised into our world of linear time, though its foreshadowings are already apparent."[21]

This resonates almost exactly with what has so far been discussed concerning an increased flow of magnetic radiations (influences), an increase in vibratory pressures, and a forced process of accelerated growth necessary for an energetic, evolutionary leap. Like a coil being wound up, our cosmic sector is set for a release of the spring. At present, we are acquiring the necessary momentum, and the influences coming in to supply this are naturally causing resistance and disturbances on physical, psychological, physiological, and emotional levels.

Such influences have also been showing up within the realms of transpersonal development, consciousness studies, and various experimental techniques such as hypnosis, primal therapy, lucid dreaming, biofeedback, rebirthing, and holotropic breathwork. The experiences of various consciousness researchers can be found in the works of such pioneers as Stanislav Grof, Christopher Bache, and Robert Monroe. Bache, a transpersonal psychologist, has made intriguing investigations into the collective psyche of humanity and our collective species' "dark night of the soul."* Bache's many and varied investigations during transpersonal sessions led him toward the revelation that humanity, in facing an environmental and species-related catastrophe, will be catalyzed into

---

*This term is a reference to the mystical writings of St. John of the Cross and his difficult spiritual journey toward union with God.

a "great awakening." He writes, "I saw that out of the seething desires of history, out of the violent conflicts and of the scheming of individuals and nations, there was now driving forward a new awareness in human consciousness. Its birth in us no less difficult or violent than the birth of a new continent through volcanic upheaval. It drives upward from the floor of our being, requiring a transposition of everything that has gone before to make room for its new organisational patterns."[22]

The focus of this transformative process, Bache tells us, is not the individual but all humanity. The awakening of consciousness applies to our entire species and leads toward a unified field of awareness. Bache understands this revelatory event as both something to be accomplished and something already accomplished. In this sense, the evolutionary transition is established as inevitable, the question being how individuals within collective humanity cope with the event. Bache continues by stating, "This quantum jump in our evolutionary status precipitated a wholesale reorganisation of global culture. It signaled a turning-point that would forever divide the human story into the before and after of THE GREAT AWAKENING."[23]

While this statement may seem somewhat dramatic, it is significant in that it refers to the human story as still continuing on a terrestrial, physical journey, one where there is a "wholesale reorganisation" of global culture. This differs from some accounts now becoming widespread among various groups that see the upcoming Earth changes as preceding some kind of ecstatic ascension. In terms that are often biblical, there are views, gaining many adherents, that suggest humankind will jump into a nonphysical dimension as a part of some dimensional exodus. The idea of leaving the physical world behind to live in a peaceful world of thought-forms and etheric bodies is very comforting for many people. However, this may not be the case.

I regard the transformative changes as altering forever the conditions of life on this planet; as such, I have suggested some means for creating and revitalizing civil and social lifestyles (see chapter 8). Many structures will be surpassed as new understandings about the life and responsibility of humanity are revealed. The new humanity that I talk of here is not so much an angelic collective as a species that has catalyzed certain latent evolutionary capacities and thus activated the inherent upgrade. This, as previously discussed, will consist of a stimulated consciousness and heightened states of perception and energetic awareness. It may, as some traditions suggest, allow the consciousness to integrate more fully with the luminous matrix of the body—the LEF. This task has been assigned, if you will, to the evolutionary future of humanity. Up until now, we have largely been isolated and ignorant of our future trajectory and functionally blind to our role. Yet we are not totally blind, as we are endowed with an intelligence within us, guiding and preparing us for the shift ahead.

Bache sees this awakening of the collective conscious as a unified field becoming more aware of itself. He visualized this as a network, or web, of flashes beginning to stabilize and connect. He writes, "I repeatedly saw extended webs of energy suddenly contract and explode in brilliant flashes. In the past these flashes had not endured long and had been swallowed by the inertia of the collective unconscious of our species. Now, however, the flashes were beginning to hold their own. Not only were they not dissolving, but they were beginning to connect with other flashes occurring around the planet."[24]

Bache reveals that this is a stage of purification for our collective species, a period when humanity is required to become more consciously aware and to rid itself of negativity and psychological trauma. We must collectively cleanse ourselves to bring in the more refined energies that are waiting, just as old wine is poured out of bottles for the new.

The transition times that we now face during this historical moment mark a momentous shift along our evolutionary journey. The key is to understand that this is a required period not only for the creation of dynamic energy for the leap, but also to purge and burn up various accretions that are no longer necessary. Using an analogy, we can say it is like a space rocket shedding its load once the rocket fuel from that container has been used up. We are burning our fuel now and ejecting some of the unnecessary baggage for our journey to the stars.

We need to be prepared but not stressed. We will lose some things deemed precious to us, yet in the losing, we will also gain something much more precious: we will be gaining our future. This future awaits us and lies within us; the evolutionary impulse of humankind is becoming activated. Our potential state, which may seem transcendental to some, is the natural heritage of humankind. Yet it requires that our human becoming be refined enough to accept this challenge. As the Mayan teachings remind us, "We are the ones who are responsible, and we can change that. If we wake up it is possible to change the energy. It is possible to change everything."[25]

It is important that we are collectively responsible to take charge of higher forms of perception. The happiness and welfare of humankind depends upon the success of our undertaking. We are called on now to act in compliance with a developed integrity. There needs to be a balanced relationship between thought, emotions, and conscience in order to harness the power of the vital force in humankind. The time is now near when this evolutionary impulse will make its presence felt.

A Tale to Finish: The Three Old Men

A woman left her house and saw three old men with long beards seated in front of her garden.

"I don't know you," she said, "but you must be hungry. Please come into my house and eat something."

They asked, "Is your husband at home?"

"No," she said, "he is not."

"Then we cannot enter," they said.

On late afternoon, when the husband arrived, she told him what happened.

"Well, tell them I arrived already and invite them to come in."

The woman went outside to invite the men to come into her house.

"The three of us cannot enter a house together," said the old men.

"Why?" she wanted to know.

One of the men pointed toward one of his friends and explained, "His name is Wealth." He pointed toward the other and said, "His name is Success, and my name is Love."

He then added, "Now go inside and decide with your husband which one of us three you wish to invite into your house."

The woman entered her house, and she told her husband what they told her.

The man, very happy, said, "That's good! If that's the way it is, let's invite Wealth, and have him fill our house with wealth."

His wife did not agree. She said, "My dear, why don't we invite Success?"

Their daughter was listening from the other corner of the house and came running with an idea. She said, "Wouldn't it better to invite Love? Our home would be full of love then."

"Let's pay attention to our daughter's advice," said the husband to his wife. "Go outside and invite Love to be our guest."

The wife went outside and asked the three old men, "Which one of you is Love? Please come and be our guest." Love stood up and began to walk toward the house. The other two also rose and followed him.

Surprised, the lady asked Wealth and Success, "I only invited Love, why are you also coming?"

The old men responded together, "If you had invited Wealth or Success, the other two would have remained outside, but since you invited Love, wherever he goes, we go with him. Wherever there is love, there is also wealth and success."

If you truly follow your heart, the rest will arrive as well.

CONCLUSION

The Evolutionary Impulse in Humankind

In everything, do unto others as you would have them do unto you.

JESUS CHRIST, MATTHEW 7:12

What is hateful to you, do not do to your neighbour.

HILLEL, TALMUD, JUDAISM, SHIBBATH 31A

Not one of you truly believes until you wish for others that which you wish for yourself.

MOHAMMED, ISLAM: HADITH

This is the sum of duty: do not do to others what would cause pain if done to you.

HINDUISM: MAHABHARATA 5:1517

If thine eyes be turned towards justice, choose thou for thy neighbour that which thou choosest for thyself.

BAHA'I/ZOROASTRIANISM,
SHAYAST-NA-SHAYAST 13.29

Treat not others in ways that you yourself would find hurtful.

BUDDHA/BUDDHISM, UDANA-VARGA 5.18

Do not do to others what you do not want done to yourself.

CONFUCIUS, CONFUCIANISM: ANALECTS 15.23

Humanity is a collective species. Individually, we have our degrees of agency with ourselves, our family, our loved ones, our friends, and our community. We are also on a collective journey that is unfolding around us at an accelerating pace. Much will be asked of us, and much will be expected. Intense times foreshadow increased opportunities for growth. First we need to be resilient, then we need to understand that we have the capacity for readaptation, and finally we need to engage with our renewal. We need to settle down and behave. It does not matter what our individual and varied religious, spiritual, philosophical, social, or any other beliefs are: in the end, we will all be forced to work toward a better future. It will, indeed, be work, but not the kind that offers financial incentives. Our incentives will be different—and much, much more significant. We will be called on to practice our sense of integrity and decency like we've never practiced it before. And how we think affects everything, for what we are is the result of everything we have ever thought. Let there be nothing to fear.

The ideas we manifest become a part of the physical world we experience. We have been informed of this many times, yet it is difficult for the reality of this statement to sink in. In a way, we are buffered against such realizations, as if some channel is cut off within us. It is my understanding that this connection, this bridge to a more expansive reality, is being reconnected once again. And if we wish to stimulate this reconnecting process, then we need to shed old and worn-out ideas and beliefs. Our mire of duality, conflict, strife, and discord no longer supports the place where we need to be. Yet we also need to have the courage to face what is manifesting in our lives in order to transform those moments within our very selves. This book has been about this relationship between our exterior and interior worlds and has attempted to stress that neither exists alone. We are partners with our physical realm, where our conscious selves must learn to operate through flesh and bone.

This book has also attempted to show that our planet is experiencing a converging set of crises. These crises were described in the early chapters, which were intended to indicate to the reader that our global society is heading toward drastic and radical upheaval. Even if the reader, having come this far, chooses to disagree with the more metaphysical aspects of the book's hypothesis, there is still ample evidence to indicate that physical disruptions are here and are likely to increase in nature. I have discussed the nature of these changes within the context of cyclic change for both social (as in the fall and rise of civilizations) and grander astronomical and evolutionary cycles. Within these epochal trigger points are periods of social unrest and uncertainty as to whether a breakthrough or a breakdown will occur. However, it was suggested that these events are framed within a grander design of guided evolution, wherein humankind may not be totally cognizant of the presence of higher influences (or cognizant at all). At such critical periods, opportunities for developmental change are offered, though these opportunities may appear random or disturbing within the scope of a person's present lifetime.

Also discussed was how humanity possesses the knowledge for readaptation. Within us, we have the capacity to facilitate a perceptual shift within our various social realities; we can, literally, change our minds. To encourage this, I have asked the reader to consider the new information being revealed by what I call the new sciences: the fields of quantum physics, quantum biology, and biophysics. These scientific investigations are now informing us as to the underlying principles enforcing our sense of reality. They tell us how we are connected energetically and consciously and how we possess the capacity for activating vital energies of development. To reiterate, we are not a finished species: we are still mutating, and there exists the possibility that we can influence this process so that mutational change can occur within an individual lifetime rather than between generations.

The final section of the book addressed what I call renewal. This involves the recognition that a spiritual renaissance within the human realm is underway. It was suggested that this renaissance has been slowly gestating within our cultures and societies for generations and that it is now emerging. Part of this renewal includes the formation of a new civic order through reevaluating our social networks, relationships, lifestyles, and communities as well as securing a more harmonious connection with our environment and resources. Finally, the book puts forth the hypothesis that new influences and interventions are preparing humankind for an evolutionary upgrade, a leap toward what could historically be viewed as a *new humanity*. The evolutionary impulse in humankind is being stimulated to awaken, and we are in the throes of a new birthing process. And with this birth labor comes some piercing pain.

The human being is a human becoming, and for a long time we have lived with the ever-present possibility of transcending our present state of consciousness by means of evolutionary processes still at work within the human race. Our religions have often been a symbolic expression of this evolutionary impulse, and in their essence, they have sought to stimulate its active functioning. At other times, the institutional side of religious power has strived to suppress the knowledge of this inherent potential and to avoid all possible conditions favorable to its activation. Yet our future state exists as a potentiality, naturally present within each human body. Should a mass activation of humankind's vital energies occur—or mainstream acceptance of its presence be acknowledged—then this would open up new directions for the focus of human energy and resources. It could serve to shift our attention from shallow materialism toward goals more attuned to the dignity of humanity. The recognition of this evolutionary impulse as a biological inheritance and process would no doubt drive our societies and cultures to facilitate the process of transformation. Our own inherent evolutionary force is carrying us collectively toward an already known state of development, of which most of us have little or no knowledge.

Gopi Krishna, a person who claims to have personal experiential understanding of this developmental process, has created a revised theory of evolution in which he states:

1. Evolution is directed by a super-intelligent force which operates through a biological mechanism in the human body known to yoga theory as "kundalini," and by many other names in a wide variety of ancient and esoteric texts.

2. Evolution, including human evolution, is therefore not "random," but a deliberate act on the part of an invisible cosmic intelligence or organizing power and has a "target."

3. The target of evolution is to produce a virtual superman or woman who will live in a permanent state of bliss, possess a genius level of intelligence, and various other attributes seldom seen in the population at large such as psychic powers.[1]

Such powers and attributes of the new human may signify a leap similar to that which occurred when our *Homo sapiens* ancestors replaced the Neanderthals, as we undergo another transitional shift in species development.

While I understand that much of what is hypothesized here is speculative, there are many threads of mythology, prophecy, tribal knowledge, and esoteric teachings that hint at and allude to this and similar propositions. And where there is smoke . . . well, one must seek to read the signs and trust one's own instinct. In the end, it will come down to each individual's inner gut instinct as to what he or she wishes to accept or feels ready to accept. It is our degree of dignity and action that will mark us, and this must by necessity start and stop within the core of each person. We are not lacking in the dynamic forces needed for our own futures; we are surrounded and swim within a sea of energy, yet it is ours for service and not for domination. There is enough available energy to support the human venture, and such energies will multiply when expressed through positive celebration, sharing, and constructive efforts. While physical energy can be diminished somewhat by use, we should remember that our resources of psychic energy will be increased and enhanced through participation and cooperative harmony. Our central focus should now be on our continued growth and development and on our increased resourceful capacities to further our limits and break old restrictive bonds. Our sacred story is now one of readaptation and renewal, not one of breakdown, collapse, or failure.

According to cultural historian Thomas Berry:

> The evolutionary vision provides the most profound mystique of the universe. Our main source of psychic energy in the future will depend on our ability to understand this symbol of evolution in an acceptable context of interpretation. Only in the context of an emergent universe will the human project come to an integral understanding of itself. We must, however, come to experience the universe in its psychic as well as in its physical aspect. . . . As physical resources become less available, psychic energy must support the human project in a special manner. This situation brings us to a new reliance on powers within the universe and also to experience of the deeper self.[2]

This "new reliance," as Berry suggests, is one that connects the human being within a living and intelligent universe. Our mythological story is of an evolving species within an evolving universe, each as a part of the other. For too long, we have had the evolutionary process guided through us as we were ignorant to its presence; now, the time has arrived for humanity to help collectively energize the process.

Evolution is grand and epic. It can be a great adventure that is both irreversible and creatively new. Our process is one of communion in which we ourselves are in a magical relationship with Earth. We are entities in growth together, and as such, we need to be in compassionate cooperation and not in aggressive competition. As intermediaries, we can integrate the material with the spiritual, the physical with the psychic, so that real work can be done that benefits all rather than creating unworkable disparities. Modern science has confirmed the unity of humans and our natural psychic and energetic bonds. It is important that we allow this to form a new basis on which to work toward a new and revitalized global Earth community. In truth, many of us will already be feeling these similar stirrings deep within our hearts. We sense that change is coming and that the inevitable approaches. Something new is happening: a new vision and a new energy are coming into being. In the end, we win.

Let It Come Down

An early dawn rises after a dark night,
just as our own personal djinns
are purged through effort
into a new cleansed state—

so too will the world soul be plunged
into its own infernal chaos before light
is drawn from its well of deep reserves
and a new epoch is created from the ashes
of a long history of struggle and strife.

Everything will know itself
in order to pass beyond its own weakness.

In the end it is a great plan, a great love.
A wonderful, human, divine purpose.

Let it come down.

KINGSLEY L. DENNIS,
JULY 10, 2005

NOTES

INTRODUCTION. STANDING AT THE PRECIPICE OF CHANGE

1. Ouspensky, *In Search of the Miraculous*, 219.
2. Cook, *Hua-Yen Buddhism*, 2.
3. Scott, *The People of the Secret*, 38.
4. Ouspensky, *In Search of the Miraculous*, 38.
5. Scott, *People of the Secret*.
6. Elgin, *Awakening Earth*, 121.

CHAPTER 1. EVOLUTIONARY TURNING POINTS

1. Loye, "Chaos and Transformation: Implications of Nonequilibrium Theory for Social Science and Society."
2. Nietzsche, *The Will to Power*, 549–50.
3. Laszlo, *The Chaos Point*.
4. Kuhn, *The Structure of Scientific Revolutions*.
5. Eldredge, *Time Frames*.
6. Margulis, *Symbiosis in Cell Evolution*.
7. Sahtouris, "The Biology of Globalization."
8. Sahtouris, "Living Systems in Evolution."
9. Laszlo, *Evolution*.
10. Artigiani, "Social Evolution: A Nonequilibrium Systems Model," 99.
11. Laszlo, "Technology and Social Change: An Approach from Nonequilibrium Systems Theory."
12. Burke and Ornstein, *The Axemaker's Gift*.

13. Goonatilake, *The Evolution of Information*.

14. Hobart and Schiffman, *Information Ages*.

15. McLuhan, *The Gutenberg Galaxy*.

16. Toffler, *The Third Wave*.

17. Carey, *The Third Millennium*, 100.

18. Scott, *People of the Secret*.

19. Ibid.

20. Strauss and Howe, *The Fourth Turning*, 210–11.

21. Ibid., 267.

22. Prigogine, *The End of Certainty*, 183.

CHAPTER 2. CONVERGING CRISES

1. Diamond, *Collapse*.

2. Homer-Dixon, *The Upside of Down*; Tainter, *The Collapse of Complex Societies*.

3. Tainter, *The Collapse of Complex Societies*.

4. Homer-Dixon, "Prepare Today for Tomorrow's Breakdown," 2.

5. Homer-Dixon, "Our Panarchic Future."

6. King and Schneider, *The First Global Revolution*, viii.

7. Meadows, Meadows, and Randers, *Beyond the Limits*, xvi.

8. King and Schneider, *First Global Revolution*, ix.

9. Pearce, *The Last Generation*.

10. Two crucial major reports are N. Stern, *The Economics of Climate Change* and Intergovernmental Panel on Climate Change report *Climate Change—Working Group I Report "The Physical Science Basis"* (2007), www.ipcc.ch/publications_and_data/publications_and_data_reports.shtml#1; recent influential popular science accounts include Lovelock, *The Revenge of Gaia*; Monbiot, *Heat*; Lynas, *Six Degrees*; Pearce, *With Speed and Violence*; Kolbert, *Field Notes from a Catastrophe*; and Linden, *Winds of Change*.

11. Townsend and Harris, "Now the Pentagon Tells Bush: Climate Change Will Destroy Us."

12. See the group's homepage at www.ipcc.ch.

13. Pearce, *Last Generation*.

14. Pearce, *With Speed and Violence*.

15. Hansen, "Scientific Reticence and Sea Level Rise."

16. Pearce, *With Speed and Violence*. For more technical analysis, see Rial et

al., "Nonlinearities, Feedbacks and Critical Thresholds within the Earth's Climate System," 21.

17. Stern, *Economics of Climate Change,* 3; Lynas, "The Effects of Potential Temperature Rises," in *Six Degrees.*

18. Flannery, *The Weather Makers.*

19. Kunstler, *The Long Emergency,* 148.

20. Lovelock, "The Fight to Get Aboard Lifeboat UK."

21. See www.peakoil.com. For a parallel analysis of "peak gas," see Darley, *High Noon for Natural Gas.*

22. Heinberg, *The Party's Over.* See also Leggett, *Half Gone.*

23. Chrisafis and Keeley, "Oil Prices: Europe Threatened with Summer of Discontent over Rising Cost of Fuel."

24. Lovett, "Russia Plants Underwater Flat, Claims Arctic Seafloor."

25. BBC News, "Russia Outlines Arctic Force Plan."

26. Bowcott, "Britain to Claim More Than 1m sq km of Antarctica."

27. Traynor, "Climate Change May Spark Conflict with Russia, EU Told."

28. Kunstler, *Long Emergency,* 65.

29. Gallopin et al., *Branch Points.*

30. United Nations, Department of Economic and Social Affairs: Population Division, "Fact Sheet 1: World Urban Population," www.un.org/esa/population/publications/WUP2005/2005WUP_FS1.pdf (accessed April 26, 2011).

31. United Nations, Department of Economic and Social Affairs: Population Division, "World Urbanization Prospects: The 2005 Revision," www.un.org/esa/population/publications/WUP2005/2005wup.htm (accessed April 26, 2011).

32. Williams, *The Future of Global Systems,* 15.

33. United Nations, *Global Trends.*

34. For more on climate change and global inequality see Timmons and Parks, *A Climate of Injustice.*

35. Rogers, *Cities for a Small Planet.*

36. Norton, "Feral Cities."

37. Mitchell, *Me++.*

38. Young, "Solar 'Superflare' Shredded Earth's Ozone."

39. See National Oceanic and Atmospheric Administration, "Solar Storms Cause Significant Economic and Other Impacts on Earth."

40. National Academies Press, "Severe Space Weather Events—Understanding Societal and Economic Impacts: A Workshop Report."

41. National Academies Press, "Severe Space Weather Events."

42. National Academies Press, "Severe Space Weather Events."

43. See www.nasa.gov/mission_pages/themis/main (accessed April 26, 2011).

44. Joseph, *Apocalypse 2012.*

45. Dmitriev, "Planetophysical State of the Earth and Life."

46. Ibid.

CHAPTER 3. MOMENTS OF TURBULENCE

1. Gribbin, *Deep Simplicity.*

2. Shah, *Reflections,* 67.

3. See National Intelligence Council, *Global Trends 2015.*

4. Homer-Dixon, *Environment, Scarcity, and Violence.*

5. Abbott, "An Uncertain Future: Law Enforcement, National Security and Climate Change."

6. Ibid.

7. McCahill and Norris, "CCTV in London (Working Paper No. 6)."

8. *Defence News,* "Met Office Climate Change Study Could Help Identify Future Security Threats."

9. Gilman, Randall, and Schwartz, "Impacts of Climate Change: A System Vulnerability Approach to Consider the Potential Impacts to 2050 of a Mid-Upper Greenhouse Gas Emissions Scenario." And see Table 3.1 in Stern, *Economics of Climate Change,* which sets out the effects on water, food, health, land, environment, and abrupt large-scale changes of varying levels of temperature increase.

10. Abbott, *Uncertain Future.*

11. Paskal, "How Climate Change Is Pushing the Boundaries of Security and Foreign Policy."

12. Lewis, "Water Shortages Are Likely to Be Trigger for Wars, Says UN Chief Ban Ki Moon."

13. Parry et al., "Millions at Risk: Defining Critical Climate Change Threats and Targets."

14. Pfeiffer, *Eating Fossil Fuels.*

15. Laszlo, *Quantum Shift in the Global Brain.*

16. Pfeiffer, *Eating Fossil Fuels,* 2.

17. Ibid., 25.

18. Ibid., 24.

19. See Reuters, "FACTBOX—Financial Crisis Sparks Unrest in Europe," www .reuters.com/article/latestCrisis/idUSLQ87702?sp=true (accessed April 26, 2011). Also see AlertNet (www.alertnet.org/) for general news of this type.

20. Williams, "Future of Global Systems," 1–23.

21. Booth, *Theory of World Security*.

22. These scenarios were initially formulated in discussions with John Urry and appeared, in an earlier form, in a coauthored book: K. Dennis and J. Urry, *After the Car* (Cambridge: Polity Press, 2009).

23. Kunstler, *Long Emergency*, 264.

24. Ibid., 266.

25. Gallopin et al., "Branch Points," 34.

26. Tainter, *Collapse of Complex Societies;* Woodbridge, *The Next World War*.

27. Information Commissioner, "A Report on the Surveillance Society." See also BBC News, "Britain Is 'Surveillance Society.'"

28. Becker, *The Body Electric*.

29. A well-known quote from Václav Havel, source unknown.

30. Elgin, *Awakening Earth*, 150.

31. Russell, "Spirit of Now" at www.peterrussell.com/SpiritAwake/index.php (accessed February 4, 2011).

32. Csikszentmihalyi, *The Evolving Self*, 293.

CHAPTER 4. GLOBAL MIND CHANGE

1. A well-known quote from Arthur Schopenhauer, source unknown.

2. Harman, *Global Mind Change*, viii.

3. Abbott, Rogers, and Sloboda, *Beyond Terror*.

4. Ornstein and Ehrlich, *New World, New Mind*, 195.

5. Rumi, *Masnavi*.

6. A well-known quote from Gandhi, source unknown.

7. Harman, *Global Mind Change*, viii.

8. Laszlo, *Macroshift*.

9. Ideas as expressed in Laszlo, *Chaos Point*.

10. Ibid.

11. Sahtouris, "Vistas—Evolving Our Beliefs to Evolve Our Lives."

12. Russell, *The Global Brain Awakens;* Bloom, *Global Brain.*

13. de Chardin, *The Phenomenon of Man.*

14. A well-known quote from Engelbart, source unknown.

15. McLuhan, *Counterblast,* 144.

16. Laszlo, *Quantum Shift,* Introduction.

17. de Chardin, *Phenomenon of Man,* 263.

18. Cited in Harman, *Global Mind Change,* 129.

19. Ibid., viii.

20. Shah, *The Exploits of the Incomparable Mulla Nasrudin,* 9.

21. Leary, *The Intelligence Agents.*

22. Taken from "The Global Brain Group"; see also Grant, "Memes: Introduction."

23. Montalk, "Fringe Knowledge for Beginners," 112.

24. Elgin, *Awakening Earth,* 157.

25. Ibid., 162.

CHAPTER 5. THE NEW SCIENCES

1. Berry, *The Great Work,* 26.

2. Laszlo, *Quantum Shift,* 101.

3. Cited in Harman, *Global Mind Change,* 52.

4. A well-known quote from Bohr, source unknown.

5. Zohar, *The Quantum Self,* 122.

6. Talbot, *The Holographic Universe.*

7. Laszlo, *Quantum Shift,* 110.

8. Capra, *The Tao of Physics,* 324.

9. Tesla, "Man's Greatest Achievement."

10. Laszlo, *The Connectivity Hypothesis.*

11. Popp et al., "Physical Aspects of Biophotons."

12. Ho and Popp, "Gaia and the Evolution of Coherence."

13. Ho, *The Rainbow and the Worm,* 210.

14. Ibid., 241.

15. Becker, *Body Electric.*

16. Strogatz, *SYNC.*

17. Ibid., 173.

18. Laszlo, *Quantum Shift,* 120.

19. Russell, *Design for Destiny.*

20. Havel, "The New Measure of Man."
21. A version of this story appeared in Shah, *Tales of the Dervishes*.

CHAPTER 6. OUR RESONATING WORLD

1. Becker, *Body Electric*, 275.
2. Becker, *Cross Currents*.
3. Blank and Goodman, "Do Electromagnetic Fields Interact Directly with DNA?" 112.
4. Brzezinski, *Between Two Ages*.
5. Narby, *Cosmic Serpent*.
6. Leary, *Info-Psychology*.
7. Fosar and Bludorf, "Spiritual Science: DNA Is Influenced by Words and Frequencies."
8. Lipton, *The Biology of Belief*.
9. Gerber, *Vibrational Medicine*.
10. Miller and Miller, "The Schumann Resonances and Human Psychobiology."
11. Cited in Miller and Miller, "Schumann Resonances."
12. Becker, *Cross Currents*.
13. For a collection of similar Nasrudin stories, see Shah, *The Exploits of the Incomparable Mulla Nasrudin*.

CHAPTER 7. SPIRITUAL RENAISSANCE

1. Cited in Harman, *Global Mind Change*, 129.
2. A well-known quote from Václav Havel, taken from a 1991 speech to a joint session of the U.S. Congress.
3. Naimy, *The Book of Mirdad*, 57.
4. de Chardin, *The Future of Man*.
5. For more information, see Banathy, *Guided Evolution of Society*.
6. McFadden, *Profiles in Wisdom*, 11.
7. Recommended reads include Shah, *Learning How to Learn* and Shah, *Knowing How to Know*.
8. de Chardin, *Let Me Explain*, 60.
9. Scott, *People of the Secret*.
10. Collin, *The Theory of Celestial Influence*.
11. McFadden, *Profiles in Wisdom*, 102.

12. Steiner, *An Outline of Esoteric Science.*

13. McFadden, *Profiles in Wisdom,* 222.

14. Ibid., 233.

15. Berry, *Great Work,* 69.

16. Brown, *The Quest.*

17. Ibid.

18. McFadden, *Profiles in Wisdom,* 21.

19. This story is attributed to the Persian poet Attar of Nishapur.

CHAPTER 8. NEW CIVIC ORDER

1. Timms, *Beyond Prophecies and Predictions,* 148.

2. Korten, *The Great Turning.*

3. Kunstler, *Long Emergency,* 238.

4. Berry, *Great Work.*

5. Ibid., 19.

6. Elgin, *Awakening Earth,* 255.

7. Spinrad, *The Solarians.*

8. Kunstler, *Long Emergency,* 248.

9. See www.newurbanism.org/newurbanism.html (accessed February 4, 2011).

10. Congress for the New Urbanism, "Charter of the New Urbanism."

11. See www.transitionnetwork.org (accessed February 4, 2011).

12. Ferry, "You Are Now Entering an Oil-Free Zone."

13. See the program's homepage at www.transitionnetwork.org.

14. Gallopin et al., "Branch Points," 35–36.

15. Ewert, Baker, and Bissix, *Integrated Resource and Environmental Management.*

16. Rogers, *Cities for a Small Planet.*

17. Howard, *Garden Cities of To-Morrow.*

18. Girardet, *CitiesPeoplePlanet,* 158.

19. Ibid.

20. Holmgren, *Permaculture.*

21. Kurzweil, *The Singularity Is Near.*

22. Mol, "Boundless Biofuels? Between Environmental Sustainability and Vulnerability."

23. Worldwatch Institute, "Biofuels for Transportation: Global Potential and

Implications for Sustainable Agriculture and Energy in the 21st Century," www.worldwatch.org/node/4078.

24. As described and advocated in Willis, Webb, and Wilsdon, *The Disrupters*.

25. For example, see the SPIN Gardening website, a self-serve, self-directed online learning series for "self-farmers," at www.spingardening.com.

26. See www.freedomgardens.org.

27. See www.slowmoneyalliance.org.

28. McFadden, *Profiles in Wisdom*, 28.

29. See the various United Kingdom examples described in Willis, Webb, and Wilsdon, *Disrupters*.

30. Lessing, *Prisons We Choose to Live Inside*, 6.

CHAPTER 9. A NEW HUMANITY

1. Scott, *People of the Secret*, 251.

2. Ring, "Precognitive and Prophetic Visions in Near-Death Experiences," 54.

3. Bucke, *Cosmic Consciousness*.

4. Nietzsche, *Thus Spoke Zarathustra*.

5. Ibid., 43–44.

6. Krishna, *Kundalini*.

7. Ibid., 90.

8. Aurobindo, *The Future Evolution of Man*, 35.

9. White, *The Meeting of Science and Spirit*, 248.

10. Sturgeon, *More Than Human*.

11. Laughlin and Richardson, "The Future of Human Consciousness."

12. Ibid., 411.

13. Krishna, *Kundalini*, 173.

14. McFadden, *Profiles in Wisdom*, 235.

15. Lipton, *Biology of Belief*.

16. Villoldo, *The Four Insights*.

17. Krishna, *Kundalini*, 91.

18. Castaneda, *Tales of Power*.

19. Scott, *People of the Secret*, 250.

20. Peterson, *Approach to Reality*, 138.

21. Ibid., 139.

22. Bache, *Dark Night, Early Dawn*.

23. Ibid.

24. Ibid.

25. McFadden, *Profiles in Wisdom,* 241.

CONCLUSION. THE EVOLUTIONARY IMPULSE IN HUMANKIND

1. See www.ecomall.com/gopikrishna.

2. Berry, *Great Work,* 170.

BIBLIOGRAPHY

Abbott, C. "An Uncertain Future: Law Enforcement, National Security and Climate Change." Oxford Research Group. www.oxfordresearchgroup.org .uk/sites/default/files/uncertainfuture.pdf.

Abbott, C., P. Rogers, and J. Sloboda. *Beyond Terror: The Truth about the Real Threats to Our World.* London: Rider, 2007.

Artigiani, R. "Social Evolution: A Nonequilibrium Systems Model." In Laszlo, E., ed. *The New Evolutionary Paradigm,* 93–129. Amsterdam: Gordon and Breach, 1991.

Aurobindo, S. *The Future Evolution of Man.* 1963. Reprint, Twin Lakes, Wis.: Lotus Press, 2003.

Bache, C. *Dark Night, Early Dawn.* New York: SUNY Press, 2000.

Banathy, B. H. *Guided Evolution of Society: A Systems View.* New York: Springer, 2000.

BBC News. "Britain Is 'Surveillance Society.'" http://news.bbc.co.uk/1/hi/ uk/6108496.stm.

———. "Russia Outlines Arctic Force Plan." http://news.bbc.co.uk/1/hi/world/ europe/7967973.stm.

Becker, R. O. *The Body Electric.* New York: William Morrow, 1998.

———. *Cross Currents: The Perils of Electropollution, the Promise of Electromedicine.* New York: Jeremy P. Tarcher, 1990.

Bennett, J. G. *Transformation.* North Yorkshire, Sherborne: Coombe Springs Press, 1978.

Berry, Thomas. *The Great Work: Our Way into the Future.* New York: Three Rivers Press, 1999.

Blank, M., and R. Goodman. "Do Electromagnetic Fields Interact Directly with DNA?" *Bioelectromagnetics* 18 (1997): 111–15.

Bloom, H. *Global Brain: The Evolution of Mass Mind from the Big Bang to the 21st Century.* New York: John Wiley & Sons, Inc., 2000.

Booth, K. *Theory of World Security.* Cambridge: Cambridge University Press, 2007.

Bowcott, O. "Britain to Claim More Than 1m sq km of Antarctica." *Guardian* (London), October 17, 2007.

Brooks, Michael. "Space Storm Alert: 90 Seconds from Catastrophe." *New Scientist* 23 (March 2009).

Brown, T. *The Quest.* New York: G. P. Putnam's Sons, 1991.

Brzezinski, Z. *Between Two Ages: America's Role in the Technetronic Era.* New York: Viking, 1970.

Bucke, R. *Cosmic Consciousness: A Study in the Evolution of the Human Mind.* 1901. Reprint, London: The Olympia Press, 1972.

Burke, James, and Robert Ornstein. *The Axemaker's Gift: A Double-Edged History of Human Culture.* New York: Putnam, 1995.

Capra, Fritjof. *The Tao of Physics.* London: Fontana, 1982.

Carey, Ken. *The Third Millennium: Living in the Posthistoric World.* New York: HarperCollins, 1996.

Castaneda, Carlos. *Tales of Power.* London: Simon and Schuster, 1974.

de Chardin, P. T. *The Future of Man.* London: Fontana, 1974.

———. *Let Me Explain.* London: Fontana, 1974.

———. *The Phenomenon of Man.* London: Collins, 1959.

Chrisafis, A., and G. Keeley. "Oil Prices: Europe Threatened with Summer of Discontent over Rising Cost of Fuel." *Guardian* (London), June 10, 2008. www.guardian.co.uk/business/2008/jun/10/oil.france.

Collin, Rodney. *The Theory of Celestial Influence.* London: Arkana, 1993.

Congress for the New Urbanism. "Charter of the New Urbanism." www.cnu .org/sites/files/charter_english.pdf.

Cook, F. *Hua-Yen Buddhism: The Jewel Net of Indra.* University Park: The Pennsylvania State University Press, 1977.

Csikszentmihalyi, M. *The Evolving Self: A Psychology for the Third Millennium.* New York: HarperCollins, 1993.

Darley, J. *High Noon for Natural Gas.* White River Junction, Vt.: Chelsea Green, 2004.

Davis, Mike. *Planet of Slums.* London: Verso, 2007.

Defence News. "Met Office Climate Change Study Could Help Identify Future Security Threats." National Archives. www.mod.uk/DefenceInternet/DefenceNews/

DefencePolicyAndBusiness/MetOfficeClimateChangeStudyCouldHelp-
IdentifyFutureSecurityThreats.htm.

Deffeyes, Kenneth S. *Beyond Oil: The View from Hubbert's Peak.* New York:
Hill & Wang, 2005.

Dennis, K., and J. Urry. *After the Car.* Cambridge: Polity Press, 2009.

Diamond, Jared M. *Collapse: How Societies Choose to Fail or Survive.* London:
Allen Lane, 2005.

Dmitriev, A. N. "Planetophysical State of the Earth and Life." The Millennium
Group. www.tmgnow.com/repository/global/planetophysical.html.

Eldredge, Niles. *Time Frames: The Rethinking of Darwinian Evolution and the
Theory of Punctuated Equilibria.* New York: Simon and Schuster, 1985.

Elgin, Duane. *Awakening Earth: Exploring the Evolution of Human Culture and
Consciousness.* New York: William Morrow and Company, 1993.

Ewert, A. W., D. C. Baker, and G. C. Bissix. *Integrated Resource and Environmental
Management: The Human Dimension.* New York: CABI Publishing, 2004.

Ferry, J. "You Are Now Entering an Oil-Free Zone." *Guardian* (London), April
19, 2007.

Flannery, T. *The Weather Makers: Our Changing Climate and What It Means
for Life on Earth.* London: Penguin, 2007.

Fosar, Grazyna, and Franz Bludorf. "Spiritual Science: DNA Is Influenced
by Words and Frequencies." Global Oneness. Extract available at www
.experiencefestival.com/a/Spirituality_and_Science/id/4161.

Gallopin, G., et al. *Branch Points: Global Scenarios and Human Choice.* Stock-
holm Environment Institute—Global Scenario Group. 1997: 1–47.

Gerber, R. *Vibrational Medicine: The Number 1 Handbook of Subtle Energy
Therapies.* Rochester, Vt.: Bear & Company, 2001.

Gilman, N., D. Randall, and P. Schwartz. "Impacts of Climate Change: A Sys-
tem Vulnerability Approach to Consider the Potential Impacts to 2050 of a
Mid-Upper Greenhouse Gas Emissions Scenario." *Global Business Network,*
January 2007, 12.

Girardet, H. *CitiesPeoplePlanet.* Chichester, England: Wiley-Academy, 2004.

Goonatilake, S. *The Evolution of Information: Lineages in Gene, Culture and
Artifact.* London: Pinter Publishers, 1991.

Grant, Glenn. "Memes: Introduction." Principia Cybernetica Web. http://
pespmc1.vub.ac.be/MEMIN.html.

Gribbin, John. *Deep Simplicity: Chaos, Complexity, and the Emergence of Life.*
London: Allen Lane, 2004.

Hansen, J. "Scientific Reticence and Sea Level Rise." *Environmental Research Letters* 2 (2007): 1–6.

Harman, W. *Global Mind Change: The Promise of the 21st Century.* San Francisco: Berrett-Koehler, 1998.

Havel, V. "The New Measure of Man." *New York Times,* July 8, 1994.

Heinberg, Richard. *The Party's Over: Oil, War and the Fate of Industrial Society.* New York: Clearview Books, 2005.

Ho, M.-W. *The Rainbow and the Worm: The Physics of Organisms.* Singapore: World Scientific, 1998.

Ho, M.-W., and F-A. Popp. "Gaia and the Evolution of Coherence." Presented at the Third Camelford Conference on the Implications of The Gaia Thesis: Symbiosis, Cooperativity and Coherence, The Wadebridge Ecological Centre, Camelford, Cornwall, England, 1989.

Hobart, M., and Z. Schiffman. *Information Ages: Literacy, Numeracy, and the Computer Revolution.* Baltimore, Md.: John Hopkins University Press, 1998.

Holmgren, D. *Permaculture: Principles and Pathways beyond Sustainability.* Victoria, Australia: Holmgren Design Services, 2002.

Homer-Dixon, T. *Environment, Scarcity, and Violence.* Princeton, N.J.: Princeton University Press, 1999.

———. "Our Panarchic Future." Worldwatch Institute. www.worldwatch.org/node/6008.

———. "Prepare Today for Tomorrow's Breakdown." *Globe and Mail* (Toronto, Ont.), May 14, 2006.

———. *The Upside of Down: Catastrophe, Creativity, and the Renewal of Civilization.* New York: Island Press, 2006.

Howard, E. *Garden Cities of To-Morrow.* 1902. Reprint, London: Faber and Faber, 1946.

Information Commissioner. "A Report on the Surveillance Society." The Surveillance Studies Network., David Murakami Wood, ed., www.ico.gov.uk/upload/documents/library/data_protection/practical_application/surveillance_society_full_report_2006.pdf.

Intergovernmental Panel on Climate Change. *Climate Change—Working Group I Report "The Physical Science Basis"* (2007), www.ipcc.ch/publications_and_data/publications_and_data_reports.shtml#1

Joseph, Lawrence E. *Apocalypse 2012: An Optimist Investigates the End of Civilization.* London: HarperElement, 2007.

King, A., and B. Schneider. *The First Global Revolution*. London: Simon & Schuster, 1991.

Kolbert, E. *Field Notes from a Catastrophe: A Frontline Report on Climate Change*. London: Bloomsbury, 2007.

Korten, D. C. *The Great Turning: From Empire to Earth Community*. San Francisco: Berrett-Koehler, 2007.

Krishna, G. *Kundalini: The Evolutionary Energy in Man*. Boston: Shambhala, 1997.

Kuhn, Thomas. *The Structure of Scientific Revolutions*. 1962. Reprint, London: The University of Chicago Press, 1996.

Kunstler, J. H. *The Long Emergency: Surviving the Converging Catastrophes of the 21st Century*. London: Atlantic Books, 2006.

Kurzweil, R. *The Singularity Is Near*. New York: Viking, 2005.

Laszlo, Ervin. *The Chaos Point: The World at the Crossroads*. Charlottesville, Va.: Hampton Roads, 2006.

———. *The Connectivity Hypothesis: Foundations of an Integral Science of Quantum, Cosmos, Life, and Consciousness*. New York: SUNY Press, 2003.

———. *Evolution: The General Theory*. Cresskill, N.J.: Hampton Press, 1996.

———. *Macroshift: Navigating the Transformation to a Sustainable World*. San Francisco: Berrett-Koehler, 2001.

———. *Quantum Shift in the Global Brain*. Rochester, Vt.: Inner Traditions, 2008.

———. "Technology and Social Change: An Approach from Nonequilibrium Systems Theory." *Technological Forecasting and Social Change* 29 (1986): 271–83.

Laughlin, C. D., and S. Richardson. "The Future of Human Consciousness." *Futures*, June 1986: 401–19.

Leary, Timothy. *Info-Psychology*. Las Vegas, Nev.: New Falcon Publications, 1988.

———. *The Intelligence Agents*. Las Vegas, Nev.: New Falcon Publications, 1997.

Leggett, J. *Half Gone: Oil, Gas, Hot Air and Global Energy Crisis*. London: Portobello Books, 2005.

Lessing, Doris. *Prisons We Choose to Live Inside*. London: HarperCollins, 1987.

Lewis, Leo. "Water Shortages Are Likely to Be Trigger for Wars, Says UN Chief Ban Ki Moon." *Times* (London). www.timesonline.co.uk/tol/news/world/asia/article2994650.ece.

Linden, E. *Winds of Change: Climate, Weather and the Destruction of Civilizations*. New York: Simon & Schuster, 2007.

Lipton, Bruce. *The Biology of Belief: Unleashing the Power of Consciousness, Matter and Miracles*. Carlsbad, Calif.: Hay House Inc., 2008.

Lovelock, James. "The Fight to Get Aboard Lifeboat UK." *Times* (London), February 8, 2009.

———. *The Revenge of Gaia*. London: Allen Lane, 2006.

Lovett, R. "Russia Plants Underwater Flat, Claims Arctic Seafloor." *National Geographic News,* August 3, 2007.

Loye, David. "Chaos and Transformation: Implications of Nonequilibrium Theory for Social Science and Society." In Laszlo, E., ed. *The New Evolutionary Paradigm*. Amsterdam: Gordon and Breach, 1991.

Lynas, M. *Six Degrees: Our Future on a Hotter Planet*. London: Fourth Estate, 2007.

Margulis, Lynn. *Symbiosis in Cell Evolution*. New York: Freeman, 1993.

McCahill, Michael, and Clive Norris. "CCTV in London (Working Paper No. 6)." Urban Eye, www.urbaneye.net/results/ue_wp6.pdf.

McFadden, S. *Profiles in Wisdom: Native Elders Speak about the Earth*. Santa Fe, N.M.: Bear & Company, 1991.

McLuhan, Marshall. *Counterblast*. London: Rapp and Whiting, 1970.

———. *The Gutenberg Galaxy: The Making of Typographic Man*. London: Routledge & Kegan Paul, 1962.

Meadows, D. H., D. L. Meadows, and J. Randers. *Beyond the Limits: Global Collapse or a Sustainable Future*. London: Earthscan, 1992.

Miller, R. A., and I. Miller. "The Schumann Resonances and Human Psychobiology." *Nexus Magazine* 10, no. 3 (April–May 2003).

Mitchell, W. *Me++: The Cyborg Self and the Networked City*. Cambridge, Mass.: MIT Press, 2003.

Mol, A. "Boundless Biofuels? Between Environmental Sustainability and Vulnerability." *Sociologia Ruralis* 47, no. 4 (2007): 297–315.

Monbiot, G. *Heat: How to Stop the Planet Burning*. London: Allen Lane, 2006.

Montalk, Tom. "Fringe Knowledge for Beginners." Montalk.net. www.montalk.net/files/fringeknowledgeWEB.pdf.

Naimy, M. *The Book of Mirdad*. London: Watkins Publishing, 2002.

Narby, Jeremy. *Cosmic Serpent: DNA and the Origins of Knowledge*. London: Phoenix, 1999.

National Academies Press. "Severe Space Weather Events—Understanding Societal and Economic Impacts: A Workshop Report." www.nap.edu/catalog.php?record_id=12507.

National Intelligence Council. *Global Trends 2015: A Dialogue about the Future with Nongovernment Experts.* www.dni.gov/nic/NIC_globaltrend2015.html.

National Oceanic and Atmospheric Administration. "Solar Storms Cause Significant Economic and Other Impacts on Earth." *NOAA Magazine,* April 5, 2004. www.magazine.noaa.gov/stories/mag131.htm.

Nietzsche, Friedrich. *Thus Spoke Zarathustra.* London: Penguin, 2003.

———. *The Will to Power.* New York: Vintage, 1968.

Norton, R. "Feral Cities." *Naval War College Review.* Autumn 2003.

Ornstein, R., and P. Ehrlich. *New World, New Mind.* Cambridge, Mass.: ISHK, 2000.

Ouspensky, P. D. *In Search of the Miraculous: Fragments of an Unknown Teaching.* London: Routledge & Kegan Paul, 1950.

Parry, M., et al. "Millions at Risk: Defining Critical Climate Change Threats and Targets." *Global Environmental Change* 11 (2001): 81–3.

Paskal, C. "How Climate Change Is Pushing the Boundaries of Security and Foreign Policy." Chatham House. www.chathamhouse.org.uk/files/9250_bp0607climatecp.pdf.

Pearce, Fred. *The Last Generation: How Nature Will Take Her Revenge for Climate Change.* London: Transworld, 2007.

———. *With Speed and Violence: Why Scientists Fear Tipping Points in Climate Change.* Boston: Beacon Press, 2007.

Peterson, A. J. *Approach to Reality.* Cambridge: Rose King Publications, 1983.

Pfeiffer, D. *Eating Fossil Fuels.* Gabriola Island, B.C.: New Society Publishers, 2006.

Popp, F.-A., et al. "Physical Aspects of Biophotons." *Experientia* 44 (1988): 576–85.

Prigogine, I. *The End of Certainty.* New York: The Free Press, 1997.

Reuters. "FACTBOX—Financial Crisis Sparks Unrest in Europe." www.reuters.com/article/latestCrisis/idUSLQ87702?sp=true.

Rial, J., et al. "Nonlinearities, Feedbacks and Critical Thresholds within the Earth's Climate System." *Climate Change* 65 (2004): 11–38.

Ring, Kenneth. "Precognitive and Prophetic Visions in Near-Death Experiences." *Anabiosis: The Journal of Near-Death Studies* 2 (1982): 47–74.

Rogers, Richard. *Cities for a Small Planet*. London: Faber and Faber, 1997.

Russell, E. *Design for Destiny*. London: Spearman, 1971.

Russell, Peter. *The Global Brain Awakens: Our Next Evolutionary Leap*. Palo Alto, Calif.: Global Brain Inc., 1995.

Roberts, J. Timmons, and B. Parks. *A Climate of Injustice*. Cambridge, Mass.: MIT Press, 2007.

Sahtouris, Elisabet. "The Biology of Globalization." Life Web. www.ratical.org/ LifeWeb.

———. "Living Systems in Evolution." Life Web. www.ratical.org/LifeWeb.

———. "Vistas—Evolving Our Beliefs to Evolve Our Lives." Life Web. www .ratical.org/LifeWeb.

Sauser, B. "Ethanol Demand Threatens Food Prices." *Technology Review*, February 13, 2007.

Scott, Ernest. *The People of the Secret*. London: Octagon Press, 1985.

Shah, Idries. *The Exploits of the Incomparable Mulla Nasrudin*. London: Octagon Press, 1985.

———. *Knowing How to Know: A Practical Philosophy in the Sufi Tradition*. London: Octagon Press, 1998.

———. *Learning How to Learn: Psychology and Spirituality the Sufi Way*. London: Octagon Press, 1996.

———. *Reflections*. London: Octagon Press, 1969.

———. *Tales of the Dervishes*. London: Octagon Press, 1993.

Spinrad, Norman. *The Solarians*. New York: Paperback Library, 1966.

Steiner, Rudolf. *An Outline of Esoteric Science*. Great Barrington, Mass.: Steiner Books, 1998.

Stern, N. *The Economics of Climate Change: The Stern Review*. Cambridge: Cambridge University Press, 2007.

Strauss, William, and Neil Howe. *The Fourth Turning: An American Prophecy*. New York: Bantam, 1998.

Strogatz, Steven. *SYNC: The Emerging Science of Spontaneous Order*. New York: Hyperion, 2003.

Sturgeon, T. *More Than Human*. London: Gollancz, 2000.

Tainter, Joseph A. *The Collapse of Complex Societies*. Cambridge, N.Y.: Cambridge University Press, 1988.

Talbot, M. *The Holographic Universe*. London: HarperCollins, 1996.

Tesla, Nikola. "Man's Greatest Achievement." Ascension Research Center. www .ascension-research.org/tesla.html.

Timms, M. *Beyond Prophecies and Predictions.* New York: Ballantine Books, 1994.

Toffler, Alvin. *The Third Wave.* London: Pan Books, 1981.

Townsend, Mark, and Paul Harris. "Now the Pentagon Tells Bush: Climate Change Will Destroy Us." *Observer* (London). http://observer.guardian.co.uk/international/story/0,6903,1153513,00.html.

Traynor, Ian. "Climate Change May Spark Conflict with Russia, EU Told." *Guardian* (London). www.guardian.co.uk/world/2008/mar/10/eu.climatechange.

United Nations. "Global Trends: Refugees, Asylum-Seekers, Returnees, Internally Displaced and Stateless Persons Report." June 2007. Revised July 16, 2007. Part of the UNHCR Global Reports, see www.unhcr.org/gr07/index.html.

———. Department of Economic and Social Affairs: Population Division. "Fact Sheet 1: World Urban Population." www.un.org/esa/population/publications/WUP2005/2005WUP_FS1.pdf.

———. Department of Economic and Social Affairs: Population Division. "World Urbanization Prospects: The 2005 Revision." www.un.org/esa/population/publications/WUP2005/2005wup.htm.

Villoldo, A. *The Four Insights.* Carlsbad, Calif.: Hay House Inc., 2006.

White, J. *The Meeting of Science and Spirit.* New York: Paragon House, 1990.

Williams, P. "The Future of Global Systems: Collapse or Resilience?" Strategic Studies Institute, 2008: 1–23. Available as free download at www.scribd.com/doc/8329024/The-Future-of-Global-Systems-Collapse-or-Resilience.

Willis, R., M. Webb, and J. Wilsdon. *The Disrupters: Lessons for Low-Carbon Innovation from the New Wave of Environmental Pioneers.* London: Nesta, 2007.

Woodbridge, R. *The Next World War: Tribes, Cities, Nations, and Ecological Decline.* Toronto: University of Toronto Press, 2004.

Worldwatch Institute. "Biofuels for Transportation: Global Potential and Implications for Sustainable Agriculture and Energy in the 21st Century." www.worldwatch.org/node/4078.

Young, K. "Solar 'Superflare' Shredded Earth's Ozone." *New Scientist,* March 23, 2007.

Zohar, Danah. *The Quantum Self.* London: Flamingo, 1991.

INDEX

BOOKS OF RELATED INTEREST

2012: A Clarion Call
Your Soul's Purpose in Conscious Evolution
by Nicolya Christi

Thomas Berry, Dreamer of the Earth
The Spiritual Ecology of the Father of Environmentalism
Edited by Ervin Laszlo and Allan Combs

The Basic Code of the Universe
The Science of the Invisible in Physics, Medicine, and Spirituality
by Massimo Citro, M.D.

Healing the Mind through the Power of Story
The Promise of Narrative Psychiatry
by Lewis Mehl-Madrona, M.D., Ph.D.

Awakening the Planetary Mind
Beyond the Trauma of the Past to a New Era of Creativity
by Barbara Hand Clow

Where Does Mind End?
A Radical History of Consciousness and the Awakened Self
by Marc J. Seifer, Ph.D.

Discover Your Soul Template
14 Steps for Awakening Integrated Intelligence
by Marcus T. Anthony, Ph.D.

Planetary Healing
Spirit Medicine for Global Transformation
by Nicki Scully

INNER TRADITIONS • BEAR & COMPANY
P.O. Box 388
Rochester, VT 05767
1-800-246-8648
www.InnerTraditions.com

Or contact your local bookseller